God And The Astronomers

GOD AND THE ASTRONOMERS

GOD AND
THE ASTRONOMERS

CONTAINING

THE WARBURTON LECTURES 1931-1933

BY

WILLIAM RALPH INGE

K.C V.O., D.D., F.B.A.

DEAN OF ST PAUL'S; HON. D D OXFORD AND ABERDEEN, HON. D.LITT., DURHAM AND SHEFFIELD
HON. LL.D., EDINBURGH AND ST. ANDREWS, HON FELLOW OF KING'S AND
JESUS COLLEGES, CAMBRIDGE, AND OF HERTFORD COLLEGE, OXFORD

LONGMANS, GREEN AND CO.

LONDON ♦ NEW YORK ♦ TORONTO

1934

LONGMANS, GREEN AND CO. LTD.
39 PATERNOSTER ROW, LONDON, E.C. 4
5 OLD COURT HOUSE STREET, CALCUTTA
53 NICOL ROAD, BOMBAY
36A MOUNT ROAD, MADRAS

LONGMANS, GREEN AND CO.
114 FIFTH AVENUE, NEW YORK
221 EAST 20TH STREET, CHICAGO
88 TREMONT STREET, BOSTON

LONGMANS, GREEN AND CO.
480 UNIVERSITY AVENUE, TORONTO

BIBLIOGRAPHICAL NOTE

First Edition - - - *September*, 1933

New Impressions :—
September, 1933   *October*, 1933   *April*, 1934

Made in Great Britain

PREFACE

A PHILOSOPHER or theologian who wishes to write on cosmology—on the relation of God to the universe—must in these days acquire some knowledge of modern astronomy and physics, two closely allied sciences in which new discoveries and new theories are being published almost every year. It is no longer possible to brush these researches aside as irrelevant to metaphysics or to theology. A hundred years ago some philosophers followed this high *a priori* road, with the result that natural science turned contemptuously away from philosophy as nothing but useless chatter. What else could be expected, after such performances as Hegel's definition of heat? "Heat is the self-restoration of matter in its formlessness, its liquidity the triumph of its abstract homogeneity over specific definiteness; its abstract, purely self-existing continuity as negation of negation is here set as activity." It may well be that the philosopher may come to the conclusion that such physical laws as entropy are not decisive of the ultimate basis of reality; but he must at least try to understand what these laws mean, and what conclusions specialists in these sciences draw from them. "The throne of the Godhead is the human mind"; but it is mainly through the external world that God reveals Himself to the human mind.

The philosopher or theologian in most cases has had no special training in science. His only chance of being able to write intelligently on the philosophical problems raised by scientific discoveries is to read carefully the best and newest books, some of which, especially in England, have been written, in a semi-popular form, in the hope of attracting the interest of the fortunately very large class who wish to know what the picture of the universe looks like in the light of the latest theories. Our leading scientists have no wish to keep the educated public at a distance, though some of them may affect to disdain "popularisers." They are also well aware that their results are found highly interesting by students of religion and philosophy. But second-hand information, however laboriously acquired, is a poor substitute for a scientific education. Errors, not, we may hope, on the heroic scale of Hegel's theory of heat, are sure to creep in; and even when the facts are correctly stated amateurishness will be apparent on every page. I should not be slow to detect these tokens of superficiality if a painstaking physicist or mathematician were to compile a treatise on classical scholarship or Greek philosophy or Christian theology. Eminent men of science have, in fact, already invaded our territory, and have been rather roughly handled by the Oxford metaphysical pundits. Their philosophy may be open to criticism ; but they are quite right in thinking that science and philosophy cannot be kept in water-tight compartments. In this book I have probably laid myself open to reprisals.

I do not deprecate severe criticism upon any faults of carelessness which may be found in my comments upon scientific theories about the origin, structure, and destiny of the universe ; but such mistakes, which I have done my best to avoid, are important only if they affect the argument of my book. It is unnecessary to expose my inadequacy to pose as an authority on subjects which are not my own, for I should be the last to claim any such authority.

The greater part of my book deals with questions with which I am more familiar. I have argued that the law of entropy, if it holds good of the entire physical universe, points to a creation in time by some Power outside the degenerative process which science observes proceeding to an inevitable end. If God is conceived of as a Being wholly immanent in the world, the acceptance of entropy as a universal law leaves His origin inexplicable and His doom certain. But a God to whom the world is as necessary as He is to the world can hardly be regarded as divine unless the world is everlasting. A God under sentence of death, at however distant a date, does not possess the attributes which religion holds to belong to the idea of God. And on the other hand, an irreversible process which must have had a beginning points to some creative agent outside itself. I have therefore

maintained that recent developments of science are unfavourable to belief in God as a mere *anima mundi*, and
are less unfavourable to the theistic hypothesis.

I have not been able to follow those who hold that
the decomposition of material particles, which were
formerly supposed to be solid and indestructible, is a
valid argument in favour of a spiritual as opposed to a
materialistic view of ultimate reality. Although I hold
that ultimate reality is " spiritual," not material, I cannot
admit that matter dissolved into radiation is more
" spiritual " than matter in a solid or liquid state. We
may refuse to call it any longer matter, but this is not a
refutation of materialism. This argument, which is used
by some Christian apologists, seems to me frivolous; it
belongs to the old notion that spirit is matter in an ultra-
gaseous condition. That matter can be literally " annihilated " I do not believe, though the word is carelessly
used by some great scientists. Nor has religion anything
to gain by speculating on a final pannihilism or acosmism.

I have crossed swords with those physicists who take
refuge, in a rather confused manner, in Berkeleyan idealism
as an escape from certain apparently insoluble problems
in their own subjects. Science, I hold, can never be
independent of the realism with which it starts, and
therefore can never become purely mathematical. A
critic has said to me, " What would your friend Plato
have said to that argument ? " I am, however, convinced that neither Plato nor Plotinus came anywhere
near to subjective idealism.

The constructive part of my argument follows the lines of Christian Platonism, which I have tried to work out in my other books. It is substantially the main tradition of Christian philosophy, and I doubt whether any definitely anti-Platonic view of reality can find room within the Christian intellectual system.

I owe a great deal to the extraordinary kindness of Professor A. E. Taylor of Edinburgh, who has read the whole book and annotated it carefully. I have generally followed his suggestions; but a few points remain in which I fear he will not be satisfied.

1. He complains that I have come to no conclusion about entropy as a universal law. I certainly have not; it is not for me to rush in where the highest authorities confess themselves baffled, or contradict one another. I have expressed a modest hope that some counteracting agency may be discovered; but at present the law seems to be impregnable. But I have pointed out that Christian theism has always contemplated the final dissolution of the material universe. It is not Christianity but modern pantheism, and the myth of unending progress, which are undermined by the degradation of energy. Professor Taylor thinks that I have wavered about the kindred question of recurrent cycles. Here again I do not profess to have any conviction, but I think this old belief may have a future.

2. I have also, he thinks, taken no firm line about determinism and free will. This terrible problem arises in connexion with the new belief in "indeterminacy,"

which is, I suppose, a mathematical demand. I do
not think that a belief in real *chance* necessarily follows,
and I am strongly opposed to the lawless, unpredictable "multiverse" of American pluralism. The notion
that "anything may happen" seems to me to threaten
the foundations of science. The free will controversy I thought hardly came within the scope of this
book.

3. I have admitted my inability to find any basis,
within the physical world, for the traditional eschatology
of the Christian religion. "Heaven," said Benjamin
Whichcote, "is first a temper, then a place." But where
shall we find either a place, or a time, in which to set the
scene of our life with God? The question cannot be
evaded; and it seems to me that we must take the words
of St. John, "it doth not yet appear what we shall be,"
more seriously than most of us do. If we face this quite
frankly, our conclusion will be, not that "death closes
all," but rather that the unseen spiritual world, the
"kingdom of values," is, as I have maintained, no mere
ideal or aspiration, but a fact, an existing reality, which
can only be pictured symbolically and poetically under
the forms of time and place. I do not know whether
this abandonment of a local, geographical, and temporal
"next world" will cause distress and indignation among
many of my readers or not; science, as far as I can
see, leaves us no alternative. "The things that are seen
are temporal; the things that are not seen are eternal."
St. Paul has already adopted this first article of the

Platonic creed. Holding fast by it, I am not afraid to allow faith and love to create their own imagery.

I wish also to thank Mrs. Cloudsley, who, while carefully typing the book for me, called my attention to sundry repetitions—that old man's failing.

To my great regret the fine Gifford Lectures of Bishop Barnes (*Scientific Theory and Religion*) were not published till this book was already in type.

Lastly, I have to thank the Warburton Trustees for allowing me to choose an unusual subject, and to embody the substance of my six lectures in a much larger book.

W. R. INGE.

The Deanery, St. Paul's.

CONTENTS

WARBURTON LECTURES

Introductory

WHEN the Trustees of the Warburton Lectureship did me the honour to ask me to give these Lectures in Lincoln's Inn Chapel, I was naturally eager to accept the invitation. But I was doubtful whether I could take any of the subjects which interest me without (so to speak) driving a coach and four through the Trust Deed. For I was informed that the prescribed subjects were Old Testament prophecy and the errors of the Church of Rome. The subject of Old Testament prophecy was not at all congenial to me, and I had no wish to devote my lectures to controversy with the Latin Church. But the Trustees were willing to give me even more than the customary latitude which is granted to the preachers of Lecture-Sermons, a latitude which is very apparent, for example, in some of the Gifford Lectures at the Scottish Universities.

The subject which I was allowed to choose is a *prophecy* certainly, though not quite the kind of prophecy which Bishop Warburton had in his mind. It is the prophecy of modern Science about the ultimate fate of the world we live in. The Second Law of Thermo-dynamics, also called the principle of Carnot and the Law of Entropy, is not a new discovery; Carnot wrote in 1825, Clausius in 1850. But it has lately become a matter of common knowledge through the books of Jeans and Eddington, of which hundreds of thousands of copies have been sold. It is safe to assume that almost all intelligent people have read and thought about them. The fact that books on astronomy, however clearly and brilliantly written, should be reckoned among the best sellers, is a very remarkable and encouraging sign. At a time when complaints are general that our civilisation is vulgarised and materialised, and that our popular press and popular amusements indicate the acme of frivolity, it is proved that the man in the street is eager to learn all he can about that branch of natural science which is furthest removed from all petty and ephemeral interests. The wonders of the infinitely great and the infinitely small, the almost inconceivable extent of time past and time future, grip the imagination and awaken the sense of sublimity. But they have little if any relation to our short earthly lives, so soon to be "rounded with a sleep." The lights which we see twinkling in the darkness started on their journey—many of them—before there were any men on this earth. The occasional catastrophes —explosions or what not—which are observed in the heavens belong to such ancient history that our pity for the possible victims of them would be hopelessly belated. Nor do the prophecies about the end of the world, to which I have already referred, touch any solicitude which we could feel for ourselves or our families. We are told that our descendants may still be living on the earth a million years hence. If they are, they will be more unlike us than we are unlike the pithecanthropus of Java, and our family interest in their welfare cannot be very acute. The curiosity which the public feels about astronomy is as nearly disinterested as any human emotion can be.

The Bedouin founders of the Hebrew nation were more familiar with the stars than we are, and the wonder of them entered into their souls. " When I consider thy heavens," says the Psalmist, " even the work of thy fingers, the moon and the stars which thou hast ordained ; what is man that thou art mindful of him, and the son of man that thou visitest him ? " What is man ? " Thou hast made him to have dominion over the works of thy hands ; thou hast put all things in subjection under his feet." The starry heavens humble and exalt us at once. The contrast between the vastness of the universe and the puny dwellers on earth is far more tremendous than the Psalmist knew it to be. But the old Hebrew poet, like Kant, found two things above all others worthy of awe and wonder—the heavens above us, and the moral nature of man within us.

The tendency to deify and worship the heavenly bodies has been widespread, and is easy to understand. But without any concessions to mythology, the imaginations of thoughtful men have been very deeply stirred by the illimitable vistas both of space and time which modern science has opened to us. Some have been most impressed by the all-pervading majesty of natural law. Shelley, who among all our poets (as Whitehead tells us) had the most scientific mind, tells us how man looked on those

> Countless and unending orbs
> In mazy motion intermingled,
> Yet still fulfilled immutably
> Eternal nature's law.
> Above, below, around
> The circling systems formed
> A wilderness of harmony ;
> Each with undeviating aim,
> In eloquent silence, through the depths of space
> Pursued its wondrous way.

George Meredith, in a remarkable sonnet, represents Lucifer rising from his dark dominion and gazing up :

> He reached a middle height, and at the stars
> Which are the brain of heaven he looked and sank.
> Around the ancient track marched, rank by rank,
> The army of unalterable law.

Wordsworth sees that the obverse of law is obedience. It is Duty, " stern daughter of the voice of God," through whom the most ancient heavens are fresh and strong—duty, obedience to the law of their being, which upholds all things, small and great, in their appointed courses. Others have felt only the sublimity of unlimited power displayed on so colossal a stage. Victor Hugo speaks of the arrogance of man rebuked by the Spirit of Earth, which itself shrinks into insignificance before the wondrous planet Saturn. Saturn pales before the Sun, the Sun before the mighty stars Sirius and Arcturus ; then the Zodiac, the milky way, and the vast nebulæ that whiten the darkness, pass before his vision. Lastly, the Infinite says, " All this multiplicity lives in my sombre unity " ;

and God sums up with, " I have only to breathe, and all this fades away."

But others have been oppressed, as Tennyson was sometimes, by the vastness of the prospect :

> As this poor earth's pale history runs,
> What is it all but a trouble of ants
> In the gleam of a million million of suns ?

So Pascal, in words often quoted, says, " Le silence de ces espaces infinis m' effraie."

Plato deprecates star-gazing. What does it matter whether we look down or up ? We shall not find God in one direction rather than another. But of all words about the stars I like best these lines of George Meredith, from the poem " Meditation under Stars," one of the gems of modern English poetry :

> So may we read, and little find them cold :
> Not frosty lamps illumining dead space,
> Not distant aliens, not senseless powers.
> The fire is in them whereof we are born ;
> The music of their motion may be ours.
> Spirit shall deem them beckoning earth, and voiced
> Sisterly to her, in her beams rejoiced.

It is needless to say that the multitudes who read Jeans and Eddington, or listen to their lectures on the wireless, are not interested in the calculations by which their results are arrived at. They know nothing of the higher mathematics, a disability which, I hasten to assure you, I share myself. Their imaginations are kindled by the vastness of creation, as was the author of the eighth Psalm, whose universe was so small and cramped compared with what the telescope has revealed to the modern man. The public feels, and rightly feels, that we are in the presence of a mighty revelation of the grandeur of Nature's God. It is, after all, refreshing to be lifted for a while above what an orator described as the petty provincialisms of this puny planet.

But the more I thought about the subject which I had chosen, the more convinced I became that it raises very deep and important questions in philosophy and religion. As Professor Muirhead has urged, " the most difficult and for the moment at least the most pressing of the problems that face idealistic philosophy is concerned with the co-ordination of its leading conceptions with the new ideas in physical science." These problems are equally important for those who call themselves realists, not idealists. The two schools are not so far apart as they formerly appeared to be ; the dispute between them no longer seems to be fundamental. I know that some thinkers hold that a metaphysician may ignore theories about the ultimate nature of matter, as lying outside his province. Strictly, this is true ; but in practice physical science and philosophy habitually encroach upon each other. Some of our astronomers present us with an idealistic scheme—a patchwork of Kant, Berkeley, and other philosophers ; and modern metaphysics is deeply entangled in historicism, in a philosophy which throws its ideals into the future, and makes inordinate claims upon the evolutionary process.

I do not think that a rigid demarcation of territory is possible or desirable. I shall have to plead with idealists, whether they are primarily metaphysicians or mathematicians, that there is an ontology of the pheno-

menal world, and that we can neither regard it as the
creation of the human mind nor as a system of symbols
with no necessary relation to reality. My own position,
I will say at once, is nearer to the realists than to the
idealists ; but I do not regard the mind as only a mirror
of happenings which are independent of it. Reality, as
I understand it, is constituted by the unity in duality of
the mind and its objects. Mind does not create the
intelligible world, nor is the intelligible world independent
of the intelligence. The real world is a kingdom of
objective " forms," which in the mind of God are the
perfect counterpart of His own thought. It is because
our apprehension of these is so imperfect that we may
speak, with Bradley, of degrees of truth and reality, a
conception which (I agree with his critics) is unintelligible if we do not accept, as he does, objective values.
(I shall explain my use of the word "value" in a later
chapter.)

The cosmology of natural science in the last century,
based on mechanicism and determinism, implied a philosophy, and one which the contemporary idealists and
theologians found most unsatisfactory. Its disregard of
the higher values must be considered later. But it also
made two fundamental assumptions—one, that everything in the nature of things can be mechanically explained, and the other that all things are built up out
of primordial and indestructible substances. " I never
satisfy myself," said Kelvin, " until I can make a mechanical model of a thing." Clerk Maxwell wrote, " Though
in the course of ages catastrophes have occurred and may
yet occur in the heavens, though ancient systems may be

dissolved, and new systems evolved out of their ruins, the molecules out of which these systems are built—the foundation-stones of the material universe—remain unbroken and unchanged." It is a detail that Maxwell's molecules have been broken up into atoms, and the atoms into electrons and protons; what is important is that both the substantiality of the universe and its indestructibility have now been challenged. The astronomers tell us as a certain fact—Eddington says it is the most certain truth of science—that the whole universe is steadily and irrevocably running down like a clock. The inevitable end, says Jeans, is annihilation—annihilation of life, of consciousness, of memory, even of the elements of matter itself. That is the doom of all that exists—annihilation, from which there can be no recovery and no return.

It seemed to me a very marvellous thing that this creed—more pessimistic than the Ragnarok or Götterdämmerung of the old Scandinavian mythology—should have co-existed with all the rosy predictions of what has been called the Century of Hope, the nineteenth century, which was to be followed, it now seems, by the Century of Disillusionment, the twentieth. For consider how the doctrine of Progress, the supposed *Law* of Progress, inevitable, endless, continually increasing and advancing Progress, was the lay creed of men of science, philosophers, sociologists, and historians, during the whole of the last century. Think how confidently it was announced, as a law of nature, by Herbert Spencer and his school, and even (more cautiously) by Charles Darwin himself. Think what an essential presupposition it was, probably to some extent even in the philosophy of Hegel, who never seems to have distinguished quite clearly enough between logical and temporal evolution, and certainly for the Italian New Idealists Croce and Gentile, for Bergson, for Professor Alexander and the late Wildon Carr. For all these writers, God is bound up with His creation. The world is as necessary to God as God is to the world. God is realising Himself in the historical process. If the Absolute did not first become self-conscious in Berlin a hundred and fifty years ago, as the critics of Hegel rather unfairly declared that he believed, He is gradually " emerging "—the evermore about to be—like the God of Professor Alexander. His fortunes are entangled with those of the Cosmos, which is merely the externalisa-tion of Himself. This notion of God is common to most of our philosophers, including even the late Professor Pringle-Pattison, who, great and inspiring teacher as he was, was never quite a theist in the Christian sense. And all the time it was certain, known to the very men who preached this optimistic and pantheistic creed, that the ultimate fate of such a God was just to die—to lose consciousness, to be for ever extinct. Why was it that neither men of science nor philosophers faced this crushing refutation of their hopes ? Why did they avert their eyes from what science was really telling them ? I sup-pose they were so obsessed with what was really the lay *religion* of the time—the this-world religion, which by its illusory optimism had almost displaced the blessed hope of everlasting life taught by Christianity—that they could not believe that their law of never-ending progress was a dream. And yet, if Jeans and Eddington

are right, this emerging, evolving, improving God is no
God at all, for surely a God under sentence of death is
no God. Modern pantheism is built on the sand, if it
seeks to find a support in the natural sciences.

As I pondered on this problem, I found myself in
deeper and deeper waters. Among the questions which
demanded an answer were these :

If the universe is running down like a clock, the clock
must have been wound up at a date which we could name
if we knew it. The world, if it is to have an end in time,
must have had a beginning in time. Is science itself
driving us back to the traditional Christian doctrine that
God created the world out of nothing at a certain date ?
That would be an amazing contradiction of some of the
presuppositions upon which nineteenth century science
was based. For consider this. Almost all processes dealt
with by mathematics and mechanics are theoretically reversible. Time strictly does not enter into them. But
the Second Law of Thermodynamics is *irreversible*. It
has a unilinear direction. All the ponderable matter in
the universe is moving in one direction, towards ultimate dissolution. Does not this throw into confusion a
picture of the world in which only mathematical and
mechanical categories are used ? Or if an absolute
beginning and end are unthinkable (they are rather
unimaginable than unthinkable), is it not reasonable to
assume that whatever power wound up the clock once
may probably be able to wind it up again ? But most
physicists and astronomers can find no trace of such a
power in nature. Whether we use this last argument or
not, the acceptance of the Law of Entropy seems to drive

us back to the traditional Christian belief in an external Creator, who made a world which had a beginning in time and will have an end in time. There may of course be other cosmic orders before and after ours, but, it would seem, entirely independent of ours. This Jeans and Eddington seem willing to admit. It is an astonishing *volte face* from the ideas of the nineteenth century. And yet the Law in question was pretty well known long before these astronomers began to write.

Other questions pressed for an answer. Is there really no escape from the final doom of the universe ? And if we have to admit that the irrevocable degradation of energy is proved, how does it affect our beliefs about God ? We Christians reject altogether the evolving emerging God who seems to be the God of New Realists and New Idealists alike. We believe that if there is a God, He must be unchangeable and eternal. But if there is such a Being, and if it is His nature to create a world, must He not create always ? Can we imagine Him literally *surviving* His creation, and living on without it ?

This leads to the old problem about the reality of space and time, on which philosophers have broken their teeth for so many centuries. The new philosophy, of which Bergson is the best-known exponent, makes Duration an ultimate reality. The universe, says Croce, *is* history. And what are we to make of the doctrine of Time as a fourth dimension, and of Professor Alexander's Space-Time ?

Again, if we have to reject the imaginary law of un-ending progress, must we reject the idea of progress altogether ? Surely not. That there is one single infinite purpose in the universe I cannot believe. An infinite purpose is a self-contradictory idea ; for an infinite purpose can never have been formed and can never be achieved. But there may be an infinite or almost infinite number of finite purposes. For example, each of our lives, we Christians believe, represents a distinct finite purpose in the mind of God. The new astronomy forbids us to find an infinite purpose in our universe. Here again we seem to be returning to the religious beliefs in which we were brought up, abandoning the romantic apocalyptism of the last century.

Then we cannot help asking whether the mechanistic science which was so tyrannical fifty years ago, and which, as we have seen, is very difficult to reconcile with the unilinear irreversible Law of Entropy, has not proved also inadequate to account for the facts of biology and psychology. There is, as we know, a very pretty quarrel raging on this subject, into which it might be prudent for a layman not to plunge rashly. But it is obviously important for philosophy, perhaps even for religion.

Some of these questions seem almost insoluble. For instance, there is the old question whether Time and Space are infinite or not. But the more we think about the whole group of problems, the more we shall be struck by the impossibility of separating *Value* from Existence. We shall, I think, be driven to seek in the idea of Value for a solution of these problems, so far as they are soluble with our very imperfect knowledge. I mean that we must recognise that reality is ultimately a kingdom of Values, and that the ultimate and eternal Values, which it has been agreed to classify as Goodness (or Perfection), Truth (or Wisdom), and Beauty, are *given* to us as much as the facts of what we call existence. These Values, which are much the same as the Ideas or Forms of Platonism, are the attributes under which God is revealed to us; they are, we may say, the contents of the divine mind as knowable by man. It is in this world of absolute Values that we find our immortality. The world of space and time and what we call existence is not unreal, but it is only a partial representation of the fully real world of which it is an imperfect actualisation. We shall have to consider the meaning of eternity as the form of perfect reality, that is to say, as something much more than an endless succession of points of time.

This, then, is a sketch of the task which I have set before myself. It is not a criticism of the new science, a thing which I should be wholly incompetent to attempt, even if I wished to do so. It is an attempt to face the view of the process of world-history as seen by our physicists and astronomers, and with the help of this world-view to expose what seem to me to be the inconsistencies in what I have decided to call *modernist* philosophy.

To some extent this book will cover the same ground as my study of Plotinus, the last of the great Greek philosophers. For I am convinced that the classical tradition of Christian philosophy, which Roman Catholic scholars call the *philosophia perennis*, the perennial philosophy, is not merely the only possible Christian philosophy, but is the only system which will be found ultimately satisfying. Plotinus, of course, was not a Christian, any more than his masters, Plato and Aristotle, were Christians. But the Christian Platonists of Alexandria, and St. Augustine, carried off to their hive the greater part of the grand philosophy of religion which was the final product of about 800 years of unfettered thought among the gifted Greek race, so that there is a real continuity between the Greeks and the medieval schoolmen who fixed the type of Catholic philosophy as it has existed ever since. The best part of scholasticism, I venture to think, is Greek—Greek rather than strictly Aristotelian, for St. Thomas Aquinas could not know all his debt to the later Platonists.[1]

In defending this religious philosophy against some leaders of thought in our day, I have found an un-expected amount of help from the new Thomist school, most of whom are Jesuits. The lucidity and precision of their arguments are very refreshing. It is possible that Bishop Warburton would not have approved of one of his lecturers admitting obligations to the unreformed Church. But there is no disloyalty to Anglicanism in doing so. Christian Platonism has been especially strong in our own Church. It is, I think, very congenial to the English mind. I have shown in one of my books how this tradition has inspired most of our great religious thinkers, and those among our great poets—Wordsworth is the supreme example—who have been religious teachers as well as poets. The modernist revolt against Plato necessarily, I think, leads away from belief in the God

---

[1] Professor Taylor reminds me that he did know that the *De Causis*, on which he wrote a commentary, is an extract from Proclus. But I think the statement in the text may stand.

of Christianity. I hope, therefore, that since the general trend of my lectures will be a defence of the central tradition in Christian philosophy, my discussion of these modern problems in the light of Christian Platonism will be neither out of place in this pulpit nor altogether at variance with the intentions of the founder of the Lectures. The form of Christian apologetic must be determined by the prevalent ideas and the pressing needs of the time.

I will ask my hearers and readers to realise that my main object is to state and defend the proper attitude of a thoughtful Christian to take up towards the world of space and time, of change and flux, of birth and death. This wonderful pageant of existence is now spread out before us more clearly than ever before, with all its inexhaustible marvels of wisdom and beauty. God is revealing Himself to our age mainly through the book of nature, fresh pages of which are opening before us nearly every year. I have no doubt that this knowledge is given us for a purpose. Science has been called, by Baron von Hügel, the *purgatory* of religion. The study of nature, he means, purifies our ideas about God and reality. It makes us ashamed of our petty interpretations of the world—ashamed of thinking that the universe was made solely for our benefit; ashamed of thinking that our little scheme of purely human values is valid for the whole; ashamed of our arrogant assumption that we are "the roof and crown of things," so that all the non-human world, including the other living inhabitants of our planet, has a merely instrumental value, " made for our use," as some have said. (Sir John Seeley, in his

Natural Religion, says that the man of science worships a greater God than the average church-goer. This is true in a sense, not because the man of science has a sound philosophy of religion—he is often rather muddle-headed outside his own subject—but because his love of truth is *disinterested ;* and this cannot be said of much of popular religion, which, as Whitehead has said, has always been tainted with egotism.

Those Christians who despise or neglect science, as having no bearing on the probation of the soul in this life, are mistaken. The world that we live in is real, though our pictures of it are very unlike the reality. It is the work of God. I sometimes think that the analogy of a poet and his work—say Shakespeare and his plays— is the most helpful in forming an idea of the relation of God to the world. The world is not a necessary condition of God's existence as God. We may even say with the dying Emily Brontë :

> Though earth and man were gone,
>   And suns and universes cease to be,
> And Thou wert left alone,
>   Every existence would exist in Thee.

The world is not as necessary to God as God is to the world. But it is the expression of His mind, and the field in which His thoughts and purposes are being actualised. (Whatever we can learn about nature teaches us something about God.)

And yet, as St. Paul says, our citizenship is in heaven. Heaven is not a geographical expression. Astronomy has disposed of that notion for good and all. We cannot picture the eternal world to ourselves without free use of symbols taken from space and time, which are the necessary forms of our thought, and I do not think we need try to banish these pictures, without which our thoughts of " heaven," the spiritual world, which is the supreme reality, inevitably become nebulous and unsubstantial. But symbols they are of a state of existence which eye hath not seen nor ear heard, neither hath it entered into the heart of man to conceive. I can think of eternity most easily as a really existing kingdom of values, remembering that as a fact which has no value is not a fact, so a value which has no existence has no value. Our heart's true home is in that perfect, unchanging world in which God's will is done, in which His thoughts are fully expressed, and which His love and beauty pervade as an atmosphere. There we have the unchanging standard by which to test and measure all that is relative and transitory, and there, as I believe, all the good and beautiful things which in the course of nature are born, bloom, and die, live for ever in their accomplished purpose and meaning in the presence of their Creator and our Redeemer. Even if the whole of the world-order that we know must submit at last to the universal doom and pass out of existence, that only means that our world-order is after all only one of the purposes of God, which like all purposes which are not frustrate has its proper beginning, middle, and end. In that case there may be, and probably are, other world-orders of which we know nothing. The idea of a dying world, which was so shocking to the Victorians, did not dismay earlier generations, who were theists, not pantheists. They believed it almost as a matter of course, and being theists they never thought of

2

God being involved in the fate of His creatures. The writer to the Hebrews quotes and makes his own the words of the Psalmist: "Thou, Lord, in the beginning hast laid the foundation of the earth, and the heavens are the works of thine hands. They shall perish, but thou remainest; and they all shall wax old as doth a garment; and as a vesture shalt thou fold them up and they shall be changed; but thou art the same and thy years shall not fail."

*

*

2

THE NEW *GÖTTERDÄMMERUNG*

THE starting-point of my inquiry in this book was the
religious and philosophical significance of the Second Law
of Thermodynamics, otherwise called the principle of
Carnot, or the Law of (increasing) Entropy. I must ask
the indulgence of my scientific readers in attempting to
state this law, in doing which I have made use of standard
works on the subject.

Mechanics is in general the study of reversible phenomena. But " Carnot and Clausius have shown that if
a determinate amount of work be expended in order
to raise the temperature of a body, we cannot return
exactly to the initial stage of the process by inverting
the cycle; there will always be a portion of the thermal
energy which is not transformed into work, which is, as
is commonly expressed, lowered or degraded." [1] This
process of change in one direction, which is a general
characteristic of the physical world, cannot be explained
by mechanical principles. The attempts which have been
made to reconcile the law of entropy with traditional
mechanics " have failed to give satisfactory results."
The attempted explanation, which has won general

[1] Aliotta, *The Idealistic Reaction against Science.*

acceptance, that " a given system tends to the configuration offering the maximum probability," seems open to the objection that it postulates, as the first stage from which the " degradation " of energy begins, a configuration against the existence of which the chances are almost infinite.

Meyerson [1] says that this law is a fatal obstacle to a mechanical explanation of the universe. The goal of all explanations is the identity of the antecedent and the consequent. Leibnitz expressly formulates this postulate of reversibility. The Second Law of Thermodynamics thus seems fatal to any *rational* explanation of the course of phenomena. It cannot be made to fit into a pan-mechanical or pan-mathematical universe. Meyerson explains the recourse to statistical probability which I have just mentioned, attributing it (before Planck) to Maxwell, Boltzmann, and Gibbs, and finds the same objection to it which had occurred to myself. " In fact, from the moment when the things change because they tend to arrange themselves in a manner more and more conformable to a probable distribution, it follows that at the beginning of time (whatever meaning we attach to this expression) they were distributed in a manner utterly improbable. This initial distribution constitutes a precise irrational (i.e. irreducible) datum. We could not escape from it except by supposing that this improbable state proceeded from one more probable ; and this would be to have recourse to the theory of cycles—the eternal return." Meyerson concludes that this attempt to " rationalise " entropy has failed.

[1] *De L'Explication dans les Sciences*, p. 203 *seq.*

It is strange to me that some philosophers have viewed this scientific impasse with indifference. Bosanquet, for example, says that " for a philosophy that knows its business the law of degradation makes no difference " ; and Pringle-Pattison, without explaining himself, says that " entropy has ceased to trouble philosophers." A theory which threatens to destroy the universal validity of the mechanistic hypothesis is, one would think, worthy of serious attention by metaphysicians. Urban [1] shows a sounder appreciation of the importance of the subject. The law of entropy, he says, introduces finality into the picture of the world—finality in the form of a magnificent dysteleology. Dysteleology is a form of teleology, just as there are negative values. The gates of the future, which Bergson and his disciples have declared to be open, are really shut. This realisation is, or ought to be, very disturbing to those who, disregarding Bosanquet's warning, throw all their ideals into the future. (Bosanquet himself might no doubt view the problem with unconcern.) " The universe," says the American, Henry Adams, in correspondence with William James, " has been terribly narrowed by thermodynamics." History and sociology " gasp for breath." I cannot, however, agree with Urban that we are faced with " a fundamental contradiction between the law of value and the law of existence " ; this, I think, is true only if we entangle our conception of value with an arbitrary interpretation of the time-process.

The historical element which the Second Law introduces into physics belongs to an entirely different order

[1] *The Intelligible World*, pp. 395-427.

of ideas from the conservation of energy, which takes no account of history.   Bergson naturally calls it " the most metaphysical of all the principles of nature," though in truth the idea of *direction*, which belongs to entropy, is foreign to Bergson's thought.   It is " metaphysical " for him, because it implies the idea of a beginning in time. This is obviously so, for it tells us that among the quantitative aspects of physical phenomena there is one which can change in one direction only.   The relation between available and unavailable energy is constantly altering irrevocably.   The process must have begun at a date which we could name if we knew it, and it must end at a future date, after which, it seems, nothing can happen any more.

It is strange that this depressing law was known at the time when Herbert Spencer, Charles Darwin, and a host of others were indulging in exultant pæans about the incluctable law of progress, which was destined, beyond a peradventure, to lead the human race onward and upward to a condition of absolute perfection.   This was the lay religion of enlightened persons in the reign of Queen Victoria.   It infected philosophy very deeply. To this day it seems to be the foundation of the historical philosophy of Croce.   Its effect upon religion was devastating.   God became the vital principle of an eternally progressing universe.   Whether He first attained self-consciousness about the time of the Napoleonic war, or whether, with Professor Alexander, He is a *nisus* towards greater perfection, the to-morrow that never comes, it was assumed that He is organic with the world, existing only as its soul, and of course condemned to share its fate.

Quite apart from entropy, this picture of universal
" progress " was ludicrously untrue. Herbert Spencer,
heaven knows why, identified progress with increasing
complexity. Man, the roof and crown of things, is
becoming more complex, and therefore " higher." He
will go on getting more complex, and therefore more
sublime, to all eternity. But some of Nature's most
successful experiments (by the test of survival, the only
one which Darwinism has the right to use) have on the
contrary become more simple. The great army of
parasites, animal and human, have shown their superiority
by surviving, while more complex organisms, such as the
stately diplodocus, the massive mastodon, and the for-
midable sabre-toothed tiger, have become portions and
parcels of the dreadful past. Under certain conditions,
such as those of modern civilisation, among the most
successful human types are those who have shed their
unnecessary organs, retaining only those which enable
them to hang on and suck.

And yet the Second Law had already rung the knell of
these fantastic hopes. We have a long lease, it is true,
but no freehold of this planet. The lords of creation
half a million years hence may be our lineal descendants or
they may not ; they may be supermen or submen, or not
men of any kind. And at last the race will die, and no
memory of its history will survive anywhere. The form
of the doctrine has no doubt varied. We used to be
told that all the matter of the universe will be collected
in a cold dead ball. Now, it is to disappear in radiation.
But these are details. In any form the doctrine preaches
a final stultification of ʻallʼhuman hopes, and it already

did so when " the century of hope " was getting drunk on draughts of extravagant optimism.

The probable explanation of this inconsistency, so far as it was not based on apocalyptic dreams, the aftermath of the ideas of 1789, or on an acutely secularised travesty of Christianity, is that the laws of physics were supposed not to apply to living creatures, or only to some living creatures and not to man. This claim, which I propose to call biologism, is still confidently made, and is supported by genuinely scientific arguments. I must consider it more in detail presently.

Entropy gives us a clear picture of the whole universe slowly running down like a clock, a picture which on the face of it implies a dysteleology of the most absolute kind, an unrelieved pessimism as to the ultimate fate of the world. Spengler calls it a new *Götterdämmerung*, a reference to the well-known Scandinavian mythology, in which the Titans will at last defeat the gods. Our northern ancestors, however, shrank from the last acknowledgment of defeat. The minor gods will be doomed ; but when Odin meets Fenrir, the gigantic -wolf, no one knows what the issue of the fight will be. Our astronomers see no hope for Odin. If he is organic with his world, and has developed with it, Fenrir will devour him, or he will pass into an unblest and never-ending Nirvana, lost to time and use and name and fame. A Buddhist might view this prospect with equanimity ; not so any energetic European or American. The conclusion is not acceptable even to pessimists, who would not be pessimists if they did not condemn the actual by comparing it with a standard which it fails to reach. The Western pessimist, in point of fact, is usually a man who enjoys being pleasantly surprised. Blessed is the man who hopes for nothing, for he will never be disappointed. But here there can be no pleasant surprises, and there is no ideal standard by which to judge annihilation. The theory which science bids us to accept seems to reduce the creation to sheer irrationality. It is not unthinkable or impossible, but it is, in the judgment of many persons, *intolerable*, an argument which Lotze is fond of using. It is, they say, a complete stultification of man as a rational and moral being, who " thinks he was not made to die."

Let us see how scientists and philosophers have reacted against this sentence of death, and what possible loopholes of escape have occurred to them. This discussion will take us into the heart of our subject.

1. It has been said, " Let us accept our doom, which is after all not a very hard one. We know that we have to die ; is it very shocking to hear that the race and its home must one day disappear in like manner ? To Christians at any rate the idea is quite familiar." And how distant the end is ! If a leasehold of a hundred years is practically as good as a freehold, so that the difference in price is negligible, much more is a lease of a million years, which our astronomers will grant us readily enough, to all intents and purposes as good as a grant in perpetuity of the use of our planet. Man recognisable as such has existed on the earth for half a million, or perhaps for a million, years ; but civilisation is a matter of eight or ten thousand years only. *Homo sapiens* is still in the stage of the rattle and feeding-bottle. He has

nearly his whole life before him. There will be ample time to try every possible and impossible experiment in government, in sociology, in economics, in eugenics, in philosophy, and in religion. We do not complain that our own lives last only seventy or eighty years ; why should we be shocked at the idea that a term is fixed to the life of humanity ? *Mortalia facta peribunt ;* such is the law for all that comes into existence.

And yet there is something in us which rises in revolt against this apparently reasonable consolation. Lord Balfour has stated it in a very eloquent passage : " After a period long compared with the individual life but short indeed compared with the divisions of time open to our investigation, the energies of our system will decay, the glory of the sun will be dimmed, and the earth, tideless and inert, will no longer tolerate the race which has for a moment disturbed its solitude. Man will go down into the pit, and all his thoughts will perish. The uneasy consciousness which in this obscure corner has for a brief space broken the contented silence of the universe will be at rest. Matter will know itself no longer. Imperishable monuments and immortal deeds, death itself, and love stronger than death, will be as though they had never been. Nor will anything that *is* be better or worse for all that the labour, genius, devotion, and suffering of man have striven through countless generations to effect."

Much to the same effect Wundt, quoted by Urban, writes : " If we could be absolutely assured of the misery of a descendant living two centuries hence, we should probably not be much disturbed. It would trouble us more to believe that the State and nation to which we belong were to perish in a few generations. The prospect would have to be postponed for several centuries at least before our knowledge that all the works of time must be destroyed would make it tolerable. But there is one idea which would be for ever intolerable though its realisation were thought of as thousands of years distant ; it is the thought that humanity with all its intellectual and moral toil may vanish without leaving a trace, and that not even a memory of it may endure in any mind." Regarding the intolerableness of this conclusion as a sufficient reason for rejecting it, Wundt accepts the validity of " a faith based on a dialectical analysis of the concept of moral end, which shows that every given end is only proximate, not ultimate—is thus finally a means to the attainment of an imperishable goal." [1]

This attitude of mind requires more consideration. Who ever supposed that our species will inhabit the earth for ever ? Is the idea of an unending series of years even intelligible ? Such is certainly not the doctrine of the Great Tradition in Christian philosophy, of which Urban, who quotes Wundt with approval, is such a doughty champion. Nor is it the doctrine of the Bible. I quoted at the end of my first chapter the vision of the end of all things which the author of the 102nd Psalm contemplated undismayed. There are several other passages in the Bible to the same effect. The idea of the end of the world is intolerable only to modernist philosophy, which finds in the idea of unending temporal progress a pitiful substitute for the blessed hope of everlasting life, and in

---

[1] Wundt, *The Principles of Morality*, p. 82.

an evolving God a shadowy ghost of the unchanging Creator and Sustainer of the universe. It is this philosophy which makes Time itself an absolute value, and progress a cosmic principle. Against this philosophy my book is a sustained polemic. Modernist philosophy is, as I maintain, wrecked on the Second Law of Thermodynamics; it is no wonder that it finds the situation intolerable, and wriggles piteously to escape from its toils. The traditional philosophy, which Aquinas and his modern Catholic interpreters base on Aristotle, but which in reality is common to him and to the Platonic school, finds nothing intolerable in the belief that a time will come when the earth will either be burnt up, as the ancients supposed, or will be cold and dead, like the moon. There will then, it need not be said, be no finite mind in space or time which will conserve the memory of human history and achievements. Those who throw all their ideals into the future are as bankrupt as those who lent their money to the Russian or German Governments during the war. Inflation, or a swelled head, will not help them. But the traditional philosophy postulates an eternal and changeless background, which is untouched by whatever fate may be in store for the visible universe.

There are, however, serious difficulties in accepting the idea of a final end of the universe. Plato in the *Timæus* asks whether, even if real existences are not inherently indestructible, it is consistent with God's goodness to destroy what He has made. Would God be *ubique totus*, as Augustine says He is, in a dead world? And if existence is not everlasting, can values be? For whom or in what could they be preserved and manifested ? If God existed alone, says Emily Brontë, every existence would exist in Him. But are non-objectified thoughts complete thoughts ? If during the existence of the universe that existence is necessary as the actualisation of God's will and purposes, can we conceive of anything happening to the Creator to make creation no longer the appropriate expression of His will and thought ? It is true that Augustine repudiates the idea that the creation must reproduce the perfection of the Creator, even in an imperfect medium ; but the difficulty is not removed.

Many have felt that if the creation is a symbol of the Creator, made, as it were, in His image, the eternity of God must have its appropriate image in the perpetuity of the creation. It is the opinion of Whittaker, in his excellent book about Neoplatonism, that the acceptance of entropy as a cosmic law would be fatal to the view of the relation of the phenomenal to the intelligible world which was held by Plotinus. I am not disposed to be quite so dogmatic. The creative will of God may, after the life of our world-order is ended, find expression in forms of which we know nothing, forms which are not set in the framework which we know. Still, it does seem to me to be probable that besides the realm of eternal and absolute values in which the life of God and of beatified spirits has its being " beyond this bourne of time and place," there will always be a created universe which in places is the abode of conscious life. I do not claim that this opinion rests on any evidence. I only say that though God might exist without a world, it is difficult to imagine any reason why He should choose to create a world for a period only, and then destroy it. This, however, raises the question about the status of Time in reality, which will be the subject of a later chapter.

Before leaving those thinkers who accept the doom of the universe, I must notice briefly three writers whose views seem to me quite unconvincing. Ostwald lays great stress on the irreversibility of the Time-process (a point which must be discussed later), and on the parallel irreversibility of valuation and values. I cannot understand what consolation he finds in this, even if it were true. An irreversible process towards greater value on one side, and an irreversible process ending in the final extinction of value and existence on the other side, can hardly be manifestations of the same law. But Ostwald's philosophy of "energetics," which is explained and criticised at length by Aliotta, has, I think, very few disciples now.[1]

William James, quoted by Urban, says: "Though the ultimate state of the universe may be its vital and physical extinction, there is nothing in physics to interfere with the hypothesis that the penultimate state might be the millennium. The last expiring pulsation of the universe's life might be—I am so happy and perfect that I can stand it no longer." This ridiculous passage is one of many which make me wonder at the high place which some distinguished philosophers, including even Whitehead, are still willing to assign to William James. The penultimate state of a dying world has been vividly pictured in H. G. Wells' *Time Machine*. Of course, if James meant that value is independent of Time, and that

[1] Bavink, however, says that "this school of thought is represented in England by Rankine and Karl Pearson."

continuance in Time adds nothing to value, he would have been at least intelligible ; but we know that he meant nothing of the sort.

The third writer who must be mentioned here is Bertrand Russell, to give him the name by which he is known to the world. His essay on " A Free Man's Worship " is beautifully written, though it does not leave much room either for freedom or for worship. It is a Promethean defiance of the cosmic process, which Huxley, in his famous Romanes Lecture, also bade us to " resist." Victor Hugo's theatrical swagger in the same posture is pilloried by Frederic Myers. Man is to renounce all hopes, and live as φυγὰς θεόθεν καὶ ἀλήτης. Like Lucretius, Russell accepts calmly the sentence of *mors immortalis*. These sonorous lines of the Roman poet are referred to by Ovid, and were evidently famous in antiquity :

> Quorum naturam triplicem, tria corpora, Memmi,
> tres species tam dissimiles, tria talia texta
> una dies dabit exitio, multosque per annos
> sustentata ruet moles et machina mundi.

Kant also faces the possibility of final failure ; but for him moral values are indestructible ; we are still within " the realm of ends." " Si fractus illabatur orbis, impavidum ferient ruinæ." His words are : " Even if it should happen that owing to special disfavour of fortune, or the niggardly provision of a stepmotherly nature, this will should wholly lack power to accomplish its purpose, if with its greatest efforts it should yet achieve nothing, and there should remain only the good will, then like a jewel it would still shine by its own light, as a thing which

has its whole value in itself., Its usefulness or fruitfulness
can neither add nor take away anything from this value." [1]

But Lotze protests against " the sham heroism which
glories in renouncing what no man has a right to renounce." " Sham heroism " is rather severe ; if the
evidence seems to point to a disastrous conclusion, it is
right to look it squarely in the face, and summon up all
the resources which Stoicism can supply. But is not this
really the attitude of those who " against hope believe in
hope ? " Does it not imply an implicit faith like that of
Job ; " though he slay me, yet will I trust in him ? "
It is either this, or a literary pose like that of Victor
Hugo, who pictured himself bidding defiance to a God
of Whose character he, Victor Hugo, cannot approve.
The step from the sublime to the ridiculous is here a very
short one. Russell's attitude would be very fine, if he
only realised that the " ought to be " which he cherishes
as an impossible ideal is not created or imagined by the
human mind, but envisaged by the intelligence or spirit,
the divine part of our nature. This, however, would
entail rather drastic changes in his view of reality.

But really these heroics are uncalled for. The real is
not so unsatisfying as we are asked to believe. The sense
of spiritual want is a witness to our relation with spirit ;
we are organic with the world, constituent parts of what
Russell and others would have us condemn as hostile to
ourselves. Those who judge the world harshly generally
start unconsciously with the assumption that the pleasure
or happiness of man is the sole object of creation. As a

---

[1] From the *Grundlegung zur Metaphysik der Sitten*.

pleasure garden this world is a failure ; but it was never meant to be a pleasure garden.[1]

2. There are some men of science who frankly admit that they see no way out of the impasse. Eddington, in his justly popular book, *The Nature of the Physical World*, says that the Second Law of Thermodynamics " holds the supreme position among the laws of nature." " If your theory is against this law I can give you no hope ; there is nothing for it (your theory) but to collapse in deepest humiliation." And yet this law is for him a unique exception to the view of the universe which as a physicist he accepts. For physics, every law is theoretically reversible ; the law of entropy is unilinear and irreversible. " So far as physics is concerned, Time's arrow (pointing in one definite direction) is a property of entropy alone." There is, of course, a very strong *a priori* improbability in a solitary exception to all other natural processes. Some scientists, however, are not content to leave it in this unique position.

Eddington sees that his irreversible law postulates a date at which either the contents of the universe were created already in a state of high organisation, or at which pre-existing entities were endowed, improbably enough, with those energies which they have been squandering ever since. An obvious difficulty is to account for the avowedly most " improbable " position at which the dissipation of energy began. It is rather strange to see physicists resorting to what they call " randomness," or even, frankly, " chance," [2] as an explanation. Alexander

[1] Cf. Radhakrishnan, *An Idealist View of Life*, p. 56.

[2] Eddington, *The Nature of the Physical World*, p. 77.

also speaks of the " restlessness of Space-Time," another quasi-personification of this strangest of Gnostic æons. Although Braithwaite [1] approves of this characterisation of entropy as the " randomness of the universe," and mentions without protest Eddington's analogy from the shuffling of a pack of cards to all infinity, my intellectual conscience rises in indignation at the admission of real randomness or pure chance into the nature of things.[2] Radhakrishnan is surely right when he says that if natural processes are themselves indeterminate, if something like chance is to be put at the basis of ordinary events of nature, all scientific enterprise will have to be abandoned. The illustration from a pack of cards is vitiated by the fact that we are not dealing with infinite time, unless indeed entropy is entirely false as a cosmic law. And if the shuffling has proceeded from all eternity, why did it end later rather than sooner ? There is nothing for-tuitous in the degradation of energy, which proceeds with the regularity of a relentless fate. Are we to believe that this was preceded by random shuffling ?

The working hypothesis of thermodynamics seems to be a naïve deistic doctrine that some billions of years ago God wound up the material universe, and has left it to run down of itself ever since. Suitably disguised, this crude deism is implied in every handbook. It is, accord-

---

[1] In *Mind*, October, 1929.

[2] Mathematicians say that the idea of " randomness " is forced upon them by the quantum physics, and that they do not wish to commit themselves to " chance " as an ultimate principle. But I think they should make up their minds about this. The question is ably discussed by F. R. Hoare in *Philosophy*, October, 1932.

ing to Eddington, one of those conclusions from which we can see no logical escape ; only it suffers from the drawback that it is "incredible." "I can make no suggestion to evade the deadlock," is given as his last word on the subject.

Suggestions, however, follow, which do not seem to me to give much help. He does not feel desperate, because he "would feel more content that the universe should accomplish some great scheme of evolution and then lapse back into chaotic changelessness, than that its purpose should be banalised by continual repetition." I have already commented upon this somewhat unusual state of mind. Most of us acquiesce in the thought of our own death, because we believe that in some sense or other *non omnis moriar*. Even those who do not cherish much hope or expectation of their own personal survival are confident that the interests which give meaning to our life, and the causes for which we labour, will not die with us, but will continue to operate and will, we hope, be victorious. But that the sum of things should end in nothingness is a painful stultification of our belief in the values of life. Of course, all our earthly interests and hopes may be essentially finite in character. This I believe myself. All purposes must be finite, unless they are eternally frustrate. But there may be an infinite succession of finite purposes, each of which when accomplished takes its place in the eternal order. This, however, is not what Eddington wishes us to believe. Continual repetition, he thinks, would bore the Creator. I do not know whether God could ever be bored or not. A man would certainly be bored at having to play an endless succession of games of patience with himself.   But anyhow, eternal inactivity, and the contemplation of " chaos," must, one would think, be more boring than continual creation, or, if we like to put it so, than the spectacle of successive dramas, none of which need exactly resemble what has gone before.

3. But Eddington's real bolthole from a law which is both supreme among the laws of nature and incredible is through mentalism or subjective idealism.   " Entropy," he says, " is of a much more subjective nature than most of the ordinary physical qualities."   Jeans takes much the same line.   The following extract is from an article in *Philosophy*, January, 1932 : " The dictum *esse est percipi* was adopted whole-heartedly—not because scientists had any predilection for an idealist philosophy, but because the assumption that things existed which could not be perceived had led them into a morass. . . . Science studies the behaviour of the phenomenal world in a mathematical way, partly so as to be able to describe and discuss this behaviour with complete exactness, but partly also because it is the only objective way."   Poetry, art, morality are all subjective, secondary qualities ; but all can agree on exact measurements. (This " idealism " begins to look very like the old materialism !)   " A particular kind of mathematical picture is successful, with a kind of success which is not shown by the æsthetic, poetic, or moral pictures of the universe. (Eliminate all values, and the residue will be free from contradictions !)   " Everything has dropped out except purely mental concepts." (Are mental concepts capable of exact measurement ?)   For example, " finite space is most easily understood as a mental

concept ; we can hardly picture it as a physical reality."
(No ; because the mental concept of a limit with nothing
beyond it is self-contradictory ; the contradiction is in
the mind, not in the phenomenal world.) Similarly,
"what can space expand into, except more space ? "
Therefore " we must treat this also as a mere mental
concept." (To say that space is finite, and that it expands
to infinity, looks to me like the enunciation of two contradictory propositions. I have stated this difficulty
lower down.)

This question, whether natural science can reconcile
itself with a philosophy of mentalism, is one of the most
important parts of our inquiry. It must be dealt with at
considerable length.

What is the external world really like ? There are a
good many representations of it which philosophy has
to harmonise if possible. There is the world of naïve
realism, constructed out of our sensations. There is the
world of physical science, which starts from observed
phenomena, but departs more and more widely from the
world as known to " common sense." There are also
the worlds of the artist, the moralist, and the mystic.
The new realists complain that scientists have neglected
the reaction against the idealism of the last century, a
reaction which has endeavoured to reinstate the world of
things—not of uncriticised sense-data, but the world as
known to thought—as having an objective existence
" independent of knowledge." [1] The modern physicist,

---

[1] Joad, *Philosophical Aspects of Modern Science*, p 11. In the pages
which follow I am greatly indebted to Mr. Joad's book, though his
realism is much more uncompromising than mine.

says Joad (he is thinking mainly of Jeans and Eddington) first destroys the everyday world of common-sense objects, and proceeds to attribute the difference between the world of common sense and the world of scientific objects to the constructive agency of the mind. "Thus between physics on the one hand and idealism on the other the common-sense world is dissolved utterly away."

The materialism of the last century was based on naïve realism and belief in mechanism. Reality consisted ultimately of tiny billiard balls called atoms, and a process was understood when a mechanical model was constructed of it. This was the real world; the whole world of values was epiphenomenal, or, as Leslie Stephen put it, "dreams" as opposed to "realities." This simple solution of ultimate problems is obsolete. The world of physical science is so unlike the common-sense world that scientists feel no interest in defending the latter. They have their own interpretation of the universe. And for various reasons, among which the desire of mathematicians to cut themselves clear of concrete facts and work only with symbolic logic is probably the chief, they are playing with Berkeleyan idealism or pure mentalism. Their attitude towards religion and metaphysics is now courteous and friendly; but we cannot help inquiring whether their procedure is legitimate. Personally, I think it is not.

Eddington is at pains to show that our everyday world is "subjective," the creation of our fancy. But the world of the physicist is also phenomenal only; there is behind it a substratum which, he says, is "spiritual." To be real is to be known by mind. The difference between the world of common sense and the world of science seems to be one of degree; sensation tells us much less about reality than mathematics does. In order to discredit naive realism, he takes the conception of " substance," which, he says, has been chased from the continuous liquid to the atom, from the atom to the electron, " and there they have lost it." We shall meet this argument again in what the Professor says about the " annihilation " of matter. I do not believe in the annihilation of anything; I believe, with Epicurus and Lucretius, *nil fieri ex nilo, in nilum nil posse reverti.* The use of the word " spiritual " reminds me of the old Stoic notion that spirit is an ultra-gaseous form of matter.

Mr. Joad shows conclusively that Eddington never distinguishes between " the entities of physics " and our knowledge of them. He nowhere makes it clear whether for him the world of mathematical symbols has any independent or objective reality. Until this ambiguity is cleared up, it is impossible to regard his philosophy as a coherent whole.

I am afraid that this vacillation is imposed upon him by the weakness of his hypothesis. Is a pan-mathematical scheme of reality in accordance with the facts which the physicist has, after all, to include, since they are the starting-point of his science? Sir James Jeans, as we have seen, says that " the secret of nature has yielded to the mathematical line of attack. It has won a success such as is not shown by the æsthetic, poetic, or moral pictures of the universe." If this means that the way to make a true picture of the universe is to abstract from all the higher values, and treat them as non-existent, we can only regret that he accepts such a fatal impoverishment of experience; I can hardly think that this is his meaning. But he leaves us in no doubt about his acceptance of pure mentalism. "The picture is one from which everything has dropped out except purely mental concepts. One physical concept after another has been abandoned, until nothing is left but an array of events in the four-dimensional continuum. Nothing seems to possess any reality different from that of a mere mental concept."

To this two objections may, I think, be made. Some of the difficulties in the way of the theory that God is a mathematician, as Jeans declares Him to be, will be dealt with presently. But are there not some things in nature, such as Planck's quanta, which do not fit into such a scheme? Indeed, are there not many things in nature which defy any rationalising explanation? Are there not many things which must just be taken as irreducible brute fact, such as the existence of the phenomenal world, and, as I should add, the higher values? We really cannot get rid of these surds by calling them mere projections of the mind. If there is one thing which our minds assert with more confidence than another, it is that they are not creations of the will, or fancy, or imagination, but solid objective facts imposed upon us, as we say, from without. Meyerson lays great stress on these "irrationals" or irreducibles. Plato, I think, was well aware of them, for all his love of mathematics; and he deals with them by the way of myth, not of science.

Secondly, I maintain that though pure mathematics is gloriously independent of concrete fact, physics and astronomy are not and cannot be. Further, that when the contradictions are in the mind itself, as when a theory like entropy, which postulates real time, is introduced into a mathematical scheme in which real time has no place, mentalism is no refuge.

But mainly I wish to urge, with all possible respect, that no science which has its starting-point in the objects made known through perception, can logically issue in pure mentalism. I maintain, with Meyerson, that science is fundamentally ontological. Its starting-point is naive realism or common-sense philosophy. It assumes, I mean, that the objects which it studies are real. Very soon it is carried far away from objects as revealed by the senses. It analyses, let us say, a drop of water into H_2O. Then it further analyses the atoms of these two elements into protons and electrons. Sir Arthur Eddington frequently forgets his subjective idealism when he is describing these discoveries. "We see the atoms with their girdles of circulating electrons, darting hither and thither, colliding and rebounding." Of course we do not see them, but Eddington surely means that they are really there. Jeans even says, "The ethers and their waves are the most real things of which we have any knowledge or experience, and are as real as anything can possibly be for us." And yet he tells us that science has been driven to accept Berkeley's *esse est percipi*. Finally, we are bidden to contemplate the possibility that the positive and negative units of electricity may cancel each other. Matter has certainly been defecated to a transparency; there is next to nothing left of it. But Jeans and Eddington are not content with "next to nothing"; they speak of the "annihilation" of matter. Radiation,

however, whatever it may be, is not " nothing." But
taking them at their word, they say that a time will come
when space will be absolutely empty. At the same
moment, " Time's arrow will cease to point " ; in other
words, Time will be empty too. The end therefore is
absolute acosmism or pannihilism, and this will occur at
a definite date in the future, after which, as I have said,
nothing can happen any more.

The last step, from radiation to a purely mental
concept, is, I maintain, illegitimate. From a concrete
object to a mental concept there is no road. Subjective
idealism must not begin with common-sense realism. It
is not true that we know only our own minds. As Mr.
Joad says, " I know less about my own brain and what
happens in it than about any other part of my physical
or mental make-up." If we start from Eddington's
presuppositions, we can know nothing about the external
world at all. But in that case, the natural sciences are
severed from their roots. The physical world of pointer-
readings, Eddington says, must have a " spiritual "
background. Is this background conscious ? If not, and
he says it is not, it is not of a piece with human consciousness. If it is, the quantitative relations and relata which
are the building material for the physical world are what
Clifford called " mind-stuff." But quantitative objects
are not mind-stuff.

When we turn to Sir James Jeans, we find a similar
but not identical philosophy. Jeans is convinced that
nineteenth-century mechanicism has shot its bolt. " The
stream of knowledge is heading towards a non-mechani-
cal reality." One is a little surprised at this animus

of mathematics against mechanics, until we discover that for Jeans the alternative to a mechanical universe is mentalism. "The universe begins to look like a great thought rather than a great machine." If Jeans belonged to the school of William James, we could understand his dislike of mechanics; but the theory which "admits contingency into the heart of things" could hardly be welcome to a mathematician. He even says, "events do not happen; we merely come across them." In that case the Time-series must be theoretically reversible; events are not in Time, though we are. But a reversible world has no special quarrel with mechanics.

The universe, he thinks, was created by a Being with a turn for mathematics; or, alternatively, it is a thought in the mind of the great mathematician. But since in mathematics as in mechanics processes are reversible, how can room be found in a pan-mathematical universe for a creation in time, which is postulated by the unilinear and irreversible law of entropy, towhich Jeans, like Eddington, gives his adhesion? He is favourably disposed to the theistic hypothesis. "The objectivity of objects arises from their subsisting in the mind of some eternal spirit." That is what I believe myself; but how does this aid him in his polemic in favour of mathematics against mechanics? "A universe of spinning-tops, cog-wheels, and thrust-bars fails to explain the simplest phenomena in the propagation of a sunbeam, the composition of radiation, the fall of an atom, or the whirl of electrons in an atom." Can these be *explained* any better by mathematics?

That nature can be exhaustively analysed in terms of

mathematics would be strenuously denied by biologists
and psychologists. I think it would not be going too far
to say that it is demonstrably untrue. And when we come
to the realm of values, the claims of mathematics seem to
be absurd. Towards a solution of our present problem,
the law of entropy, Jeans gives us no more help than
Eddington. And yet the Second Law makes a big hole
in his pan-mathematical universe.

It is easy to understand and to sympathise with the
trend towards subjective idealism which has led modern
astronomers and physicists to their not altogether happy
incursions into metaphysics. Every specialist is anxious
to ward off encroachments upon his preserves by other
sciences. Theology, for example, surrounds itself with a
circle of barbed-wire entanglements, the real object of
which is to keep the enemy's guns out of range of the
citadel. The vigorous controversy between " mechanicists " and " vitalists," to give them the names fastened on
them by their opponents, has no other origin. A pan-
mathematical or pan-mechanical world leaves no room
for the phenomena in which biology, psychology, and the
study of the imponderable values are interested. And
these studies, on their side, threaten to introduce confusion into any mechanical system. Besides this, the
physicist and astronomer are almost obliged to minimise
the importance of life and mind in the cosmic scheme.
The very existence of our earth and its inhabitants, with
all their thoughts and theories about the universe, their
science, their philosophy, and their religion, is, from their
point of view, an accident, and a very strange accident.
The chances against the emergence of a planetary system

attached to a star have been roughly estimated at 100,000 to one. There was a time when Jeans thought that the splitting up of our solar system into sun, planets, and satellites may be a unique phenomenon in the whole universe. " Viewed from a strictly material standpoint," he says in *The Mysterious Universe*, " the utter insignificance of life would seem to go far to dispelling any idea that it forms a special interest of the great Architect of the universe." While we confine ourselves to the interpretation of the phenomenal world in and for itself, the physicist and astronomer are obliged to relegate life to a very subordinate position. It is the rarest of accidents in a lifeless universe. This conclusion is as unwelcome to the scientist as to anyone else. He feels that this cannot be the last word about reality. Accordingly, he is very ready to accept what the materialists of the last century denied, that the natural sciences are after all an abstract study, and that, in the words of Jeans, " all discussion of the ultimate nature of things must necessarily be barren unless we have some extraneous standards with which to compare them." I have given reasons for thinking that mentalism is not the way of escape. It ends by discrediting the very researches which are among the special glories of our time. The correspondence between pure mathematics and one important aspect of the physical world is evidence, not, I think, that we ourselves have put mathematics into nature (this Kantian view is much approved by many men of science), but that our minds are of a piece with the intelligence which created (not merely thought of) the universe.

Since writing these paragraphs, I am delighted to

find that Whitehead agrees. " A favourite solution is to maintain that the molecules and ether of science are purely conceptional. . . . But if there are no such entities, I fail to see how any statements about them can apply to nature. The current answer is that though atoms are merely conceptual, yet they are an interesting and picturesque way of saying something else which is true of nature. But surely if it is something else that you mean, for heaven's sake say it. Do away with this elaborate machinery of a conceptual nature which consists of assertions about things which don't exist in order to convey truths about things which do exist. Scientific Laws, if they are true, are statements about entities which we obtain knowledge of as being in nature; and if the entities to which the statements refer are not to be found in nature, the statements about them have no relevance to any purely natural occurrences. . . . The electrons are only hypothetical in so far as we are not quite certain that the electron theory is true. Their hypothetical character does not arise from the essential nature of the theory in itself after its truth has been granted." [1]

I have followed Joad in some of his criticisms of Eddington and Jeans as disciples of Kant and Berkeley. The alternative philosophy which he advocates is a pluralistic realism. He defines the issue clearly on page 192 of his book. We may hold either (A) that sense-experience, scientific knowledge, and mystical consciousness are three different ways of knowing a reality which is fundamentally the same; or we may hold (B) that there

---

[1] *The Concept of Nature*, pp. 44 *seq.*

is one way of knowing what are in effect three different orders or realms of reality. On the first hypothesis reality is a unity, and sense experience, scientific knowledge, and mystical consciousness reveal it to us under different aspects; on the second, reality is plural, and different reals are revealed to what in all types of experience is essentially the same faculty of knowing or apprehending. Joad accepts the second (B) of the two theories of knowledge.

The uncompromising realism of his position is shown by such utterances as these: " Knowledge, I am convinced, does not in any way contribute to the nature of its objects." " The features of significance which we discern in things are in no sense dependent upon the mind that discerns them." " The only logical alternative to the annihilation of the individual soul is to maintain its complete otherness from that which it contemplates." " The mind achieves a nobility from its capacity to be swayed by reverence for that into which there enters no element of self."

Joad's opinion is that all our experience comes to us through the same faculty of knowing and apprehending, but that there are different orders of reality. The world as known to science is objectively real, and so is the world of values. They must not be allowed to discredit each other. This demarcation of territory is very convenient, but the problem remains how these different reals are related to each other; for they must be related. I think also that he treats the perceiving mind too much as a kind of photographic plate on which " real" objects are registered. He is very suspicious of the mystical claim that at the summit of knowledge the knower and the known are unified. But surely the mind expands *pari passu* with the things which it perceives and knows. The " Soul," to use the language of the Platonists, is no stable register of events ; it is in a sense (not in the mentalist's sense) the creator of the world. " Degrees of reality " mean mainly degrees in the apprehension of reality as a kingdom of values; and these values are not merely exhibited to the soul as something outside and alien to itself ; they are, and increasingly become, the life of the soul, which as it ascends to the spiritual world, finds the absolute values less and less external to itself. The division between subject and object is never wholly transcended in experience ; but the externality of the spiritual mode of experience has ceased in beatified spirits. A complete correspondence of the subject and object of knowledge is eternal life. This doctrine, which is the most precious part of Neoplatonism, I have explained at length in my book about Plotinus. It is the philosophy of mysticism, with which Joad has a good deal of sympathy. But I think Plotinus could have satisfied him, as he did Porphyry, that it is possible to hold οὐκ ἔξω νοῦ τὰ νοητά without falling into subjective idealism.

3. In my chapter on the Time-philosophies I shall express my doubts whether the fusion of Space and Time, advocated by Alexander and others, gives us much help towards solving the terrible problem of the status of Time in the real world. We are here concerned with the relation of the theory to the fate of the universe. In the January (1932) number of *Philosophy* Sir James Jeans writes : " At first Einstein thought that the closing up

of the universe was like a cylinder, so that in one direction
there was no closing up at all. This one direction he
identified with Time, so that space became finite while
Time remained infinite. Recent work by Lemaître and
others suggests that the cylinder must be replaced by a
cone or horn-shaped surface, with Time for the open
axis. Space is still finite, but it for ever expands as Time
advances. Time has a beginning in the past, but there
is no end in the future, Time running steadily on to
eternity, with the spatial universe expanding all the
time." Is it not plain that in order to bring Time into
the " horn " it has been completely spatialised ? In this
guise it is like a string with only one end, which to me is
an utterly impossible conception. Moreover, since the
universe is (according to Jeans) finite, how can it go on
expanding to eternity ? I wish our authorities had been
a little more explicit about their " expanding universe."
I have ventured to complain of their incorrect use of the
word " annihilation " ; are they not also using " universe "
and " space " in an unfamiliar sense ? They seem to
mean, when they speak of an expanding universe, that
the circumference of the sphere which encloses all the
ponderable matter of the universe is moving further from
its centre ; in other words, that matter is encroaching
upon the surrounding vacuum. This, however, is not an
expansion of the universe or of space, which includes
Lucretius' " void " as well as his " atoms." If it is
answered that this objection depends on the discredited
Euclidean geometry, I have no doubt that the eminent
men whom I am daring to criticise could soon
draw me out of my depth. But I am also utterly

unable to reconcile the " expanding universe " with
" annihilation." [1]

While I was puzzling myself over these questions,
which perhaps would not offer quite the same difficulties
to a trained mathematician, I was much interested to
hear from Professor Piaggio of Nottingham that Einstein
himself in 1931 abandoned his theory of a universe expanding to all eternity, and substituted for it the theory
that the ponderable matter of the universe alternately
expands and contracts. This, if it is Einstein's settled
view, is a revolutionary change, for it means a return to
the old theory of cosmic cycles, which has long attracted
me. Jeans and Eddington say that it is utterly impossible ; but if I may take refuge behind Einstein, I am
content. In that case the universe may be perpetual as
its Creator is eternal ; and there must be some hitherto
unknown agency which counterbalances entropy.

4. Another expedient is to throw doubt on the cosmic
significance of the Second Law. This may be done in
several ways. I shall here crave indulgence for making a
quotation, somewhat abbreviated, from Meyerson,[2] since
the matter is very technical, and I should probably make
mistakes if I tried to put it in my own words. " The

---

[1] Professor de Sitter has lately dealt with the notion that the universe
is expanding. He explains (says a review in *The Times*) the theories put
forward by Einstein and himself, which are not opposed but complementary. The expansion of the universe is postulated to account for the
observed recession of the spiral nebulæ. But Professor Milne has recently
proved that any system of bodies moving at random must after sufficient
time all be moving outwards. This makes expansion of the universe seem
an uncalled-for hypothesis.

[2] *De l'Explication dans les Sciences*, p. 35.

science of thermodynamics may perhaps be brought down to two very general statements, the principle of the conservation of energy and the principle of Carnot (= entropy). Neither of these seems to bring in any material or semi-material image. It cannot be gainsaid that thermodynamics plays a considerable part in general physics, and at one time seemed destined to play a greater part still. It was therefore not unreasonable to hope that the whole of science would approach more and more to this model, so conformable, at least in appearance, to the positivist schema." (By " positivist " he means the philosophy of Comte, opposed to ontology and to the admission of the " irrational," or irreducible, in nature.) " But these hopes have been falsified. Thermodynamics has failed to account for certain phenomena, such as the blue colour of the sky, which the kinetic theory can explain perfectly, and the Brownian movement, which those who use the microscope have known for nearly a hundred years." He quotes from Henri Poincaré, who laments the disappointment of his hopes from the triumph of thermodynamics. But in reality, Meyerson proceeds, " thermodynamics is not less ontological in its essence than any other part of physics, and the contrary opinion is an illusion." The last sentence is plainly true ; there is no justification for Eddington's statement that entropy is more subjective than other parts of science. The former part of Meyerson's statement I must leave to those who are better qualified to discuss it.

More important, or at least more intelligible to the layman in these matters, is the revolt of biology against the mechanical and mathematical picture of the universe.

4 *

(I cannot help connecting these two, in spite of the rejection of mechanicism by Jeans.)

Urban states the problem clearly, though I do not entirely agree with him. " A law of progress is a necessary presupposition of an intelligible history and sociology. But in a world which is growing old progress can be only an illusion, or at best of a very limited significance." A law of " universal necessary progress " is by no means a necessary presupposition of intelligible history. That the progress of humanity, whether it is a truth or an illusion, is " of very limited significance " in the cosmos as a whole, is a conclusion which it is very hard to escape. We can regain the significance of our lives as moral and spiritual beings only by placing them where they belong, in the imperishable world of values.

The biological protest against making entropy the dominant cosmic principle may be summed up in the words of Brunkes : [1] " From our point of view the degradation of energy would prove nothing against the fact of evolution. The progressive transformation of species, the realisation of more perfect organisms, contains nothing contrary to the idea of the constant loss of useful energy. On one side, therefore, the world wears out ; on the other side, the appearance on the earth of living beings more and more elevated, and, in a slightly different order of ideas, the development of civilisation in human society, undoubtedly gave the appearance of a progress and a gain. Only the vast and grandiose conceptions of the imaginative philosophers who erect into an absolute

[1] Brunkes, *Degradation*, Paris, 1908.

principle the law of progress could no longer hold against the most fundamental ideas that physics reveals to us." The last sentence seems to convey a caution against the untenable optimism which might be based on those which go before it. I shall have more to say about the nineteenth century belief in a law of progress in a later chapter. The law of entropy is really fatal to it, in the crude forms which it took in the happier times which are now no more. My only complaint against Urban is that he does not fully realise this. He says epigrammatically, " the world bank is the one bank of which it may be said that if it is ultimately insolvent it has always been so." This is, I think, to confound perpetual survival in Time with the eternal life of the higher values. The world bank may be for the transaction of finite business. This business settled, it may be wound up without bankruptcy.

A much more serious defence of the biological position is that undertaken by Professor J. S. Haldane. He lays stress on the idea of reality as a concrete whole. Now science not only gives us what is admittedly an abstract view of reality, neglecting for its own purpose the values of goodness and beauty, but it analyses every whole which it studies, breaking it up into a collection of parts. It would be possible to analyse the human body into a physico-chemical machine made up of an aggregate of parts. A body so analysed and put together again could do everything but live. The living body, on the contrary, is governed by an activity which is not the activity of any part. " We find in the living body," he says, " definite mechanical structures so arranged as to conduce to the maintenance of normal vital activities, or to

protect normal living structure; but on close examination
these are found to be themselves alive, either partly or
wholly—that is to say, they are constantly being actively
maintained by a co-ordinated activity; and in individual history they have all been originally formed by
co-ordinated activity for which there is no mechanical
explanation.[1] To the same effect, J. Johnston (*The
Mechanism of Life*, 1921) says: " If we regard the laws of
the conservation of energy and augmentation of entropy
as of universal validity, we come to an impasse. For the
latter law tells us that the changes that occur in the
universe tend towards absolute degradation of energy,
and therefore towards cessation of all physical phenomena.
But since there can be no limit to past time, this ultimate
degradation ought to have already occurred, and we
know that it has not occurred.[2] Therefore, the Second
Law is not of universal significance. We must postulate
that it may be reversed, so that in certain circumstances
energy that has become unavailable may again become
available. In living processes the increase of entropy is
retarded—this is our 'vital' concept." (Obviously *re-
tardation* does not answer the objection that it ought to
have occurred sooner, if time had no beginning.)

The quarrel between biology and mechanism is, I
think, much the same as the quarrel between " religion
and science " in the last century, in so far as this was not
based on mere conservatism and prejudice. Material-

[1] *The Sciences and Philosophy*, p. 69.

[2] It is not, however, self-evident that " there can be no limit to past
time."

istic science denied the reality of all that religion cares for. It not only neglected but ruled out of court the values in which the life of religion consists. In the same way, the physico-chemical explanation of life fails to account for those characteristics of living bodies in which investigators like Professor Haldane are interested. There is, as we have seen, a mechanistic biology, as there is a behaviourist psychology; but many biologists, like Haldane and Lloyd Morgan, and, I suppose, most psychologists, say that their opponents simply fail to account for the facts. There are technical aspects of the controversy into which the layman would be wise not to enter. But it is easy to see that the introduction of an unknown and unpredictable agency, whether we call it, in discarded language, " vital force," or entelechy, or the organic, or emergent evolution, must be very disturbing to the biochemist. Fortunately, I am not obliged to take sides in this most difficult question. Biological mechanism, as Bavink says, is consistent with any world-view whatever. What we have to consider in this chapter is whether the organic view of life, as expounded by Haldane, Lloyd Morgan, and others, is incompatible with the Second Law of Thermodynamics as a cosmic principle.

I cannot see that it is so, if we admit that organic evolution is a local, sporadic, and temporary phenomenon. Such it certainly seems to be. The existence of living organisms appears to be confined to a few corners of the universe, during a short episode in their existence. There can be nothing contrary to natural law in the appearance of life under certain conditions, for as a matter of fact it has appeared. Nor should we make much of the fact

that while the general course of evolution is dysteleo-
logical, there has been and is an emergence of higher
values at certain isolated spots. Higher and lower are
value-judgments ; for us men the conditions for " higher
modes of existence " are those which have produced our
noble selves, and which will enable us, for a time, to go
further along the road which we wish to follow. The
scientists whom we are now considering are on much
more dangerous ground when they attempt, as some of
them do, to erect the course of organic evolution, as they
observe it on our planet, in our present geological epoch,
and especially in our own species, into a cosmic principle,
which may be set against the law of increasing entropy.
We have then an alleged law of cosmic progress, which
may be set against the law of degradation. Here we
surely have a flat contradiction. One theory or the
other must be untrue.

Meyerson, as we have seen, argues that the " principle
of Carnot " is " irrational," as it fits very badly into
a mechanical or mathematical scheme. It is irrational
in the sense of being irreducible and inexplicable, a unilinear process which has all the appearance of being
teleological. The same obviously applies to the alleged
law of progress as a cosmic principle. They are both
intractable surds in a physico-chemical or mathematical
universe, and they contradict each other. Are our values
threatened if either of them is true ? My contention in
this book is that the attempt to erect progress in time
into a cosmic principle has failed and must fail ; that
organic evolution gives us very inspiriting prospects for
a long period, but not for eternity ; that the doom of

our present world-order is fixed, for a very distant date ; that for a long period before the final extinction life will probably have to assume simpler and what we call " lower " forms ; that all the religions and philosophies which depend on any other view of the destiny of the cosmos are becoming untenable ; and that the world-view of the Platonist, or Christian Platonist, remains untouched.

Finally, it has been suggested, I think by Boutroux, that this and other physical laws may themselves be the result of evolution, and so that their stability may be contingent and transitory. This is, I suppose, theoretically possible, and Whitehead would probably be willing to accept it.

I have hitherto assumed in this chapter that the unilinear process of entropy is an embarrassing exception to the law of reversibility which holds good in physics generally. But this is not universally admitted. The assumption implicit in Newton's laws is that the elementary processes in Nature are reversible, or would be if they were isolated. An irreversible process would yield an objective criterion of past and future, and this criterion is not needed in a mathematical scheme. If any elementary processes are irreversible, a breach is made in Newton's system. Einstein, I think, believes that the nature of physics is mathematical, and Eddington follows him, while admitting an inexplicable exception in entropy. Bergson, Lloyd-Morgan, and (if I understand him) Whitehead hold that nature is creative—which means that some processes are irreversible. It is said that quantum processes are irreversible, and that the apparent reversibility of the classical processes is only an approximation due to the fact that their irreversibility happens to be negligible.[1] Mr. Whyte suggests the following classification of natural processes. (1) Processes which are reversible, and whose laws can be expressed independently of the age of the system, e.g. gravitational and mechanical motions which do not involve light or heat. (2) Processes which are irreversible, the laws being best expressed in terms of the total time which has passed since some initial state, e.g. chemical combination, growth, evolution, radioactivity, and all changes involving light or heat. Time, then, is negligible for some aspects of physics, all-important for others. If this is so, we seem to be involved in an intractable dualism.

Biologists who refuse to accept the law of entropy as decisive against their theory of organic evolution have more than once told me that I ought to consider the significance of Planck's quantum theory, the essence of which is the rejection of the old adage that *natura nihil facit per saltum*. This theory, or rather, discovery, for it has now won its way to general acceptance, is considered by many good judges more revolutionary even than Einstein's law of relativity. It has driven another nail into the coffin of the old mechanicism; and as entropy is based on the " classical laws," Planck may be said to have proved that the law of entropy is not of universal validity. I have tried to follow this advice; but the utterances of our leading scientists are enough to drive a poor layman to despair. Planck himself says: " There are parts of physics, among them the wide region of the

[1] Born, quoted by L. L. Whyte, *The Future of Physics*.

phenomena of interference, where the classical theory
has proved its validity in every detail, even when sub-
jected to the most delicate measurements; while the
quantum theory, at least in its present form, is in these
respects completely useless." So the old theory is used
for some purposes, the new for others, though they can
hardly both be right. Sir William Bragg says pictur-
esquely: "We use the classical laws on Mondays, Wednes-
days, and Fridays, and the quantum laws on Tuesdays,
Thursdays, and Saturdays." On Sundays perhaps a
truga Dei is proclaimed. So Eddington says: "We have
turned a corner in the path of progress, and our ignorance
stands revealed before us appalling and insistent. There
is something radically wrong with the fundamental conceptions of physics, and we do not see how to set them
right." I suppose we must say with Meyerson, "On
ne peut donc qu'attendre l'avenir." If physicists and
astronomers are honest enough to own that they are
completely stumped, there is not much for a philosopher
or theologian to say. But it is difficult to acquiesce in
final agnosticism—in the verdict *ignoramus, ignorabimus,*
when the subject is the fate of the visible universe.
Meyerson's expedient of adding one more, and then
another, to his long list of "irrationals," irreducible given
facts, leaves the empire of science sadly curtailed. Must
we really, as Jeans seems ready to do, capitulate to
Bergson, and admit that the future is not unalterably
determined by the past? Must we give metaphysical
importance to Heisenberg's "principle of indeterminacy,"
a real wobbling of nature within the limits of "Planck's
constant"? Is determinism, in large scale events, only

a matter of statistical averages ? Is the uniformity of
nature only an instance of the mathematical laws of
chance ? These are concessions which some of our
scientific prophets are willing to make.

As I am not writing for scientific experts (such pre-
sumption never entered my head), I will give a brief
summary of those parts of Planck's popular book, *The
Universe in the Light of Modern Physics*, which throw
light on the dilemma just mentioned, and will then add
such reflexions as suggest themselves to me in connexion
with the subject of this chapter.

All the ideas employed by physics are derived from
the world of sense-perception. But reason tells us that
the laws of nature existed long before there was life on
this earth, and will survive mankind. There is therefore
a real world existing independently of man. Besides the
world of sense and the real world there is a third, the
world of physics, which has a double function—to apprehend the real world and to describe as simply as possible
the world of the senses. Some, however, are chiefly interested in the internal consistency and logical structure
of the world of physics, thereby running a risk of losing
contact with the world of reality. All, however, wish to
find a law which connects the world of sense with the
real world. In times when the physical world presents
a stable appearance, men are confident that the real is
rational ; when this appearance is unstable and confused,
as at present, they fall back on the world of the senses,
and become " positivists." Science, however, recedes
further and further from naive realism, and so becomes
more mathematical.

The principle of uncertainty which is characteristic of quantum physics " seems to imply a surrender of the demands of strict causality in favour of a form of indeterminism." If this step proved necessary, " it would be a disadvantage whose importance it is impossible to overestimate." " As long as any choice remains, determinism is in all circumstances preferable to indeterminism." But " in Heisenberg's principle of uncertainty there is no question of indeterminism." " The element of indeterminism is due to the manner in which the question is asked." The question " is based on corpuscular mechanics," " in wave-mechanics it has no place."

Planck comes to grips with the problem of entropy when he says that all the laws of physics can be divided into two groups, reversible and irreversible. " In the laws belonging to the second group the time-order is of essential importance." " Irreversible events always lead to a definite final state ; the class of reversible events knows neither beginning nor end." " If we wish to introduce unity into the physical view of the universe we must find a formula to cover both these contrasted types of law." Perhaps one group of laws is a derivative of the other ; if so, which is to be considered the more simple and elementary ? Planck decides that the reversible processes are the simpler, the irreversible composite, so that the laws governing them are only roughly valid. The laws governing the irreversible processes seemed to be absolute only because of the enormous number of events of which they are composed. They are statistical averages. Against those who hold that all the laws of nature are only statistical, Planck " considers it necessary to hold that the goal of investigation has not been reached until each instance of a statistical law has been analysed into one or more dynamic laws." " No one doubts that the alleged accidental variations, e.g. of population statistics, are subject to strict causality." (Planck therefore will have nothing to do with such ideas as are advocated in William James' " wild universe.")

Of the two sensational modern discoveries, relativity and the quantum theory, he says that the former falls " within the body of classical physics," of which " it is in a manner the crowning point." But the quantum theory is really revolutionary. As long as the two theories subsist side by side, each valid in some fields and invalid in others, it seems impossible for any cosmological system to be regarded as established. I do not think Planck would agree that his theory has discredited the " principle of Carnot," but only that that principle, which is based on the " classical laws," cannot find room for the new laws. And there, I fear, a layman must be content to leave the question. I am, however, glad to find this great authority saying, " that two opposite substances, positive and negative, should completely neutralise each other is unthinkable." We may therefore dismiss the word " annihilation," as used by our astronomers.

The late Professor Hobson, in his important Gifford Lectures (*The Domain of Natural Science*, 1923), thinks that " the theory of the dissipation of energy is open to the very serious criticism applicable to all statements made about the physical universe as a whole. . . . The range of validity of the principle, even as applied to an isolated finite system, has not really been ascertained. Kelvin

himself expressly excluded living organisms in his statement that it is impossible, by means of inanimate material
agency, to derive mechanical effect from any position of
matter by cooling it below the temperature of the coldest
of the surrounding objects. Moreover, the view is held
. . that the increase of entropy is only a statistical
principle, based upon the laws of probability." He
thinks that " the law of thermal equilibrium between a
black-body and the surrounding medium, obtained by
Planck from thermodynamical considerations, is inconsistent with the total, or almost total, absorption of
energy by the ether." This argument would take me
out of my depth ; it is sufficient here to note that in the
opinion of some good judges the theory of the complete
dissipation of energy conflicts with Planck's discoveries,
and that the latter are better established than the former.

Whitehead, in his *Process and Reality*, bids us to
remember that " the modern quantum theory, with its
surprises in dealing with the atom, is only the latest
instance of a well-marked character of nature. The
theory of biological evolution would not in itself lead us
to expect the sharply distinguished genera and species
which we find in nature. There might be an occasional
bunching of individuals round certain typical forms ; but
there is no explanation of the almost complete absence
of intermediate forms." Nature tried many intermediate
forms—reptiles which looked like birds, and other reptiles
which were almost indistinguishable from mammals ; but
these experiments were scrapped as unsuccessful ; just as
the American marsupials have disappeared, except the
opossum, who lives by his wits. But Whitehead's next

parallel—the ninety-two possibilities for atoms, is more instructive. The absence of intermediate elements implies a unit of definite magnitude, and therefore " discontinuity," which is what Planck asserts.

The familiar principle that nature abhors perpetual motion makes me suspect, against my will, that there may be something which forbids perpetual activity in the universe. If this is so, we must accept creation *ab extra*, or perhaps a series of creations.

Nothing puzzles me more than Jeans' belief that the downfall of mechanicism, over which he almost exults, favours a pan-mathematical theory of the universe. There are, as Meyerson and others have shown, many " surds " in nature, which can no more be explained mathematically than mechanically. It seems to me that this surrender leads logically, not to a coherent mentalism —for a mentalism which accepts acosmism is simply solipsism ;—but rather to utter scepticism, the " as if " of Vaihinger. " There is nothing new or true, and no matter." (If we follow " no *matter* " to the bitter end, we may reach the other two articles of the pan-nihilist creed !)

5. But are we so sure that the Second Law may not be balanced by another process, under which dissipated energy may be recombined and again made available ? Are we sure that there is no creation (say) of hydrogen atoms out of radiation ? A discovery of such a balance between creation and destruction would be extremely welcome to most of us. It would end the necessity for believing in the creation of the universe in Time. It would satisfy our very natural feeling that a perpetual

continuance of the universe would be more in accordance with what we may imagine to be the will of God than its temporary existence and final annihilation. On the other hand, we have the unpleasant experience that every closed system of our construction leaks somewhere. " There is a crack in all that God has made," as Emerson says. Perhaps endless continuance and infinite extension are contrary to the possibilities of Time and Space. We cannot answer the question *a priori*.

The possibility of a counter-movement to that of the degradation of energy has been mooted, it is hardly necessary to say, many times. Aristotle, who before the age of modern science had many followers, believed that " the heavens " are subject to different laws from the " sublunary " universe. Change and decay do not touch them. Even in modern times Hegel thought that we have no right to extend the laws which prevail on earth to the universe of stars. Hegel, as is well known, was reactionary and unwisely dogmatic in these matters. Comte, in spite of his great admiration for Newton, thought it " rash " to extend the principle of gravitation beyond the solar system. Haeckel, in his *Riddle of the Universe*, says the same. The Swedish astronomer Arrhenius, while admitting the universality of the Second Law, thought that rare exceptions may occur, leading to the rebuilding of worlds. He recalls the famous " demon " of Clerk Maxwell. To which Poincaré replies unanswerably that even if this were true, it could only retard the death of the universe. Besides, Maxwell's demon was supposed to be conscious and intelligent ; it is a very different thing to suppose that a reverse movement

5

of this kind could be due to an unconscious and mechanical agency.

Quite lately, Professor Millikan claims to have discovered a rebuilding process in the depths of interstellar space. One of the most remarkable of recent discoveries is that of the " cosmic rays," which are said to be very short and of great penetrative power. These rays, we are told, do not emanate from the sun or from any other heavenly body. The orthodox view is that they are disintegration products ; but Millikan thinks that they are caused by the release of energy in the reconstruction of matter out of radiation. The theory is very attractive, but it seems to have made very few converts. It was decisively rejected by the most influential speakers at the British Association in 1931.[1] I do not know whether

---

[1] Some arguments against it will be found in Jeans, *The Mysterious Universe*, pp. 22, 23, 74-76. And Professor A. S. Russell has lately written (October, 1932) : " Since 1930 there has been a return to the view that the cosmic rays may be terrestrial in origin, connected in some way with thunderstorms. This most prosaic and local theory, contrasting ill with the atom-building or atom-annihilation processes suggested by other workers, was first put forward tentatively by Professor C. T. R. Wilson, of Cambridge, and is now being developed and extended by Professor Lindemann, of Oxford. In thunderstorms there is the possibility that electrons with the enormous energies of a thousand million volts might be summoned into existence, and that such electrons might behave like the penetrating rays." Professor J. B. S. Haldane (*The Inequality of Man*, p. 263) has written in 1932 : " At least two physical alternatives are open. One is the possibility, discussed by Poincaré and others, and persistently ignored by Sir James Jeans, that the universe is a fluctuation, i.e. that it has run down in the past and built itself up again by random processes. Another is suggested by a recent paper of Mosharaffa on the duality of matter and radiation. According to, Mosharaffa's views it seems plausible that a universe where the matter had mainly dissolved

Einstein's new theory of alternate expansion and contraction of "the universe" has any bearing on Millikan's theory. A layman can only say that to all appearance, though no finality has been reached, we have at present no right to believe in any physical agency which in the cosmic process can neutralise entropy.

6. For the sake of completeness, I add some further arguments from Bavink's great work, *The Anatomy of Modern Science*, though they do not appeal to me much. "If we assume a world infinite in space, the levelling of energy in it will undoubtedly take infinite time." (This is not self-evident to me.) "The law of entropy itself contains the express assumption that we are dealing with a finite system closed in itself." (But so we are, for all practical purposes.) "The contents of the entropy law are exhausted by the statement that the free energy of a finite system continually decreases; it makes no statement as to the rate at which this decrease takes place." He tells us that Nernst has enunciated, as the Third Law of Thermodynamics, that the specific heat of all bodies approaches zero at the absolute zero of temperature. The operation of entropy, then, can only approach zero asymptotically. (I imagine, however, that the "approach" will be near enough to extinguish all life, and "the subsequent proceedings" will "interest us no more.")

7. There is only one other way of escape which we need notice. Bradley objects to any philosophy which

into chaotic radiation would proceed once more towards aggregation as did the world of chaotic gas which Jeans believes was the initial state of our present universe."

5 *

exalts the future.   If the gates of the future are open, as
Bergson claims, they are closed to perfection.   Bosanquet
echoes this doctrine in words which I have quoted already,
and adds, " reliance on the future has become an actual
disease."   It follows that if futuristic hopes are found
to be illusory, nothing is lost.   Bosanquet bids us to
give up the coincidence of termination and end, and to
think, not of the last term but of the whole.   " We must
give up," he says, " the whole finite analogy of means to
ends, and fall back on the characteristics of value which
apart from sequence in time and selected purposes attach
to the nature of reality which is perfection."   This is to
detemporalise finality completely.[1]   Fichte, on the other
side, claimed that " not only must the purpose of our
earthly life be realised, but there must be a time in which
it shall be accomplished, as surely as there is a world of
reasonable beings existent in time with respect to which
nothing earnest and rational is conceivable besides this
purpose, and whose existence is intelligible only through
this purpose."

I am in sympathy with the protest of Bradley and
Bosanquet against the popular Time-philosophy, but we
must beware of a monism which leaves Time no significance at all.   This is the objection which modernist
philosophy makes against the school which we are now
considering.

Can we say that since Time does not belong to reality
it does not matter whether entropy is true or not ?   I
have rejected the notion that the life of the universe is

---

[1] *Urban*, p. 362.

comprised in a single unitary purpose. All purposes are necessarily finite, having beginning, middle, and end. An infinite purpose would be eternally frustrate. It may be answered that this is an argument in favour of a creation of the universe in Time and its dissolution in Time, which is what the Second Law seems to indicate. If so, and if we believe Time to be a constituent of ultimate reality, on which I shall have more to say, either there must be other world-orders before and after the one which we know, or there must at last be a will-less God presiding in an eternal slumber over an empty universe. But there is not the slightest reason to think that there is one purpose only in the universe. The notion belongs to the discredited superstition of everlasting and universal progress. We must distinguish between the fate of the macrocosm itself and that of individual objects and lives within it. For the whole, I believe, Time has no significance. The whole is the realm of the absolute values. But the case is different with individuals, whether they are persons or races or civilisations or species or worlds as units. These all have a beginning, middle, and end. Only so can the values of life be actualised and achieved. But whatever may be the truth about the fate of the material universe, all earthly lives, we know very well, are but for a time. They achieve some limited purpose, or fail to achieve it, and then pass away, as far as existence in space and time is concerned. I must consider the status of Time in the real world in another chapter.

My conclusion, then, is that the philosophy of the Great Tradition may view the prospect of " the new

Gotterdämmerung " without deep concern, just because
the fate of its own God is not involved. " Nothing that
really is can ever perish " ; but it is not in Time that all
that has value and true existence on earth is preserved.
Nevertheless, though we have no fear that our higher
values can ever be destroyed, nor the spirits who are the
bearers of them, I prefer to suppose that there will never
be a time when there will be no universe. If, as the
Platonists assert, Time is in the universe, not the universe
in Time, the question answers itself.

But it does seem to me that our astronomers have got
themselves into a philosophical impasse by trying to fit
real Time, and entropy, which presupposes real Time,
into a purely mathematical universe, in which Time has
no place. The Second Law leaves them with an ultimate
acosmism and pan-nihilism. They cannot escape by subjective idealism, because the contradictions are in the
mind itself, and because physics and astronomy are not,
and cannot be, independent of concrete fact, assumed to
be real. This at least is what I have tried to establish in
this chapter.

3

THE PROBLEM OF TIME

THE Great Tradition in Philosophy has always conceived of the spiritual world, the highest reality, as non-spatial and non-temporal. It follows that the solution of the riddle of life in space and time lies outside Space and Time. And yet no philosophy which reduces the world in which we have to live to a meaningless phantasmagoria can be satisfactory.

A philosophical position, says Bosanquet, is definitely characterised by its attitude towards Time. "The problem of Time is the central crux of philosophy."[1] Unless we except the problem of evil, it is the hardest in all philosophy. Augustine knows that he cannot solve it. "Quid est tempus? Si nemo a me quaerat, scio; si quaerenti explicare velim, nescio."[2] His well-known suggestion that Time and the creation began together is intended to answer the question what God was doing before He made the world. A similar solution has been

---

[1] So Bergson says: "Le clef des plus gros problèmes philosophiques est là"; and Eddington: "In any attempt to bridge the domains of experience belonging to the spiritual and physical sides of our nature, Time occupies the key-position."

[2] *Conf.*, XI., 14.

offered by Plato (in the *Timæus*), by Philo, and in modern times by Leibnitz, Renouvier, and others. But I am afraid it does not really remove the difficulty. We shall see in a later chapter that Christian theology has never been at ease about the creation of the world at a definite date.

In accordance with the fundamental principle of this inquiry, the question " Are Time and Space real ? " comes to mean, " Are they an essential part of the kingdom of absolute values ? " The Great Tradition says that they are the necessary frame in which these values are manifested. Space and Time are important for description and explanation, but not final for interpretation. In themselves, apart from their concrete filling, they are meaningless.

We have been earnestly exhorted by Bergson and Alexander to "take time seriously," and the older philosophers are blamed for not taking it seriously. The controversy thus aroused has drawn attention to certain important differences between Space and Time, differences which have been strongly emphasised by Bergson, for whom Space is only an instrument of description and explanation, incapable of interpreting reality in an intelligible manner, while Time, or Duration, as Bergson prefers to call it, is reality itself. This is to identify being with becoming, though the picture of the world as mere becoming, without direction and without the illusion of progress, is (as von Hügel says) the philosophy of Buddhism. Bergson, however, rightly rejects such a world as destitute of real meaning. This must be considered later. But there are curious differences between

Space and Time which cannot be disputed. For instance, most of us wish to be immortal, but no one wishes to be ubiquitous. The idea of empty Time seems to be unthinkable; that of empty Space (though this has been denied) is not unthinkable. We may dispute as to the amount of value which belongs to duration; but some value it certainly has, unless our judgments of value are erroneous, whereas Space, though a necessary condition for the manifestation of most (not quite all) values, is itself irrelevant to value.[1] The connexion of psychic states and activities has a time-relation but no spatial relation.[2]

In ancient philosophy the question took the form of the problem of rest and movement, which was earnestly debated by the Ionians. Heracleitus, the father of those who believed that all things are in constant flux, had indeed little in common with the evolutionary time-philosophy of the present day. For he believed in a cosmic balance; "the way up and the way down are the same"; the world is an "ever-living fire," which gives back all that has been consumed. All things are held together by a tension like that of a bent bow or a strung lyre. There is therefore a principle of stability behind the flux, a directing wisdom which "wills and wills not to be called by the name of Zeus." Parmenides conceived of reality as something like the "matter" of nineteenth-century physicists. It never began to be; it never changes; and it has no "secondary qualities."

---

[1] Herbart's "intelligible space," in which "substances come and go," is not really spatial.

[2] Windelband, *Introduction to Philosophy*, p. 98.

The real is a finite, motionless, spherical, continuous plenum. Nothing comes into existence or passes out of it. It seems to follow that change and movement are not even the appearances of anything real. These two opposing philosophies, if their doctrines have been rightly reported, belong to the infancy of speculation; they state in violent disagreement two aspects of the truth. Plato was perhaps the first to grapple seriously with the problem of reconciling them.

Plato says in the *Timæus* that Time came into existence " with the heavens " ; the World-Soul therefore had no beginning in Time. " When the father and creator saw the creature which he had made moving and living, the created image of the eternal gods, he was glad, and in his joy determined to make the copy still more like the original ; and as the original was eternal, he sought to make the universe eternal, so far as might be. But to bestow this attribute in its fullness upon a creature was impossible. So he resolved to have a moving image of eternity, and when he ordered the heavens he made this image eternal but moving according to number, whereas eternity itself rests in unity ; and this image we call time. For there were no days and nights and months and years before the heaven was created, but when he made the heaven he made them also. They are all parts of time, and the past and future are created species of time, which we unconsciously but wrongly transfer to the eternal essence ; for we say of him that he was, is, and will be, though in truth ' is ' alone is properly attributed to him. ' Was ' and ' will be ' belong only to becoming in time, for they are motions. That which is

immovably the same is not subject to any of these
states." " Time then came into being with the universe,
and if there shall ever be a dissolution of them they will
be dissolved together. It was framed after the pattern
of the eternal nature, that it might resemble this as far
as possible; for the pattern exists from eternity, and
the created heaven has been, is, and will be, for all
time."

Time, for Plato, is the continuum involved in the
conception of motion ; it cannot be known in abstraction
from motion. I do not think he really contemplates an
end of the phenomenal world, for perpetuity is the
" copy " of eternity. Space is the inert formless matrix
on which forms are impressed. Plato's " matter " ($\H{\upsilon}\lambda\eta$)
is in fact empty space ; his philosophy would not have
been affected by the evanescence of solid matter in
modern physics.

Plato has been accused of transferring timeless values
and meaning out of the world of events altogether by his
separation of the temporal and eternal worlds. I do not
think that this is just. Thought fixes the flow of events,
and unites sections of them in a " specious present,"
which is not, as modern historicists hold, a part of Time,
but is taken out of the time-series altogether, past, present,
and future surviving only in their inner reciprocal relation
of earlier or later. To my thinking, one of Bergson's
chief errors is in not recognising that his " la durée " is
not in Time at all.

Aristotle assumes that just as things and events really
exist, whether we perceive them or not, so Time is independent of our awareness of it. Time is inseparable from

motion or change.[1] We only perceive that Time has elapsed when we see that something has happened.[2] But Time is not identical with change or motion. There are different speeds, but as we compare them, they cannot be different velocities of Time. Time is the numerable aspect of movement,[3] and also of rest; a stationary body may still be in Time, for it is movable though not in motion. Past, present, and future are in Time; things that always are, are not in Time. Aristotle, while bringing the world of forms into closer connexion with the world of change than Plato had done, leaves the former its changelessness. There is no evolution in the macrocosm, and the growth of individuals and of groups has its term, its τέλος, which when it has attained, it becomes a changeless activity.

Plotinus penetrates more deeply into the problem. " Time is the activity of an eternal soul, not turned

---

[1] The question here arises whether, as Hyslop asserts (*Encyclopædia of Religion and Ethics*, s.v. " Change "), the Greeks failed to distinguish between motion and change, having only one word (κίνησις) for the two ideas. I rather agree with Lutoslawski that Plato's extension of κίνησις to include change was " a wonderful anticipation of modern philosophy." The Greek language is not here to be blamed for poverty. Under the general word for change (μεταβολή) are included movement (κίνησις) and change of properties (ἀλλοίωσις).

[2] Lucretius (I., 459-463) agrees :—

> Tempus item per se non est, sed rebus ab ipsis
> consequitur sensus transactum quid sit in aevo,
> tum quae res instet, quid porro deinde sequatur.
> nec per se quemquam tempus sentire fatendumst
> semotum ab rerum motu placidaque quiete.

[3] Gunn, *The Problem of Time*, p. 24.

towards itself nor within itself, but exercised in creation and generation." It is " the life of the soul as it moves from one manifestation of life to another." Time is, in fact, the form of the active Will, and belongs entirely to that sphere of reality in which " Soul " energises. The Soul " desires always to translate what it sees in the eternal world into another form," and therefore " the Soul took upon herself the form of a servant and the likeness of a creature of Time, and made the creation also subject to Time in all things." [1] But neither Soul nor (of course) the higher order, Spirit (νοῦς), is really in Time; Time is rather within them. This is very far from the modernist doctrine of Time as reality. Time for Plotinus is more than the measure of the impermanence of the imperfect; it is the form of willed change—activity directed to some end beyond itself. This is so much the character of Time that in the eternal world, where nothing changes, " movement does not need time." What is real in Time is the potentiality of qualitative change.[2]

Temporal differences " Here " are differences of order or logical development " Yonder." In other words, past and future are real only to our experience as subject to Time; earlier and later correspond to real relations, though in the world " Yonder " these are rather logical than temporal. Differences of quality in the eternal world are polarised into spatial and temporal differences Here.

The conviction which underlies these early speculations about Time is that, as Münsterberg says, " Things

[1] *Enn.*, 3. 7. 11.
[2] See my *Philosophy of Plotinus*, Vol I., pp. 169-187.

have their space-shape, but are not parts of one Space; they have their time-shape, but do not lie in Time." If we take our stand within Time, we cannot overcome the power of Time.[1] Nothing is more characteristic of thought than the power to look at things out of relation to Time, "under the form of eternity." So Greek thought attached primary importance to stability, permanence, the immortal, and in the complete attainment of this it found the distinguishing difference between divine and human life. Plato and all his disciples found in the conceptions which thought uses the permanent forms which have this quality of stability. They constitute a higher world, a kingdom of absolute values, which never changes; but these forms create the world of phenomena, and give a fixed goal to every aspiration.

Modern writers have misrepresented this preference given by the Greeks, and by those who have followed them, to stability over change. It is not true to say that the Great Tradition seizes motion only to arrest and petrify it. After Aristotle, all thinkers made much of potentiality (δύναμις) and actuality (ἐνέργεια). These are really value-concepts, by which alone the meaning of movement can be grasped. If we reject the idea of "intelligible movement," which is not the contradiction of stability, we are left, it seems to me, with directionless movement, unless, indeed, with Alexander and others, we smuggle in some kind of *nisus*, an entirely mystical principle acting within nature itself, which has no place in the idea of becoming as known to inorganic science.

[1] Eucken, *Life of the Spirit*, p. 105.

This mysterious *nisus*, as we shall see, is presented to us as the begetter of Deity. Theism, when expelled by the door, sometimes comes in by the window.

Bradley argues that not only past and future, but direction, is relative to our world. "It is not a self-contradictory supposition that there are beings the direction of whose lives in the Absolute runs opposite to our own. Death would come before birth—the wound before the blow." This idea is familiar to many readers of Lewis Carroll, who have never studied philosophy. I once, greatly daring, read a paper to the Aristotelian Society on the subject, " Is the Time-Series Reversible ? " But Bradley's statement seems almost ultra-Parmenidean. If events could occur in the reverse order, it might be held that we live in a world where nothing ever happens at all; and this, I suppose, is what critics of the Greeks object to when they accuse them of petrifying movement.

McTaggart, who also disbelieves in the reality of Time, holds that though our experience of a temporal series is a misperception, there is a real series, and that there is some correspondence between the two.[1] What seems to us to be direction towards the future is in the real series the direction towards the final term, which is also the whole. This is obviously incompatible with the idea of reversibility, and involves a definite belief in finalism. I do not myself think that a series can be thus summed up in its last term. As Bernard Shaw says, " Shakespeare did not make *Hamlet* out of its final butchery, nor *Twelfth Night* out of its final matrimony."

[1] See Miss H. Oakeley on " The Status of the Past," *Proceedings of the Aristotelian Society* for 1932.

If, however, " the last term " means the full expression of the meaning of a unitary process, his position is nearer that of Royce.

A comparison between Bradley and McTaggart suggests the question whether Royce is right in saying that " Time is the form of the Will." Our temporal form of experience, he says, " is peculiarly the form of the Will as such." [1] Space, he adds, furnishes the stage and the scenery of the universe, but the world's play occurs in Time. Our experience of Time is essentially an experience of longing, of pursuit, of restlessness ; it is this character of finite existence which Indian thought finds intolerable. " Even the Time of physical science gets its essential characters, as a conception, through considerations that can only be interpreted in terms of the Will, or of our interest in the meaning of the world's happenings." That Time is the form of willed change I have asserted in reference to Plotinus ; but we might object that the Will has no necessary connexion with " interest in the meaning of the world's happenings." Our thinking about events in time is intellectual, not conative. For instance, when we try to understand a past epoch by tracing the development of ideas and events within it, the Will is silent. Meaning is one thing, purpose another. There is also an artistic presentation of a time-sequence, as in music. Time, in short, is not exclusively the form of willed change. It is a necessary condition for the manifestation of all the higher values, except when we are engaged in pure contemplation of the eternal, or in

[1] Royce, *The World and the Individual*, Vol. II., p. 124.

the appreciation of immobile beauty, or in working out logical or mathematical problems.

The question whether, if we could see phenomena *sub specie aeternitatis*, we should find that Time had vanished, is not easy to answer. The dualistic solution of positing two worlds, one changing and temporal, the other changeless and eternal, was not the real intention of the Platonic philosophy; but this persistent misunderstanding of Plato suggests that the tendency of the phenomenal and the real to fall apart has not been fully obviated in his thought. We might, I think, say that in the view of Platonism, Heracleitus, the prophet of flux, is right from the standpoint of phenomenology, but not of metaphysics. This distinction may be helpful in the course of our discussion.

Christianity, here true to its Jewish antecedents, thought rather in terms of a single cosmic drama than of a cyclic movement; but for many centuries it was more detached from life in this world than the Greeks had ever been. This was not the result of the distinctive world-view which belongs to Christianity as an intellectual system; the cause must be sought in the deplorable condition of Europe during and after the dissolution of the Roman Empire. Christianity had indeed brought the eternal into Time more thoroughly than the school of Plato, or even of Aristotle; but the eternal world, with its ideal values, was now definitely envisaged as a *future* life, and the popular pictures of heaven and hell, as places of future retribution in kind, sucked the vitality out of secular interests more completely than the contemplative life of Greek philosophy had done. Among other things,

6

the idea of permanence in the external world simply disappeared. Mysticism, in which the religion of the Middle Ages [1] found its highest expression, sought simply to rescue the soul from the world of change and chance, and to give it a home in the eternal Now. " Eternity, be thou my refuge," is the motto of all the mystics. But the mystic quest, though it excludes the " practical " life, in the vulgar sense of the word, involves a lifetime of earnest striving, and the stages of the inner ascent (*introrsum ascendere*) require time for their accomplishment. Rest is undoubtedly regarded as the goal of movement ; but the possibility of growth, which means movement, is assumed and acted upon. The more philosophical mystics, like the later Greek thinkers, were aware that movement and stability are complementary ideas, which imply each other. " Only the permanent can change," as Kant says. Movement being identified with change, and change being an inner state of the permanent— Plotinus says that " thought is a kind of movement "— there is no contradiction between stability and movement in the eternal world, where, as Plotinus reminds us, " movement does not need Time." In the temporal world, continuous and regular movement is a form of stability. Change is always within a given unitary whole, the persistence of which through all its changes alone gives those changes any meaning. Christianity, like Platonism, is committed to belief in a supreme Being

[1] I mean the whole period between Augustine and Machiavelli. For most purposes, we ought to distinguish between the dark ages and the middle ages in Western Europe. It is only after A.D. 1000 that we can speak of a Christian civilisation in Western and Central Europe.

who never changes; if this is offensive to modernist philosophy, it cannot be helped. But it is not true that the world of Plato, or of Christianity, is a world in which nothing ever happens. Time is as real as the activities for which it serves as a framework, and these are a manifestation of spiritual reality, a kind of sacrament of eternal life and law. When Hegel rather harshly bids us to " banish from our minds the prejudice in favour of duration, as if it had any advantage as compared with transience," he is really arguing in favour of the Platonic position. For " duration " is only a poor surrogate of the idea of eternity, which assures us, in the words of Plotinus, that " nothing which truly is can ever perish." Nevertheless, I think that Hegel goes too far. Just as perpetuity is the time-form of eternity, so duration is the time-form of whatever values are to be realised in this world. We speak of " survival-value "; and we cannot help thinking that one business of the true, the good, and the beautiful is to preserve themselves in being! But duration must not be identified with the eternal mode of existence. Even the most historical of religions, such as Judaism, are emphatic in asserting that God is not organic with the Time-process. " Before ever the earth and the world were made, Thou art God from everlasting, and world without end." Augustine, whose thoughts about Time are very acute, though he is aware that he has not solved the problem, is very emphatic that God is outside Time. For Him, *futura iam facta sunt*. Time cannot be ultimately real, for the past is no longer, the future is not yet, and the present has no duration. Thomas Aquinas, adopting, though not without

6 *

modification, the idea of eternity as a timeless present which is developed by Boethius, finds the essence of Time in motion numbered by earlier and later—very much like Aristotle's view. I postpone a discussion of his conception of *aevum* till the last chapter, which will deal with eternal life.

Spinoza is of special importance on this subject.[1] In the order of nature eternity is prior to duration, and duration to Time. Duration is "existence so far as it is conceived as a certain form of quantity"; we can measure duration by such convenient standards as the motion of the stars. Time is the measurement of duration by such comparisons; from which it follows that Time is not a real thing, but an *ens rationis*, a mode of imagining duration. Duration itself cannot be ultimately real, since it involves an absolute direction—the unilinear relation of before and after. This, he says, cannot be a quality of the real. The case of extension is different, since any direction in space is reversible. This dislike of irreversible movement is intelligible in a mathematician; we have seen how inconvenient entropy is in a pan-mathematical universe. In the Being of Substance (ultimate reality) there can be no earlier or later, still less any past or future. Thus duration, and *a fortiori* Time, has no footing in the real, though Spinoza admits that we can only "imagine" eternity under the form of duration. A more modern philosopher would hardly regard it as self-evident that a changing thing cannot be real; the controversy about movement in the real world was to come later. But the

---

[1] I have found much help in Hallett's *Aeternitas, a Spinozistic Study* (1930).

arguments by which Spinoza disposes of the reality
of Time are not very unlike those by which Bradley con-
victs it of being only appearance. Bradley, however, is
no Spinozist ; for he demolishes extension even more
summarily.

Duration as experienced—*vécu*, as Bergson says—contains a growing past, an ever-moving present, and a
diminishing future. Direct experience is confined to the
present, which alone can be " enjoyed," in Alexander's
phrase. But the idea of the present is ambiguous and
contradictory. Strictly, it is a mere line with no magnitude, which divides the past from the future. This
moving line can have no content of its own. When we
speak of the present, we mean what modern psychology
calls " the specious present," a not very happy phrase,
first used, I think, by William James. The specious
present is not the present at all ; it is a synthesis of memory
and anticipation with reference to the unitary idea. As
Royce says, the present, in our inner experience, means a
whole series of events grasped by somebody as having
some unity for his consciousness, and as having its own
single internal meaning. We may speak of the present
year, or the present century, or the present geological
epoch. So for Spinoza, our " present," or pure duration,
is composed of a bit of the past which is remembered, and
a bit of the future which is anticipated, and these are
rigidly arranged in an order of earlier and later. It is not
true to say that we regard the present as more real than
the past or the future, but what we perceive comes to
us more vividly and seems to us more trustworthy than
what we remember or expect ; and the specious present, as

our field of action, makes a special claim on our attention. Earlier and later must not be confused with past and future. They remain as the fixed framework of events, whereas past and future have no meaning except in relation to the individual subject, who passes along with the stream of time.

This part of Spinoza's thought about Time pleases me far better than the often-repeated assertions that the past is dead and non-existent, and the future either contingent or, as Broad seems to say, unreal and nothing at all. I am nearer to Bertrand Russell, who says that the difference between past, present, and future can be resolved into differences in our cognitive relations to different events.[1] Then what we call past and future are merely parts of our " elsewhere." We do not suppose, as we travel to Scotland, that Carlisle must pass out of existence before Carstairs can become real; we know that before long, when we return to our duties, we shall pass these stations in the reverse order. Similarly, the years 1900, 1930, and 1940 may be equally real, each holding its fixed position in an unchangeable series. We happen to be moving away from 1930 and towards 1940, just as the earth happens to revolve in one direction and not in the other. I suppose that no explanation can be given of the direction of the earth round the sun, nor of the moon round the earth, a direction which is reversed in the motion of certain satellites, nor of the linear motion

---

[1] Gunn, *The Problem of Time*, p. 312, objects to Russell's view on the ground that " the creative advance of the universe brings new events into being." This is, of course, the point at issue; perhaps the events are not really new, but only appear so as they swim into our consciousness.

of the whole solar system. We cannot therefore expect to explain why we are moving forwards and not backwards through time. When we remember a series of events, we keep its order, but we fix it, taking it out of the time-stream. We turn it into a logical or a teleological series. When we say that God lives in an eternal Now, we mean that reality is a coherent system which may be viewed indifferently from any point within it. We deny the unreality of the past and future. Or, and this is nearer the thought of the mystics, we mean that the consciousness of God is always immediate. He does not remember or anticipate ; He sees. But an event which is intuited immediately is taken out of the time-stream. The specious present embraces a period of Time ; it is not in Time. Our consciousness of the present is our point of contact with supra-temporal existence ; to identify this experience with the moving line which divides past from future is an error. Immediacy belongs to a supra-temporal mode of intuition ; mystical intuition is generally of objects which have little or no relation to Time.

But it may be said that a fact is a series of events linked together as cause and effect, and cause and effect are not reversible. The conception of cause in the or- dinary sense undoubtedly involves the idea of real tem- poral succession. It also involves the idea of a transaction between two things, of which one is active, the other passive. The conception of force, now discarded, belongs to this conception of cause. Force is efficient action exercised by one thing upon another. This conception of causation has been almost driven out of natural science ;

perhaps it would be a good thing if it were driven out of philosophy also. Newton long ago laid it down that "action and reaction are equal and opposite "; and Bertrand Russell (at present, I think) wishes to make a clean sweep of the whole conception of cause. He calls it a relic of a bygone age, and points out that " in astronomy the word never occurs; physics has ceased to look for causes, because there are no such things." It was the realisation that events cannot be causes that led to the Cartesian doctrine that all " efficiency " belongs to God. Berkeley also thought that God is the sole cause.

If earlier and later are reciprocally determinate, the Time-process is not essentially irreversible. The cinema has made it easier for us to imagine movement in the opposite direction. We say that we can alter the future, but that we cannot alter the past. But what does this mean ? Of course we cannot make the past other than it was, and it is equally certain that we cannot make the future other than it will be. This is a mere application of the law of contradiction. But there is no absurdity or contradiction in saying that our past would have been different if our present state of mind were different. Our past could, I suppose, be theoretically built up from our present. If I am a necessary consequent, given the atoms, the atoms are a necessary antecedent, given me. So the eclipses of next year already appear in our calendars. The ultimate ground of any event must be sought in all the rest of reality, future as well as past ; all is part of an intelligible, coherent system.

Does this argument make all change illusory ? The idea of change, as Bradley has shown, is full of difficulties.

It is only true as negating a staticism which would turn Time into a second and incomprehensible spatial system. When we speak of change, we only mean that Time is not the same as Space.

To return to Spinoza. Eternal existence is conceived by him in much the same way as by Plato and Plotinus. Eternal existence is the object of true knowledge, and the objects of true knowledge are individuals which are so apprehended as to be also universals. So for Plotinus in the intelligible world every part represents the indissoluble whole.

There can be no past and future for God, Who lives in an eternal Now. But is the distinction of earlier and later also non-existent for the divine mind? If we assume, with the majority of thinkers, that the Time-process is necessarily irreversible, can we remove the point of reference given by the position in Time occupied by the individual observer, and still retain the successiveness and irreversibility asserted by perception? If we hold that successiveness belongs only to perception, and not to what Spinoza calls "intuitive knowledge," we are left with the bare form of externality, and irreversibility disappears together with Time. If, however, Time and duration are appearances of reality, and we can hardly claim less than this for them, we cannot get rid of them by eliminating all that they stand for.

What is called absolute or objective duration is an attempt to liberate duration from the standpoint of a supposed observer. In history the problem is simplified by considering the past only; history deals not with the relation of past, present, and future, but only with earlier and later. The later is assumed to have a causal dependence on the earlier, and a reversed direction of " Time's arrow " would be dismissed as an absurd notion. This retention of earlier and later is really borrowed from our perception of ourselves as sliding along with the moving focus of experience which we call the present. If this point of reference is removed, will Time still flow ? What would be left of the idea of Time after the elimination of past and future ? Personally, I am content with the distinction of earlier and later, which have no reference to any particular observer, since the relation of earlier and later belongs only to parts of the series which we are treating as a unity. But Spinoza, I think, would accept the destruction of Time, substituting for it a logical order, " the order of the intellect." In this order there is no before or after ; if the premises of an argument are said to come before the conclusion, this applies only to the timeless processes of logic.

I agree with Spinoza and his interpreter Hallett that we cannot even imagine the macrocosm as finite in duration. Time is an inadequate expression of the real world, but not because it is an episode in the life of eternity. As for those who identify eternity with the concrete process of Time, my disagreement with them is complete. Some thinkers of this school even equate eternity with the last stage in the process, so coming near the popular notion that a man who is born into Time on one date, is " launched into eternity " on another. Philosophy can make no terms with such ideas as this.

Time is the arena in which any purpose is achieved or frustrated ; that is its main character as we know it.

Time then belongs to the psychic stage in the hierarchy
of existence. It is as real as the conflict between good
and evil. In our higher activities, and even in the exercise of the moral Will itself, we vanquish Time. We
ourselves, as the Platonists have taught us, have a footing
in both worlds, and we can choose which we wish to live
in. In so far as we live in the temporal, and "mind
earthly things," we are temporal; in so far as we "have
our conversation in heaven," we are eternal—not, however, *the* Eternal, for we never put off our individuality
or merge ourselves in the Absolute. This doctrine, that
we are what we love and care for, is perhaps the central
point in Spinoza's ethics, as it must be, I think, in any
truly religious philosophy.

In a later chapter Hallett, still interpreting Spinoza,
repeats Plato's definition of Time in modern language:
"Time is the phenomenon of eternity." Eternity, the
infinite existence, is imperfectly expressed in duration.
To take Time seriously, as we are now bidden to do, is
not the same as to treat it as an uncriticised *datum*,
accepting it without examination as a metaphysical
ultimate. Hallett finds the source of nearly all modernist
errors in the confusion of phenomenalism with metaphysics. This school talks of " empirical metaphysics,"
taking Time at its face value, and most unjustifiably
supposing that the spiritual world—the κόσμος νοητός
of the Platonists—is " a ghostly apparatus of thought-
objects," or in Bradley's phrase " an unearthly ballet
of bloodless categories." "We are not presented," says
Hallett, " with two reducible interpretations of a single
reality, but with two realities, one of temporal facts and

the other of eternal realities, and also with the necessity of relating them in such a way as to explain the nature of the moral person who mysteriously and necessarily belongs to both realms, and without radical bifurcation." The phrase "two realities" is open to criticism; but Hallett is on firm ground when he says that "the solution is impossible so long as a divorce of fact and value is maintained." Reality and perfection are one and the same. Not only is the higher reason concerned with values, but so is also the phenomenal understanding as it constitutes the world of nature. This contradicts the obstinate error that religion and philosophy deal with values, science only with facts.[1] Valuation is everywhere present. That science, for its own purposes, abstracts from some intrinsic values is evident; but those who make an irreducible dualism between fact and value fail to understand either.

I have followed Hallett in his attempt to bring out the permanent value of Spinoza's thought about time and eternity. This is the most useful way of dealing with the great philosophies, instead of passing summary criticisms on some parts of their systems. It is what I tried to do for Plotinus some years ago. But we may now return to the precursors of the philosophy of movement, in the hope of understanding genetically how the revolt against the *philosophia perennis* came about.

Copernicus and Galileo were pioneers in substituting

---

[1] The indecision of scientific writers on this point is curiously illustrated in Hobson's *Gifford Lectures*. On p. 462 he says rightly, "for a philosopher or a man of science truth is itself a value of the highest kind"; but six pages later he declares that "natural science has no concern with values."

empirical and mathematical science for the idealistic physics of the schoolmen, who were absorbed in the problem how potentiality can pass into actuality. Galileo believed in objective mathematical Time, unilinear and irreversible. Time is independent of our perception of it, and thus has a place, together with the three dimensions of space, in reality. Hobbes held the mischievous notion that the future is unreal. " The present only has a being in nature; things past have a being in memory only, but things to come have no being at all, the future being but a fiction of the mind." [1] Barrow anticipated Newton in his definition " Tempus est quod aequabiliter fluit " ; it does not imply either motion or rest, but runs on whether we sleep or wake. He distinctly makes Time a dimension, to be represented always by a straight line.

For Newton, real Time is a homogeneous entity, independent of events or motion ; we try to measure it by the heavenly bodies, without being sure that they exhibit perfectly equable motion. But we cannot doubt that absolute motion exists, since it is present to the Divine mind. It is not strange that this idea of absolute Time, so supported, was attacked by Locke. Locke distinguishes mental Time and physical Time, a distinction which perhaps had never been so clearly made before ; but he contents himself with saying that the two methods of measurement " I guess vary not very much in a waking man." He " guesses " also that the relations of Time and Space " may afford matter to further speculation," since " such a combination of distinct ideas is, I suppose,

---

[1] Quoted by Gunn, p. 51.

scarce to be found in all that great variety we do or can conceive." Berkeley, in accordance with his general principle, declares that we can form no notion of absolute Time. Time for us is subjective, relative, and private; but for God there is an absolute Time. It is unnecessary to emphasise how completely this last sentence alters the character of his philosophy. There is, he maintains, an absolute standard; there is one real Time; but we have no means of using it as our standard. His view must not be identified with that of the modernists, who deny that there is or can be any uniform standard.

Leibnitz attacks the problem of the everlastingness of the world. If there were no creatures, Space and Time would be only in the ideas of God—by which he does not mean that they would be non-existent, but only that they would not exist as Space and Time. He holds the curious view, which we find also suggested by the astronomer Jeans, that Time may have had a beginning, but no end. He is one of the first to use the argument from progress. If it is the nature of things to grow uniformly in perfection, the universe of creatures must have had a beginning. Time began with the creation of things, but space is unlimited. But though change and duration are real, " Time can be only an ideal thing," because " it exists in instants, and an instant is not even itself a part of Time." [1] His doctrine of the ego as a " windowless monad " gives a peculiar form, not acceptable to those who think as I do, to his idealism. Space and Time are mental entities, private to individual persons, and not part of ultimate

[1] Quoted by Gunn, p. 75.

reality. Space is only the position of bodies in relation to each other; if the position were reversed it would make no difference. "It is the same," he says, "of Time." He means, I think, that if the world has no beginning or end, earlier and later have no meaning, which I believe to be untrue. Leibnitz probably intends to say that if there is a meaning in Space and Time, it must be found outside Space and Time. This I believe to be true, as I said at the beginning of this chapter.

Windelband says quite truly that the predilection for a finite or an infinite universe is a matter of temperament. Some welcome the idea of eternal rest after labour, of eternal fruition after achievement; others, with Tennyson, desire only " the wages of going on, and not to die." But everlasting rest, if consciousness survives, would be intolerable; and a never-ending struggle condemns the Will itself to the doom of Sisyphus. If we look clearly at them, says Windelband, it is difficult to say which idea is the more intolerable. The paragraph ends with the valuable thought that " things which are certainly real in the finite world of experience become impossibilities the moment they are converted into absolute realities by metaphysics." We only pause at the word " impossibilities," by which he means what is unintelligible and intolerable. The last word which, as I have said before, is a favourite argument with Lotze, depends on the assumption, which we probably have a right to make, that reality cannot be a stultification of our moral and intellectual convictions. In other words, the argument depends on the identification of reality and value. Those who make this identification approach the problems of metaphysics with different presuppositions from those who try to banish ideas of value from their scientific constructions.

The subject of this chapter is not a historical summary of the views held by famous thinkers about Time, but the genesis and implications of the modern philosophy of movement. I cannot therefore follow the debate in all its ramifications. But a few words about Hegel seem necessary, since both sides in the controversy are able to appeal to him. In a deep but cryptic sentence, he says : " The whole of reality is quite distinct from Time, but also essentially identical with it." This dictum indicates a desire on Hegel's part to give Time a footing within reality, which some earlier thinkers had denied to it. It is well known that he was one of the pioneers of the theory of evolution, and he attributes a great importance to history, in which the World-Spirit, which is eternal, " slowly achieves for itself a philosophy." This appreciation of history has been seized on eagerly by Croce and his school, while others have argued truly that Hegel on the whole stands with the Platonists in his estimate of Time and its relation to reality. Hegel certainly did not mean that the logical development of his dialectic corresponded accurately with any concrete historical process. Whether he was careful to preclude this interpretation of his meaning is not so certain. He teaches clearly that there is an eternal Spirit Who gives value and meaning to the Time-process, which is as it were the language of a non-transient and supra-mundane wisdom.

James Ward's criticism [1] of Hegel's teaching on the

[1] *The Realms of Ends*, pp. 468-477.

temporal and the eternal is instructive only as showing how completely an able writer may misunderstand a school of philosophy with which he has no sympathy. Taking as his text Hegel's words that " God is the eternal reality of which the world is the temporal expression," he can think of eternity only as duration without beginning or end. He realises that for Hegel, as for Spinoza, God, as the eternal, is timeless. " Then," says Ward triumphantly, " He cannot be real at all ; He can only be an idea, not a spirit." He assumes as self-evident that the supra-temporal cannot be real, and dismisses with a flat contradiction those who have taught the opposite. He wishes to make this world a " realm of ends " in the pluralistic sense, and condemns Augustine's words that in the knowledge of God " futura iam facta sunt "[1] as " an obvious contradiction." So I suppose St. Paul was talking obvious nonsense when he said, " I, yet not I, for Christ liveth in me."

Lotze has given so much attention to the problem of Time that his arguments cannot be omitted ; but it is very difficult to reduce them to consistency. He insists rightly that the problem is metaphysical, not psychological ; it concerns nothing less than the nature of reality itself. He reminds us—and this is a most important point—that the mind could not arrange events within a specious present unless the mind itself transcended successiveness. The differences within a specious present are qualitative ; the mind " expands its impressions into

[1] I do not think that determinism necessarily follows from these words of Augustine. God may foreknow the future as that which is going to happen, not as that which could not have been otherwise.

a system of spatial and temporal ' juxtaposition '." And yet he feels that this does not do justice to our consciousness of a real succession, which cannot be explained away. Is there any succession in the real, to account for the appearance of succession to us ? Even if reality is timeless, it must be such as to be capable of being translated into temporal succession. " There would be no meaning in the statement that things exist in Time if they were not modified by so existing in a way which they would not be if they were not in Time." Perhaps his clearest utterance on the subject is in his *Three Books on Metaphysics* [1] (1878) at the close of his life. He there says that Time-succession is valid for finite beings, but that God, Who is definitely characterised by him as personal, is timeless. This is the doctrine of the Platonists and of the Great Tradition in Christian philosophy. But Lotze does not adhere to it consistently.

Ever since the Renaissance there has been an increasing tendency to exalt movement and to disparage stability. This tendency has been on the whole antagonistic to traditional Christian teaching, which profoundly distrusts any tendency to entangle the Being of God with the flux of phenomena. The incompatibility of the modernist philosophy of movement with Christianity has become more and more apparent as its advocates have found confidence to develop their principles to their logical conclusion.

It would not be true to say that with the birth of the new ideas attempts ceased to find some fixed and stable principle as a background to the flux of change. It was

---

[1] Referred to by Gunn, p. 131, who, however, dates the book wrongly.

believed that philosophy on the one side, and the laws of nature on the other, provided such a background. Descartes found it in the thinking ego, though in truth it was thought itself, not the individual, to which this stability could be assigned. So we find a revival of Platonism in the hypothesis of " innate ideas." Not only did Spinoza and Leibnitz defend these eternal truths, but the " Reason " of the Deists and of the German *Aufklärung* was a fixed standard of reference of the same kind. With Hegel and Fichte thought claimed absolute sway, but soared away beyond concrete experience ; and presently the historical school, with its relativism, claimed to have overthrown the edifice, and with it the last refuge of immutability. Bradley, who stood forth as the champion of what at the time seemed a losing cause, declared, in a defiantly Parmenidean phrase, that " nothing perfect, nothing genuinely real, can move " ; but Bergson won more votes for his counter-assertion that " duration is the very stuff of reality." If I am not misled by my own wishes, there are clear signs that a reaction in favour of the old philosophy is now approaching.

I shall say more in a later chapter of the belief in automatic predestined progress which was the lay religion of the Century of Hope. Its connexion with the philosophy of movement, which is its rather belated theoretical justification, is obvious. The cosmology which corresponded with the Greek view of finite processes in which the creative power of unchanging ideas was actualised, was the theory of recurrent cycles. Since the circle is the perfect figure, in which the heavens revolve, temporal change must also be circular. The theory of the Great

7 *

Year, at the end of which the heavenly bodies have returned to the same positions which they occupied at the
beginning, is described in the *Timæus*. But the theory
is older than Plato. It has had a long history in Western
Asia, Persia, India, and China. Aristotle, as is well known,
adopts it, and the Pythagoreans and Stoics went further in
fancying that there will be an exact recurrence of events.
We shall be reincarnated some ten thousand years hence,
and shall then act exactly as we are acting now. This idea
favoured a strict determinism, and gave some justification
to astrology, since all events on earth, it was believed,
follow the motion of the heavens. In this form the
theory of cycles is obsolete. In our experience history
resembles itself always, but repeats itself never. But the
idea of a succession of world-orders, a series without a
beginning and without an end, has commended itself to
many thinkers down to our own day. It is maintained
by Origen ; Nietzsche accepted it, and Arrhenius the
Swedish astronomer. I have mentioned already that
Einstein in 1931 was inclined to abandon his theory of an
expansion to all eternity of the sphere which bounds the
universe, and to favour the theory of alternative expansion
and contraction, thus returning, it would seem, on a
much larger scale, to the old dream of a Great Year.

If the Greeks had had a symbol for zero, and that
symbol the sacred circle,[1] would it have made any difference in their philosophy ? As it was, the round o was
their symbol of perfection. Plato says that the circular
orbits of the heavenly bodies must be the work of a good

---

[1] I am told, however, that the invention of this symbol is now attributed to the Greeks, at which period I do not know.

God, because circular motion is the best. Bodies left to themselves move in a straight line (Aristotle wrongly denied this), but the heavenly bodies have not been left to themselves; a " good Soul " directs them and causes them to move in a circle. So, it was thought, human affairs, if they are guided by Providence, must take the same course. According to Theophrastus, who must have known, Plato in his old age repented of having made the earth the centre of the universe, a position to which it had no right.[1]

A Platonist may hope that this theory, rather than that of an irreversible dissipation of energy, may establish itself; but the fate of the universe is not of vital importance to the philosophy of the Great Tradition, which holds that God is not organic with His creation. Empty Time is in any case unthinkable; Space and Time, we may assume, will be the frame of events while there are events, and we cannot even imagine a condition in which there are no events.

The *philosophia perennis* does not claim to have solved the old antinomies which arise from the conception of infinite Space and infinite Time, and the alternative conception of a Space and Time which are not infinite. But it regards this impasse as a confirmation of what I said at the beginning of this chapter, that the solution of the riddle must lie outside Space and Time. The forms of succession and co-existence belong to a world of origin, purpose, and destiny, in which the eternal counsels of God are actualised on a lower plane than that of the

---

[1] Plutarch, *Quaest. Plat.*, 1006.

spiritual world, the realm of absolute values. Why and how this lower world was created are questions which, I am convinced, can never be answered. As Bradley says, only the Absolute could answer them. The created world is for us an irreducible given fact ; but an ultimate fact it cannot be, for it is not intelligible in itself. This is where we part company from modernist philosophy.

In most religions, and very notably in traditional and popular Christianity, confusion has been caused by the crude intercalation of value schemes, transmuted into brute facts or flat historical recitals, into the existential frame. Traditional orthodoxy has never been the creed of philosophers, but of the masses. In order to give them a rough ready-reckoner, good enough for practical purposes, the realm of values was ruthlessly spatialised and temporalised. A theological geography or cosmography, and a theological history, were set in the background of common experience, and presented to the half converted a readily understandable code of conduct, enforced by external rewards and punishments. In this way Time and Space were embedded in the spiritual world, and made the framework of spiritual truths exactly as they are of phenomenal truths, and so " the next world " became merely a revised and corrected edition of this. The decay of this picture-book theology, which was never satisfactory to Christian philosophers, though they accepted it as having a symbolic value, has caused the greatest disturbance in popular religion. If heaven is not in Space, nor eternity in Time, have they any existence or reality at all ? Are they not merely ideal values, which we set before ourselves as desirable ends, without supposing that they exist ? Or alternatively, if the real is supra-temporal and supra-spatial, what reality remains to the world of phenomena ?

The problem is really axiological; it belongs to the philosophy of value; and this does not at all mean that it has no reference to concrete actuality. It is indeed a very practical problem. If we hold that the kingdom of values is spaceless and timeless, can we allow any intrinsic importance to Space and Time, or either of them, without introducing confusion into our view of reality ? The answer might be in the negative if we were considering Space only; but duration, as we have said, does seem to enter into value. Wherever a process is concerned, whenever purpose can be traced, Time is essential. So intimately does the idea of something to be done or realised, not in a moment but gradually and progressively, enter into our idea of value, that we are almost tempted to say that as Plotinus was driven to admit " intelligible matter " into his higher world, so there must be a kind of intelligible Time, χρόνος νοητός, in heaven. This is very different from Bergson's assumption that movement in itself, without direction, is the essence of value and of meaning. Thinkers of this school unconsciously pack the idea of Time with values. They make evolution itself creative, and Time, which is the mere framework in which events happen, they make the warp and woof of reality itself.

Time can be measured only by something other than itself, and this other must be motion in Space. Devices for the measurement of Time by the sand-glass, water-clock, sundial, watches and clocks, are familiar. For

longer periods, the movements of the earth and of the
heavenly bodies have been taken as the standard from
very early times. These, as is now known, are not absolutely uniform ; the solar year is lengthening at the
rate of one minute in several million years. Newton's
system of physics has been proved to be not quite exact.
In this book we are concerned only with the philosophical
implications of these discoveries. Clerk Maxwell long
ago said : " In space there are no milestones ; one part
of space is precisely like any other part, so that we cannot
know where we are. We find ourselves in a waveless sea
without stars, without compass or sun, without wind and
tide, and cannot say in what direction we move." [1]

The protagonist of the new philosophy of movement
is Henri Bergson, who for many years enjoyed a great
reputation, based, I cannot but think, less on the intrinsic merits of his philosophy than on its conformity
with what many wished to believe, and on a brilliant,
persuasive, and lucid style. Bergson offers to liberate
us from two philosophical bugbears—determinism and
intellectualism. It is no wonder that William James,
the great psychologist, whose raids upon metaphysics
are animated by a violent prejudice against these two
principles, becomes lyrical in his praise.

For the traditional philosophy, Time, and development in Time, are aspects of events within the universe,
not the containing element in which all reality exists, and
through which it advances. This latter is what Bergson
has been understood to teach. His enemy is the theory

---

[1] Quoted by Gunn, p. 188.

that *tout est donné*, that the future is predetermined. Not
only naturalism, but teleology or radical finalism, which
is only "inverted mechanism," falls under his condemnation. The future is really uncertain—not merely unknown to us; "its gates are always open." Reality is
a ceaseless springing up of something really new; contingency, as James Ward boasts, "has been admitted into
the heart of things." William James is not afraid of the
word "chance," an idea with which the newest physics
is beginning to coquet.

Nothing is more distinctive of Bergson's thought than
his sundering of Time and Space, which earlier philosophy
had closely joined. (Spinoza, it is true, gives "extension"
a higher rank in reality than "duration"; in this few
have followed him.) We have seen that, according to
Bergson, Space is only an instrument of description
and explanation, unintelligible in itself, and incapable
of making the world intelligible.[1] Time, on the other
hand, is not only real but the only reality. The key to
all intelligibility is the absolute nature of Time. Bergson
identifies being with becoming.

All depends on the credentials of this conception of
Becoming, thus exalted to the supreme throne in the
hierarchy of reality. Bergson falls back on *intuition*. We
have, he says, an intuitive knowledge of pure becoming.
This seems to be simply untrue. We have no intuition
of becoming apart from direction; and direction is what
Bergson wishes to eliminate. Apart from direction, mere
sequence has no meaning and no value. To use the

[1] See p. 72, and Urban, *The Intelligible World*, p. 248.

language of ancient philosophy, the only movement which the mind grasps is "intelligible movement," the passage of potency or potentiality into act. Here we are obviously in the region of values, and we may say that without valuation, without the introduction of values which are not to be found in movement as such, movement has no meaning. We are in fact threatened with a new mythology. "Time," says Guyau, "is too often made a sort of mysterious reality designed to replace the old idea of providence, and made almost omnipotent." [1] Time without direction is unintelligible, and Space by itself is equally unintelligible.

The famous *élan vital* is mere indeterminateness, the chaotic activities of James' "wild universe," whose incalculable behaviour administers a series of shocks even to its Creator. The extreme crudity of this doctrine of flux may be realised best by a quotation from his enthusiastic English disciple, Wildon Carr. "Reality is a flowing. This does not mean that everything moves, changes, and becomes; science and common experience tell us that. It means that movement, change, becoming, is everything that there is; there is nothing else. You have not grasped the central idea of this philosophy, you have not got the true idea of change and becoming, until you perceive duration, change, movement, becoming, to be reality, the whole and only reality." [2] It seems hardly credible that any trained philosopher should thus make an absolute out of the abstract form of change or move-

[1] So Janet protests: "Time is not really destructive, conserving, or creative, and should not be divinised, as it is by Bergson." Gunn, p. 245.

[2] Carr, *Henri Bergson*, p. 28.

ment taken by itself, and I should not think it fair to make Bergson responsible for all the extravagances of his disciples.

" Creative evolution " has been revived in England under the name of emergent evolution ; it is advocated by Lloyd Morgan, Alexander, and others. Philosophically there is no objection to it, as long as it is recognised that it is a process *within* the whole, not a movement *of* the whole. There is nothing contradictory in the idea of changes within an unchanging whole ; the alternative would be petrified immobility. The objections to making " emergent evolution " a cosmic principle seem, to me at least, quite fatal ; but they are based on what we know of the actual facts of nature, in which involution is as common as evolution.

In a later chapter I shall show what great confusion has been caused by the failure to distinguish between two wholly different and mutually contradictory meanings of evolution—the idea of a mechanical unpacking of what was there, at least in germ, from the first, and the idea of real change, growth, and progress. At the root of the controversy about the status of Time in reality is a revolt against the former conception of evolution, which, it is said, excludes the phenomena of *life*. Modernism in philosophy is so determined to rectify this error that it wishes to make life the ultimate category. This really means making the biological categories world-categories. The enormous difficulties under which this philosophy labours leap to the eyes. It threatens to throw all mathematical physics into confusion ; it makes the conditions which are found to exist for an (astronomically) very short period in one corner of the universe normative for the whole ; and it introduces the unintelligible idea of a changing and " progressing " Absolute. We shall be on safer ground if we say that biologism does justice to certain facts of experience for which mechanism fails to account. How to reconcile it with the fundamental principles of physical and mathematical science is a problem of which the solution is not yet in sight.

Bergson thinks that Newton was in error in making Time a homogeneous medium (*tempus est quod aequabiliter fluit*). This, he thinks, is *spatialised* time. His " real Time," or duration, is " wholly qualitative multiplicity, an absolute heterogeneity of elements." But this, I maintain, is not Time at all ; nor can we know " absolute heterogeneity," with no element of permanence. If life is only change, there can be nothing which changes, and nothing to change, since if there were anything to change, change would not be everything. He never seems to distinguish between Time as it is and our awareness of it. In other words, he makes psychology do duty for ontology, and yet he cannot dispense with ontology, for he believes in objective evolution. Subjective idealism is incompatible with belief in an absolute *durée*.

Bergson's attitude towards physical and mathematical science is interesting, and certainly acute. Mechanical explanations, he says, hold good of the systems which have been artificially cut off from the real continuous flux of the world. The essence of them is to assume that the future may be calculated from the past. A perfect intelligence would survey past and future at one glance ; our failure to do this is merely the result of our weakness.

This, says Bergson, is to deprive Time of every vestige of meaning and reality. The Time of science is a homogeneous scheme conceived by analogy to mathematical Space; psychology knows nothing of such a Time. The physicist aims at the complete spatialising of Time; but the philosopher ought not to follow his footsteps. The mathematical form of physical law is thoroughly artificial. The art of measuring is purely human; nature neither measures nor counts. The success of these calculations would be inexplicable if the mathematical order were something positive and objective. Thus he turns the amazing success of scientific method into an argument for scepticism. He strangely regards the mathematical order as the form to which the *interruption* of the evolutionary movement automatically tends; the mind, tired of creating, turns to *calculating!* His disparagement of the intellect prevents him from seeing that the intellect itself creates.

It might be suggested that Bergson's " intuition " is really imagination, and that his philosophy might be classed with the " imaginism " of Froschammer and Fawcett. In any case, I do not think that Aliotta's judgment is too severe. " Bergson's fantastic mysticism reduces the universe to a perennial stream of forms flowing in no definite direction, a shoreless river whose source and mouth are alike unknown, deriving the strength of its perpetual renewal from some mysterious, blind, and unintelligent impulse of nature, akin to the obscure Will of Schopenhauer." At the same time, I think we may be grateful to him for insisting that reality contains an element of unceasing flux or change.

Professor Alexander would not wish to be classed as a Bergsonian, but his famous Gifford Lectures are unquestionably a philosophy of movement. Without displaying, like Bergson, a kind of animus against Space, he makes it quite subordinate to Time. " Time is the soul of Space-Time, with Space for its body." " Space even to be Space must be temporal." " Space must be regarded as generated in Time and by Time." " Time is not a fourth dimension, but repeats the other three." " Space is the trail of Time." He praises Bergson for being the first to take Time seriously ; and when Bertrand Russell says, " a certain emancipation from slavery to Time is essential to philosophical thought ; both in thought and feeling, to realise the unimportance of Time is the gate of wisdom," Alexander retorts by an indignant contradiction. " To realise the *importance* of Time as such is the gate of wisdom." [1]

Out of several views of the nature of Space and Time he prefers that which makes them the stuff out of which events and things are made. The finites are complexes of Space and Time. Things are modes of extension and duration. Physical extension is continuous and infinite ; so is duration. Their infinitude expresses not their uninterruptedness but their single wholeness. There is no empty space ; the vacuum is full of Space-Time! Space and Time are abstractions from Space-Time. The real existence is Space-Time, the continuum of point-instants or pure events. Space and Time are the simplest characters of the world. " Space-Time as a total is absolute and independent of its observers." " Reality and truth

[1] *Space, Time and Deity*, p. 36, etc.

are not identical; the reality is Space-Time." "There are no degrees of truth or reality." "Mind is a complex of Space-Time stuff." [1]

These extracts, short and inadequate as they are, are enough to prove the affinity of Alexander with Bergson, though Bergson would have shrunk from the downright materialism of the last sentence. His is a philosophy of movement, and movement is his absolute. Movement does not involve anything which moves; it is prior to things, which are complexes of movements, and it breaks itself up into these complexes, which it embraces in a single unity. Space is a continuum, because Time secures its divisibility, and Time is a continuum, because Space secures the connexion of its parts. How Time can be held to differentiate the parts of Space I do not understand. Nor do I see how point-instants, which do not move in the system of points, can generate things whose points do move and occupy different Space-Times.

Time, for Alexander, is characterised by duration in succession, by irreversibility, and by transitiveness. Physical and mental Time are aspects of one Time, but "mental Time is a piece of the Time which physical events occupy." It is clear that in his fusion of Space and Time into one absolute he is influenced by the physical speculations of the relativists, especially, I am told, by Minkowski, whom I have not read. But whereas the physicists and mathematicians are content to measure, Alexander gives their measurements a metaphysical significance, as if measurement could determine the nature of Space and Time, a question which lies outside

---

[1] *Space, Time and Deity*, II., 244; and I., 93.

the purview of science when it confines itself to its own domain. This is fully recognised by Alexander. The new theories or discoveries "leave Time and Space and Motion in their ancient reality," and (he adds as a realist), "independent of their observers." But it may be questioned whether the purely physical theory of relativity ought to be brought in to support a Time-metaphysics.

The elevation of Space-Time into an absolute is really mythological. This mysterious pair of Siamese twins is *creative*. It is almost identical with Spinoza's *natura naturans*, and with Bergson's *élan vital*. Reality, for Alexander as for the Italian school, is historical through and through—an agreement, by the way, which shows how right Bosanquet was in saying that the differences between the New Idealists and the New Realists are almost superficial. The categories are, as it were, "begotten by Time on Space." So these two strange entities are really married—a Gnostic sygygy. Time, however, is the "restless" partner, who drives Space to produce, in an ascending scale, life, mind, and Deity. Space-Time, or rather Time-(Space) seems to be simply movement invested with quasi-divine attributes. It need not be jealous of "Deity," who has not yet appeared on the scene, and apparently never will. It is hardly necessary to say that these creative powers do not reside in Space or Time taken separately. They must be added by the hyphen.[1]

[1] I recall the election story of how a popular statesman, recently deceased, put to his audience the question, "What is unearned increment ? Can anybody tell me ? " To which came the devastating answer, " It is just the 'yphen between Joynson and 'icks ! " The unearned increment in the union of Space and Time is enormous.

The objections of Gunn to this marriage of ideas seem to me unanswerable. Time is not directly allied with Space but with events. Space is not dated, but events are. The continuity of Space lies in co-existence, not in succession; there is no succession-element in Space, though Alexander would deny this. The co-existence which is the essential character of Space does not depend on Time at all.

My widest difference from this philosophy comes to light when Alexander says that " the universe is a growing universe, and is through and through historical." We might have thought that F. H. Bradley had finally disposed of the notion that there can be growth or development in the macrocosm. The idea is philosophically self-contradictory, if the universe is the all, for the all cannot grow. Science will have nothing to say to it. Even apart from entropy, which negatives it decisively, there is not a tittle of evidence for it, when we contemplate the world as a whole. The theory of evolution is legitimate when applied to certain parts of the universe, such as the recent history of the species to which we happen to belong. To assume that this local and temporary phenomenon is the primary law of the macrocosm is the extreme of provincialism.[1]

To me at least it is refreshing to turn from this philosophy, with its entirely incomprehensible Absolute

[1] Sheen (*God and Intelligence*, p. 261) says: " The modern God of evolution is nothing but the transfer, without correction, of biological categories to the spiritual world. The laws and methods of one science are not indifferently transferable to another. There is no more reason for applying biology to God than there is for applying music or chemistry, or even mining engineering."

and its resurrection of Clifford's mind-stuff, its God who is the to-morrow that never comes, and its picture of the inhabitants of the world doomed for ever to be the slaves of Time, and so condemned to the doom of Tantalus until the final and irrevocable extinction of themselves, their world, and their God, to the confession of faith with which Bradley concludes his *Essays on Truth and Reality* :

" As regions of mere fact and event, the bringing into being and the maintenance of temporal existence, our world and every other possible world have no value. It counts for nothing where or when such existence is taken to have its place. The differences of past and future, of dream and waking, of on earth or elsewhere, are all immaterial. Our life has value only because and in so far as it realises in fact that which transcends time and existence. Goodness, beauty and truth are all there is which in the end is real. This reality, appearing amid chance and change, is beyond these and is eternal. . . . For love and beauty and delight, it is no matter where they have shown themselves, there is no death nor change. These things do not die, since the Paradise in which they bloom is immortal. That Paradise is no special region, nor any particular spot in time or place. It is here, it is everywhere where any finite being is lifted to that higher life which alone is waking reality."

These eloquent words were written without special reference to any modernist philosopher. But quite recently an able Roman Catholic writer, Mr. Sheen, has criticised *Time, Space, and Deity* in a way which seems to me decisive, both in his earlier book to which I have just referred in a note, and in his *Religion Without God*. I do not follow Sheen in all his opinions. For instance, when he says that " the laws of biology are more universal than those of chemistry, because life is more universal than chemical elements," he is saying what is obviously incorrect. But in dealing with Space-Time as an absolute, he says truly, as I think, that one props up the other, a very insecure foundation for a universe. Time is not empty only because it contains Space, and Space is not empty only because it contains Time. The two " earn a precarious living by taking in each other's washing." [1] The real filling of the system seems to be supplied by the *qualities* that occur in them. Quality, Alexander allows, " is the great mystery " ; but for qualities to be evolved from Space-Time is more like an impossibility than a mystery. The whole system depends on rejecting two elementary facts, viz. that there can be no movement without something which moves, and that the greater cannot come from the less.[2] The former is Bergson's error ; it tries to support itself by the new splitting up of matter into something which no longer behaves like the matter which we know. But the last step, which dissolves matter into pure mental concepts, is quite illegitimate. The second seems to be a residuum of the discredited theory of automatic progress. Finally, Sheen asks, What can we say of a system which makes God a creature, who " owes his being to pre-existing finites ? " Either God

---

[1] This is telling criticism ; but of course Space and Time are actually given to us in close combination.

[2] To which Alexander would probably answer : " the greater always comes from the less."

is greater than man or He is less. If He is greater, the greater comes from the less; if He is less, He is not God. And, treating several other modernist writers as tarred with the same brush, he adds, " language loses its meaning when we call black white, religion a *libido*, God a creature, and man a creator."

It seems almost discourteous to omit any discussion of living philosophers whose reputation stands so high as Whitehead and Broad. But I find both these writers, and especially Whitehead, so obscure that I have thought it best not to attempt to summarise or criticise their arguments. I find, however, towards the end of Whitehead's most difficult book on *Process and Reality*, an excellent passage about " the two notions, permanence and flux." " In the inescapable flux there is something that abides; in the overwhelming permanence there is something that escapes into flux. Permanence can be snatched only out of flux; and the passing moment can find its adequate intensity only by its submission to permanence. Those who would disjoin the two elements can find no interpretation of patent facts." Broad, if I understand him rightly, regards the future as simply non-existent, for God as well as for ourselves. I have already said that I cannot agree with this. Taylor, I think, is right when he says that no events, past or future, are outside God's knowledge, which views all *sub specie aeternitatis*, but with awareness of the order which we call earlier and later.

I have already made a long quotation from Bradley, whom on this subject as on almost every other I find extremely helpful. For him the Absolute is eternal in the fullest sense, exalted above durational existence. But His nature is truly though inadequately expressed in the system of " appearances " among which we live. Bradley escapes from dualism or acosmism by his famous theory of degrees of truth and reality. This, I think, makes his philosophy really a philosophy of values, for there are certainly degrees of value, but it is difficult to attach much meaning to degrees of existence, though there are many degrees in our approach to a true knowledge of existence. In dealing with Time in his *Appearance and Reality*, he insists that however we look at Time it is self-contradictory. " It is so far from enduring the test of criticism that at a touch it falls apart and proclaims itself illusory." These objections are valid only against those who give an absolute reality to Time. He does not deny that it must " somehow " belong to the Absolute. (Bradley's " somehow " is an honest confession of failure to answer the question " how ? " or perhaps a warning that experience contains elements which cannot be rationalised.) I should have welcomed a frank recognition that Time, with its relation of earlier and later, is a fundamental datum which we must accept. It cannot itself be " contradictory," though our attempts to explain it may easily be so ; it cannot be ultimate, for the reasons given by Bradley.

I do not find McTaggart helpful on this subject. He is regarded as a champion of the unreality of Time.[1] But he bases his argument on the assertion that the past is dead and the future unborn, while the present is a line

[1] See a detailed criticism in Taylor's *The Faith of a Moralist*, Vol. I. pp. 112-117.

without breadth.   The conclusion ought, I should have thought, to be pan-nihilism or acosmism.   But he strangely believes that the time-series will go on for ever, or will somehow pass into eternity.   This process, he seems to think, is the result of the gradual and progressive triumph of good over evil.   It is probable that this argument has never before been used by a disbeliever in theism.

Bosanquet has long been one of my teachers.   He resembles Bradley, but shrinks at times from the harshness of the destructive dialectic of *Appearance and Reality*. His famous protest against throwing our ideals into the future tears up the tree of modernism by the root. Equally important is his advice to take refuge from mechanistic determinism, not by going to history, which (as he says) is incapable of a high degree of truth or reality, but to art and religion.   This means that the road of escape is by a value-philosophy ; that the three intrinsic values, Truth, Beauty, and Goodness, are all liberating ; and that while Art and Religion will show us genuine Beauty and Goodness, history will only give us imperfect and distorted Truth.   Critics of Bosanquet have objected that though in our experience of Time we undoubtedly transcend Time, and indeed could not be conscious of Time if we were entirely within the move-ment of Time, yet the Time-experience is an integral factor in the life of the conscious self, and cannot be treated as illusory.   The soul, as Plotinus says, is the link between the temporal and eternal worlds, participating in both.   We must be on our guard against simplifying the problem by treating either Time or Eternity as unreal.

Bosanquet lays his finger on an important point when

he says that the overvaluing of Time is closely connected with a too exclusively moralistic view of the realm of values. Time, it is often said, is the form of the Will, and it is the moral Will which cannot dispense with a real process in Time. Moral goodness, however, is only one of the absolute values. Neither Truth nor Beauty depends on Time to anything like the same extent. Sorley's excellent book on "Moral Value" suffers, I venture to think, from its apparent identification of Value with the pursuit of the moral good, though no doubt the author deliberately limited himself to this one aspect of reality. Archbishop William Temple, who might, I think, be called a Kantian, gives the Will a more central place than Hegel, for example, would allow it, and, for this reason, is suspicious of any philosophy which denies the importance of Time.

Hobhouse, while insisting, in a very valuable phrase, that the distinction between Time and Eternity is qualitative, not quantitative, holds that the special function of Time is to make possible the development of the imperfect to the completion which belongs to it. When a process takes its place in the eternal order, it is not immobilised in endless petrifaction, but is part of a living harmony in which all things are alive and operative. This is not far from Plotinus' picture of life in the spiritual world.[1]

---

[1] Dr. C. S. Myers, in his interesting Hobhouse Memorial Lecture (May, 1932), summarises what he believes to be Hobhouse's position as follows : " Living matter is characterised by an inherent activity different from that inherent in lifeless matter—an activity not blindly mechanical nor involving the expenditure of mechanical activity, viz. *directive*

Royce's Gifford Lectures, on which I have already commented, contain much that is interesting and instructive on the subject of Time. I think, however, that he is too anxious to include what he considers valuable in several divergent philosophies, and that he sometimes vacillates when a clear-cut decision is desirable. His conception of eternity is defective from the standpoint of the *philosophia perennis*. " The eternal insight," he says, " observes the whole of Time and all that happens therein, and is eternal *only by virtue of the fact that it does know the whole of Time.*" This surely makes eternity quantitative, not qualitative. Awareness of the successive stages of a process as a *totum simul* is not enough as a description of the Divine knowledge. Royce in other places admits this. Emphasising as he does the supreme importance of Will and purpose in reality, he thinks that God views the cosmic process as a system of fulfilled purposes. As an advocate of free will, he says that God cannot foresee what a free agent will do. I see no reason why the Divine foreknowledge should preclude human freedom.

There is no writer on the philosophy of religion with whom I am in more general sympathy, and from whom I have learned more, than Friedrich von Hügel. His *Eternal Life* was written during the apogee of Bergson's popularity, and I think von Hügel has read more into the

activity. The system of the whole universe exhibits a diffuse directive activity, but in the living organism it is inherent within the system of the individual. The activities of what we artificially separate as living matter and mind are identical, each comprising the same directive and peculiar mechanical activities. The highest directive activity in the living organism is that of the self."

doctrine of *la durée* than can legitimately be found there.
He finds great value in the scholastic doctrine of *aevum*,
which I shall discuss in a later chapter, and says that the
life of man on his temporal probation is lived mainly on
this intermediate plane between the " pure simultaneity
of God " and " mere clock time." If I am right,
Bergson's " duration " has already been taken out of the
Time-flux ; it is an axiological category. This explains
why it is that through our consciousness of duration we
rise to the understanding of eternity. The reality and
meaning of the temporal world lie in the fact that through
temporal events the eternal values are displayed and
externalised. Our existence here is inescapably durational ; but in the spiritual life there is a strong *nisus* or
ἔφεσις to reach the supra-durational form of eternity
itself. When von Hügel says that " Time is the abstraction of unachieved purpose," he recalls the view of
Hobhouse.

Eucken, in his verbose but excellent books, constantly
reverts to his central thesis, the autonomy of the spiritual
life, as a higher stage of being to which we may attain
even while we live here. The doctrine of Time which
belongs to this fundamental principle is not unlike that
of von Hügel.

Urban points out that denial of the reality of Time
always follows and results from a conviction of its unim-
portanc· from a metaphysical or religious point of view.
This supports us in the belief that the problem is really
axiological at bottom. The question may be put in this
form. Do the eternal values, or any of them, positively
require Time for their actualisation ? The answer,

already given, is that whereas Truth, as an object of discovery, requires only a logical, not a temporal process, and whereas Beauty, in most of its forms, requires to be appreciated in a specious present, but (if we except music) is mainly spatial, not temporal, moral Goodness, as the aim of the Will, is integrally bound up with real temporal succession.   But is the moral Will active in the eternal world, except as creating values on a lower sphere ? It seems to me that every moral purpose, when fully achieved, passes out of the plane in which morality itself is active.   Time, therefore, belongs to soul-life, not to spiritual life, though the creative activity of the latter is operative in Time.

For the Platonist, the juxtaposition of things in space, and the sequence of events in Time, are symbols of the mutual inclusion and compenetration of real existents in the intelligible world.   Nothing in this world is intelligible without transcending the mutual externality and exclusiveness of points and moments, which the phenomenal world gives us.   Space and Time are, as it were, the " matter " ($\mathring{v}\lambda\eta$) of values.

The notions of omnipresence and a timeless present are obviously and almost deliberately self-contradictory. They are our best attempts to express in spatial and temporal language the inadequacy of Space and Time to characterise reality.   We shall find the same objection to Höffding's " conservation of value."   We cannot conserve what is in its nature imperishable.   But if we remember the limitations of language we may use such expressions —and we can hardly escape using them—without falling into confusion.

In our way of thinking, Space and Time are not intelligible in and for themselves. Their meaning and value are non-spatial and non-temporal. If it is asked how we are aware of non-spatial and non-temporal value, the answer is that we perceive them and know them with as much right and as much certainty as we perceive and know the things of sense. We need not even quote the words of Plotinus about a faculty which all possess but few use; for we all assume that we know non-temporal values, in art, in religion, and in science itself. "The things that are seen are temporal, but the things that are not seen are eternal." Yes; and whenever we think or speak about the things which are not seen, the "imponderables," as Bismarck used to call them in politics, we use the idea of timelessness. As Urban says:[1] "Of the things in Space and Time we say, this thing is outside that, they cannot coincide and amalgamate; this thing comes after that, the former must disappear before the latter arrived. But our minds tell us that there is a large class of objects of which these statements are not true, and the meaning of which are incommunicable in these terms. These things do not interfere with each other. They are alive and active, but they are neither born nor do they die. They are constant without inertia, they are active but they do not move. Our knowledge of this order is as direct and certain as our knowledge of the spatio-temporal order, and we have an idiom to express that knowledge."

The quarrel of the new philosophy with the philoso-

[1] *The Intelligible World*, p. 267.

phical language of tradition is that the latter seems to exalt the permanent and unchanging above the flux of phenomena. I think we must admit that it does. But when we think in terms of value, we cannot help it. Everlastingness is a character of all absolute values. The denial of this eternal mode of existence, by participation in which the world of becoming derives what meaning and value it can have, has made the world seem so petty an affair that modernism has attempted to find in the *future* a new world to redress the balance of the old. Hence the unscientific and unphilosophical myth of universal progress which I shall discuss in a later chapter.

That events in Time are relevant to the eternal order is the belief of Christianity. Things of lasting moment really happen; souls are saved and lost. Whether the eternal mode of existence can really be deflected in any way by happenings in Time, is a question which I shall not attempt to answer. The philosophical difficulties in the way of an affirmative answer are great; but Christians have always believed that in the personal life the consequences of right and wrong conduct on earth are decisive for the condition of souls in eternity. It will be seen that I end this chapter on a note of indecision, though the problem raised in this last paragraph is of great importance.

4

GOD IN HISTORY

I have called this lecture " God in History." Some of our Modernist guides would substitute " God as History." This I consider a very grave error, which has had pernicious effects on the religion of our day. I want to consider first what the real meaning and value of the Concept of Evolution are, and what false ideas have been based upon it ; then, to discuss the kindred idea of Progress, which has been the lay religion of western Europe, especially in England, all through the last century ; and finally to inquire whether any signs of unitary purpose can be found in History.

It is a commonplace that for nearly a hundred years we have used the concept of Evolution as a general framework in which to set our ideas about history, natural science, civilisation, and politics. The idea of evolution has taken possession of philosophy and religion, and has been predominant in all the thought of our time. That it has often been used in an illegitimate manner goes without saying. It has become a favourite catchword, which is brought in to adorn pretentious and thoughtless writing on every subject, though the word " relativity," used with equal want of comprehension, is beginning to displace it.

The word Evolution, or *Entwickelung* in German, appears for the first time towards the end of the seventeenth century, but it did not become popular till the second half of the eighteenth. In the sense of *self-development* it came into use with the growth of the German humanistic movement, to express the soul of reality and the constructive forces of nature. The word is so used by Goethe and Herder. Evolution and Involution are common words in Leibnitz, and the physiologists of that time used them in the sense of the later preformation (or "box") theory. Kant distinguished evolution in the proper sense from epigenesis. It would be well if the nineteenth century had not so frequently confused the two ideas. "The system of generated things" (says Kant) "as mere *educts* is called that of individual preformation or the theory of evolution ; that of generated things as *products* is called the system of epigenesis."

How far was either of these recognised in Greek and Catholic-Christian thought ? By Plato and Aristotle the world was regarded as a living work of art controlled by an unchanging principle of order. Science (ἐπιστήμη) was occupied in bringing this truth into clear relief, in contrast with the passing shapes of mere opinion (δόξα). "Becoming," as such, was an unreal polarisation of true Being, with which alone Science is concerned. The unchanging Forms continue through the whole process of time. The world, they taught, is full of rhythmic but not unilinear movement. Finite movement accomplishes itself, and so, as Aristotle said, things reach their " nature " and then cease to evolve. We can enter into the eternal here and now, because the eternal already exists, and is the true home of the soul. This is the consistent teaching of the Platonic-Aristotelian schools, which passed almost entire into Christian philosophy. It was not intended to deny reality to the world of experience, but only to the flux of phenomena as a passing show. Plotinus in a remarkable sentence says, "All things that are Yonder" —in heaven, we may say—"are also Here." But in response to the hopeless and wretched condition of the world which accompanied the collapse of the ancient civilisation, the idea of permanence took the form of flight from or renunciation of the world of becoming.[1] It was individualised into a craving of the soul to find rest and fulfilment in God, and so, especially in the mystics, the inner journey banished all thought of the progress of humanity. Even in secular knowledge, it was thought, the great men of old had discovered all that was worth knowing, and, as the Christians believed, divine truth had been "once for all committed to the saints."

This almost complete absence in historical Christianity of any idea of evolution in man, and of progress for society, is a matter of great importance for the understanding of Church history. It has been brought out most clearly by Weber and Troeltsch. The great *Soziallehre* of the latter is now at last accessible to English readers. It is no use to look for any ideas of evolution and progress in Christianity before the modern period; they are not there, or are to be found only in the independent sects

---

[1] It is fair to admit that Plato, in certain moods, welcomed the idea of "flight."

disowned by the Great Church. In historical Christianity, down almost to our own day, evolution is purely individual, and is confined to the present life, which is to be followed, perhaps after a disciplinary period of purification, by a *static* condition either of rest and enjoyment, or of unending torment. The great changes are catastrophic, not evolutionary. We can hardly deny that in this view of the world the idea of permanence or stability was overstressed, and the values of change, movement, and progress unduly neglected. I have discussed this in my chapter on the modern philosophy of movement, which in my opinion has gone further astray in denying the existence and the value of permanence or stability altogether. The necessary effect of the modern attitude is to disparage the past; and in religion, instead of St. Paul's exhortation to " grow up *into* Christ in all things," the Catholic Modernists accept the idea of a Church which has grown, almost by a historical accident, *out of* the career of Jesus of Nazareth into an organisation of a kind which He can hardly be supposed to have contemplated while He was on earth.

And yet we must not undervalue the deep tranquillity and security which in earlier times surrounded the Christian, often in the midst of turbulent external conditions. " He to whom time becomes as eternity and eternity as time, is free from all stress." And may we not think of the splendid medieval churches, built not for a time but for ever—" they thought not of a perishable home who thus could build ? " Art, which is the wide world's memory of things, expresses the æsthetic value of rest and permanence ; in painting and sculpture movement is necessarily arrested. Nevertheless, the time came when this over-emphasis on the unchanging was felt to be paralysing. At the Renaissance Western Europe revolted against it. In Eastern Christendom there was no Renaissance and no Reformation—no Renaissance, because there classicism, though senile, had never died; no Reformation, because there a new spiritual awakening meant only a return to monastic asceticism. The conditions were wanting for an outburst of spiritual activity. The western revolt could appeal to one aspect of Christianity, for not only was Jewish thought about the world always based on history and critical events in the time-order, but the Church was built on critical events. The idea of history as a unilinear movement, though it belongs to modern thought, is not alien to the Christian view of the world, which never forsook its Hebrew antecedents.

The idea of evolution in the literal sense, as the unfurling of a scroll on which the eternal purposes of God are inscribed, is frequent in Christian theology. The scientific distinction between evolution and epigenesis did not trouble the old thinkers, because it was then assumed that the direct action of God may either use existing materials or introduce new forces. But the whole course of nature, it was taught, was planned from the first. Augustine's words on the subject are characteristic : " Just as in every seed there were invisibly and at once all that were afterwards to grow into a tree, so we are to consider that the world, as soon as God created all things, had in itself at once all things which were made in and with it. When the day was created, the later products of creation were

9

already there, *potentialiter atque causaliter*." Mystical philosophy, such as that of Eckhart, regarded the world as a differentiation of the Absolute or the Godhead, and so a partial manifestation of His Being. This, on the whole, led to treating phenomena with more respect, as symbolic of eternal truth.

There was, however, something in Christianity, and certainly in the temper of the peoples who accepted Christianity, which prevented them from being satisfied with a pantheistic and static theory of emanations. If the world is comparable to a work of art, there must be an idea or ideas being realised in it. This is rather different from the ancient idea of progress ($\epsilon\pi\iota\delta\sigma\sigma\iota s$ is by no means strange to Plato and Aristotle, and the Stoics laid great stress on self-improvement ($\pi\rho\sigma\kappa\sigma\pi\eta$)). The old teaching, which is an integral part of Neoplatonism, is that all things come from God, and are drawn by a natural longing, conscious or unconscious, to return to God. In this universal upward striving the world has its life. But the "return" is only in inner experience, a progress in the knowledge of God, which means increasing likeness to Him. That remarkable thinker and pioneer of modern science, Nicholas of Cusa (1401-1464) says : " To be able ever to understand more and more without end is to resemble the divine wisdom." " Could a man wish to understand better what he understands, and to love more what he loves, the whole world would not content him, because it could not satisfy his desire to understand." Leibnitz has a more modern sound when he says, " The perfection of all creatures, including man, consists in a strong and unhampered forward impulse towards ever new perfections." Why, men began to ask, should there not be traces of this upward striving in the processes of nature and the history of societies, on a larger scale than the life of individuals ?

So some thinkers came to regard history as the process of the absolute reason. Hegel insisted strongly that the process on which he laid so much stress must be regarded as logical, not temporal or successive. It is certain that he wished to avoid the error, as he thought it, of giving absolute value to succession in time. But it does not seem to me that he quite succeeds, and in any case naturalism was eager to understand him in the sense which he repudiates. The present condition of the world was to be explained by its past history. Reality was essentially an unfinished process. Becoming, not Being, was the essential character of the real world.

We need not here speak of the precursors of the evolution theory, Linnæus (1707-1778), Buffon (1707-1788), Erasmus Darwin (1731-1802) and Lamarck (1744-1829). Lamarck was the inventor of the unfortunate word biology, which ought to mean the science of human society, now described by the barbarous hybrid "sociology." Biology ought to be called zoology, or zoticology (the science of τὸ ζωτικόν). It is more important to note that Lamarckism is not so dead as it appeared to be fifty years ago, though Bavink, who was for a time deceived by Kammerer, thinks that the theory of the transmission of acquired characteristics has now received its death blow.

Charles Darwin came exactly at the right time to put the keystone into the arch. Hitherto organic forms had not been brought within the general law of evolution,

9*

and man in particular still stood outside it. Darwin
supplied a principle which seemed capable of compre-
hending all natural processes under a single law. Having
established the validity of the concept of evolution in
organic life, he made it possible to treat it as a law which
could explain life as a whole. Nevertheless, he wrote
always as a naturalist, not as a philosopher ; he was, I
believe, no more desirous than Einstein is said to be that
his discoveries should be taken out of their proper setting
and erected into laws for the macrocosm.

The confusion which underlies popular ideas of
Darwinism has been mercilessly exposed by F. H. Bradley.
For Darwinism, properly understood, there is no valuation,
no good or evil. It often recommends itself because it is
confused with a doctrine of evolution which is radically
different. Humanity is taken as a real being, whose
history is development and progress to a goal. That
which is strongest on the whole must therefore be good,
and the ideas which come to prevail must therefore be
the right ideas. " This doctrine," says Bradley, " possesses my sympathy, though I certainly cannot accept it.
For good or evil it dominates our minds to an extent of
which most of us, perhaps, are dangerously unaware."
The one criterion for real Darwinism is the abstract
success or prevalence of whatever happens to prevail,
without any regard for its character. This leaves us
with no criterion at all. Nevertheless, Darwin himself
unhappily fell into the confusion. He concluded his
treatise with the words : " We may look forward with
some confidence to a secure future of inappreciable (he
means ' incalculable ') length. And as natural selection

works solely by and for the good of each being, all corporeal and mental environments will tend to progress towards perfection." How little even the greatest men can rise above the fixed superstitions of their age !

This confusion about the meaning of evolution is even more apparent in Herbert Spencer, whose philosophy illustrates in a startling fashion the influences of social and political movements on what should be pure thought. He makes social progress an instance of a cosmic law, and indulges in the most grotesque pæans about the inevitable progress of our species to perfection.[1] An egregious specimen of this language may be found in J. B. Crozier's *Civilisation and Progress.* " The progress of civilisation figures merely as one illustration more of a law that has necessitated alike the formation of solar systems from misty nebulæ ; of mountain and river and meadow from the original murky incandescent ball of earth ; and of the bright and infinite variety of animal and vegetable forms from a few primitive simple germs ; the great law of evolution, whereby all things that exist must pass from the simple to the multiform, from the incoherent to the coherent, from the indefinite to the definite ; the law which while determining that the worm, striving to be man, shall mount through all the spires of form, determines also that human society itself . . . shall eventuate in those complex settled states of modern civilisation where labour is carried to its minutest subdivision and every function finds its appropriate social organ."

The new doctrine of perfectibility, fortified, as was wrongly supposed, by natural science, differed widely

[1] Examples are quoted in my *Outspoken Essays,* Vol. II., p. 163.

from the romantic progressism of writers like Condorcet, and also from the Hegelians, in that the latter placed the human mind above the rest of nature, and found in the logical process of reason the principle of cosmic development. But the naturalists were bound by their own presuppositions to regard human development as part of the blind, non-purposive operation of a mechanical law. It should follow from this that reason itself has been evolved only in response to human needs ; it has no longer any absolute or sovereign authority. Spencer, a non-conformist and an individualist Liberal, could not draw from the survival of the fittest the obvious conclusion that there is no right but might, and that, as Empedocles said, strife, including war, is the parent of all things. He thought that industrialism is in the line of true development, and militarism in the line of retrogression. That the two may be different forms of the same struggle was an inconvenient truth on which he preferred not to dwell.

The universe, according to Spencer, evolved out of a nebula, which is as near *nothing* as he can get. Since everything is evolved out of something simpler than itself, the process ought to begin with an entirely un-differentiated jelly, and the nebula was almost featureless enough for his purpose. His well-known formula is that all development is from " an indefinite unstable homo-geneity to a definite stable heterogeneity." We have already seen that the Second Law of Thermodynamics proclaims a process in precisely the opposite direction, ending in the maximum of homogeneity. But Spencer and his contemporaries were judicially blind to the doom thus proclaimed to their romantic hopes. It is true that Spencer himself was attracted by the theory of recurrence; but the optimism of his generation was too strong to allow him to work this out.

The redistribution of energy, as described by Spencer, gives us really no clue as to the *direction* of the cosmic process. As far as the principle of conservation is concerned, it is a matter of indifference whether we pass from the homogeneous form of heat to other forms of energy, or whether the process is reversed, since in either case it remains unchanged in its totality. For the physicist the world is always the same in its totality, and unchanged in its regular mechanical laws. Mechanism and evolution are two concepts which contradict each other. One asserts quantitative permanence and the determinism of mechanical law; the other qualitative transformation and the genesis of individual forms. Spencer, I think, was not blind to this fundamental difficulty. His recognition of the Unknowable, which in his later years seemed to be taking on the character of the One of Plotinus and the Godhead of Eckhart, showed that he could not picture the order of nature as an entirely closed system.

The strangest assumption of Herbert Spencer and his school was to identify progress with increased complexity of organism. Complexity is often a false step in evolution; irrelevant complexity is a sign of maladaptation. Man is less specialised in some ways than the apes. The modern aeroplane is much simpler than some of the awkward flying-machines which preceded it. Civilised languages are much simpler than savage languages.

There has been a further tendency to call movement in any direction progress. Progress, in the sense of desirable change, is a value-judgment ; no doubt the word may be used without implying change for the better, as when we speak of the progress of a disease ; but this is not the sense in which those who believed in the perfectibility of the species used the word " progress."

From the religious point of view, evolution is only the name of the method by which it has been found that God works. It is neither hostile to religion nor favourable to it ; it merely substitutes belief in regular action for the catastrophic theories of the divine activity which were formerly held. But the philosophical doctrines of determinism, of universal relativism, and of materialism, which were grafted upon it, justly excited the opposition of the religious world. On the other hand, the theory of perfectibility has brought with it an unprecedented emancipation and hopefulness to the human spirit, which confronting no longer a changeless and fixed order, has thrown itself with ardour into the quest of making the world a better place for men and women to live in. It has, in fact, transferred the aspirations of the individual life to a larger stage, with the vision of a perfected humanity in the far future, in place of the hope of the final deliverance of the soul from the trammels of existence in the world of change and chance. This may be admitted, and should not be forgotten when we bring to light the ambiguities and contradictions of the popular conceptions of evolution. I have no wish whatever to pour cold water on the secular hopes of our time. We may look forward to a higher state of civilisation, with a more equitable distribution of the instruments of happiness, than the world has yet seen. But we have here no continuing city, neither we ourselves nor the species to which we belong. Our citizenship is in heaven, in the eternal world to which even in this life we may ascend in heart and mind. There is a sense in which it may be said truly that otherworldliness alone can transform the world.

It is not necessary for the purposes of this book to enter into the controversy about natural selection. Some continental naturalists have spoken, I think with great exaggeration, of the "abandonment" of Darwin's theory.[1] It was pointed out long ago by von Hartmann that " selection can accomplish no positive achievement at all ; it can only operate negatively by exclusion." Driesch and others emphasised the importance of " mutations " —sudden and considerable changes—in opposition to Darwin's theory of the cumulative effect of inherited minimal variations. The controversy is often connected with the old question whether acquired characteristics can be transmitted. Bergson and his followers naturally advocate the Lamarckian *élan vital*, an inner impulse towards change, in opposition to the merely mechanical doctrine of Darwin, which does not admit of qualitative alteration. It must, however, be admitted that for a metaphysician a minimal change is as great a problem as a mutation. We·cannot admit the excuse of the girl who palliated the appearance of her baby by saying that

[1] Bavink (1932) says : " Biology has been returning to natural selection to a greater extent than one would have supposed possible ten or twenty years ago." " Lamarckism has been badly beaten along the whole line."

it was a very small one. The opponents of mechanicism
have, I think, been too ready to assume that mechanicism
excludes teleology. Lichtenberg, in a striking phrase,
says that mechanism may be the teleology of the inorganic. It may conceivably be the teleology of the organic
also, if we hold that there is a divine purpose behind the
regular operation of evolution. The question whether
there is an inner teleology favouring the production of
what we call higher forms is not an easy one. The
Platonists held that there is a *nisus* towards the spiritual
life, unconscious in the inorganic world and partly
conscious in all the varied forms of living creatures. It
is extremely doubtful whether such a *nisus* can be
admitted as a general law of nature.   The so-called
higher forms, when we are below the range of the eternal
values, are superior, from the point of view of the evolu-
tionist, only as long as the environment gives them a
superior survival value. The external conditions may
change—the climate becomes more severe, desiccation
destroys the forests, new enemies appear—and the species
which for thousands of years has been perfecting its
weapons of offence and defence leaves only fossils to
perpetuate the memory of its existence. Instead of the
uniform success of the more highly organised species we
find numerous examples of the reverse process in the
" degradation " (to use a word which is out of place in
biology) of freely moving organisms into parasites ; and
the time will almost certainly come when only the
simpler and less differentiated forms of life will survive,
for a time, amid the rigours of a dying world. The
triumphs of evolution, as we consider them, will then

vanish, and man will follow the dinosaurs and the dodo into extinction. The purely scientific problems will be solved more readily if value-judgments are excluded from them. It is the intrusion of meta-physical idealism which has led to the conception of evolution as a cosmic principle instead of as a useful scientific theory. There cannot be any evolution of the whole of reality. Evolution presupposes the interaction of the environment and the environed ; but there can be no environment of the whole of what is.[1] We cannot think of the whole of reality moving in a unilinear direction, whether of space or time or space-time. The very notion of such a movement, when there is by hypothesis no environment, is meaningless. We do not get rid of this impossibility by saying that Time itself is reality, even if there were no fatal objections to this theory.

As soon as we try to erect evolution into a cosmic principle, we are in the region of the eternal values, which are supra-temporal and supra-spatial. We are measuring change against an eternal background. And when we thus measure the changing against the unchanging, does the changing bear the appearance of a single whole, or a single and uniform process ? I maintain that it does not, and that we have no warrant for assuming a single purpose in the universe. To make this assumption (as Professor Taylor says) would be like supposing with the ancients that all astronomical movements must form a single rhythm with a single period, because each of these separately considered has its periodic rhythm.

[1] A. E. Taylor, *Evolution*, p. 450.

Before leaving the subject of evolution in general, and passing on to the more restricted topic of human progress, it seems necessary to say something about the attempt which is just now popular with some (not all) biologists, to find in the idea of *emergence* a reconciling principle between mechanism and teleology.[1]   I have a great respect for the eminent men who have found this concept valuable ; but I fear it is of no use as a principle of explanation.   It is an attempt to intercalate the value-scheme into the existential.   Values certainly " emerge " —they become visible ; I do not think the word has any place in natural science.   Professor Lloyd Morgan, who borrows the phrase from Professor Alexander, wishes us to " acknowledge " emergent qualities with " natural piety," an unexpected appeal in a scientific discussion.[2] There is no natural piety in using a word which asserts and denies the reality of change in the same breath.   Do the emergents emerge out of what they are not, or are we to take evolution in its earlier and proper sense, of an unpacking of what was potentially there all the time ? The advocates of emergent evolution wish to allow for the appearance of something really new, without surrendering to teleology or breaking too sharply with the mechanicists.   They have, I am afraid, only succeeded in finding an ambiguous word.[3]

[1] W. R. Matthews, *God in Christian Thought and Experience*, p. 146.

[2] I find myself much nearer to Professor Lloyd Morgan, an advocate of " emergence," when at the end of his chapter in *Contemporary British Philosophy* (pp. 304-306) he enunciates a doctrine of the Logos, " of which the evolutionary process is the manifestation."   Here he returns, after all, to Plato.

[3] Urban, *The Intelligible World*, pp. 305-329.

The idea of emergence could be justified on the hypothesis of an external Creator, but not as a natural self-explaining process.[1] It seems to postulate the appearance of something *new* at certain stages of evolution, e.g. when life first appeared. Whether the old canon *omne vivum ex vivo* will continue to be accepted it is not for me to predict; it seems to me very improbable; the gap between living and non-living has, I believe, been very nearly closed. Similarly, with the mutations of which Driesch made so much. They are unaccounted for, and may remain for ever unaccountable; but that they have no natural " causes " few would venture to maintain. Some who love to take refuge in gaps, and temperamentally prefer the indeterminate to the certain, find comfort in the discontinuity of Planck's quantum theory; but here again the assumption of real discontinuity seems to lead to greater difficulties than it solves. Nor is it a legitimate parallel to speak of the emergence of water from oxygen and hydrogen. This is a typical reversible chemical process, quite different from the biological doctrine of emergence. The biologists can only explain emergence by making progress (in a more or less Spencerian sense) a cosmic law, which, as we have seen, it cannot be. Either we must return to the old theory of separate creations, the *fiat* of a divine will, which is an ultimate

[1] Boodin (in *Philosophy*, October, 1931) says: " Materialistic emergence owes its plausibility to antiquated science. The science of to-day makes necessary the conception of cosmic control or cosmic structure. The uniformity of nature is possible only because of the universal cosmic control." " It is not possible to account for the order of emergence on the basis of accident."

cause, or we must give up the attempt to separate life as another order, from those mechanisms with which the inorganic sciences deal. Mechanism may be quite unable to predict or explain the phenomena of life; but some kind of continuity there must be, unless we call in a *Deu. ex machina* to confound the mechanicists. Lotze notices the natural repugnance of the mind to ascribe consistency to the divine activity. We wish, he says, to secure " freedom " for God as well as for ourselves, and so draw a boundary line between nature as the realm of necessity. and history as the realm of freedom.[1] But such boundary lines are worse than suspect.

We pass now to the question of human progress, which may seem to be only a particular instance of the supposed *nisus* of all created things, or all conscious organisms towards a better future. In reality, human progress is the primary assumption, which the scientific theory of development was brought in to support. A popular religion is a superstition which has enslaved a philosophy. In this case the superstition was belief in the perfectibility of the species; the philosophy was a misreading of the biology of Darwin. This biological theory, as we have seen, has in itself no relation to value; the secular religion based upon it is a theory of value, which depends upon the assumption that the more complex is of a higher worth than the simple, and the later in time of higher worth than the earlier.

The idea of progress means the faith that the human race has moved, and will move still further, in a desirable

---

[1] Lotze, *Microcosmus*, Vol. II., pp. 133-135.

direction. But which of the goods which men have regarded as desirable do we choose as our criterion ? Do we maintain that life is becoming more enjoyable ? Is the net surplus of pleasure over pain growing greater ? Or have we some standard of well-being other than the hedonistic ? Are we advancing in intrinsic excellence of body, mind, and character, as Coué wished us to persuade ourselves that we are ? Or is increase in knowledge the test ? Clearly we must have some standard of what is desirable before we can decide whether the changes which we observe in ourselves and our environment can be pronounced desirable or otherwise. Have we before our mind's eye some perfection proper to our species, which when we have attained we can say that evolution, as regards ourselves, has reached its final phase ? Have we ever considered what is the minimum time which would satisfy us in which to enjoy our realised aspirations ? Science now guarantees us ample time; formerly, a prolonged future for humanity on this earth was neither expected nor desired. The intellectual climate has in this respect changed completely.

It is often said that the Greeks had no idea of progress. They put their golden age in the past, we put ours in the future. They were the degenerate descendants of gods; we are the creditable descendants of apes. These epigrams do not express the whole truth. Æschylus has a fine description of the savage state, before Prometheus taught men the arts of living. The myth in Plato's *Politicus* and the opening of the Third Book of the *Laws* may also be remembered. Lucretius may have found something of the same kind in Epicurus; we do not know the source

of his brilliant description of primitive barbarism.   Still,
the prevailing opinion among the Greeks, derived partly
from the poems of Hesiod, who was much revered in
antiquity, was that progress and decadence recur in
cycles ; they believed that they were living in a period
of decline.   In Plato the cycle seems to be (it is not
certain), 72,000 years, equally divided between advance
and decline.   Aristotle thought that all the arts and
sciences have been discovered and lost " an infinite
number of times."   It follows that the cramped chronology
of the Christian tradition was not derived from Greece
or Rome.   The ancients had an outlook into the past
and future as ample as our own.   But they did not
believe in permanent progress as a cosmic principle.
Both advance and retrogression were merely temporary
phenomena, alternating with each other.   This belief
has been advocated in modern times by Goethe, Shelley,
Kierkegaard, and Nietzsche.   It can be called pessimistic only by those who see nothing but evil in the
world they live in.

And yet we must ask why the Greeks believed that
they had happened on a period of decadence.   I suppose
the condition of the cultivators in the time of Hesiod
was really hard, but why were the Greeks of what we call
their golden age not more optimistic ?   Or to put it
differently, for the Greeks were not really pessimists,
why did they believe that there was a truly golden age
in the past ?   The Hebrews had their legend of the
Garden of Eden, but it does not seem to have affected
their religion much.   And they regarded the Fall as a moral
lapse, whereas for the Greeks it was just fate.   I do not

find the question easy to answer. Perhaps they thought
that the existence of a perfect society in the remote past
was a guarantee of a new golden age in the remote future.
The temper fostered by the belief in cycles is not pessimism, but what Clough calls " a Stoic-Epicurean acceptance." "The rational soul," says Marcus Aurelius,
"wanders round the whole world and the surrounding
void, and gazes upon infinite time. It considers the
periodic destructions and rebirths of the universe, and
reflects that our posterity will see nothing new, and that
our ancestors saw nothing greater than we have seen. A
man of forty, possessing the most moderate intelligence,
may be said to have seen all that is past and all that is to
come."

It seems curious that the Epicurean Lucretius, who
describes so brilliantly the ascent of man from savagery,
should not have dreamed of further progress. The fact
that he did not only shows how difficult the ancients
found it to think of Time as a friend. Epicureanism was
notoriously individualistic and devoid of public spirit;
but when Lucretius speaks of the final[1] doom of our
universe, he might, one would think, have allowed himself
to think of a golden age before the ultimate catastrophe.
This, however, was contrary to the general pejorism of
outlook common to him and his contemporaries. And
yet we must not forget the famous Fourth Eclogue of
Vergil, in which the poet expresses confident hopes that
the "Saturnia regna" were about to return under the

[1] A. E. Taylor (*The Faith of a Moralist*, Vol. II., p. 329) shows that
Lucretius (V., 243) did think of a rebirth of the "maxima mundi
membra." His second quotation is a conflation of two passages.

peaceful sway of Augustus. "The world's great age begins anew." "Magnus ab integro saeclorum nascitur ordo." The Christians regarded this poem as an inspired prophecy.

Troeltsch in his great book on the Social Teaching of Christianity has shown very clearly how completely absent the idea of progress was from the mind of the Church until modern times. The idea that we have duties to posterity can hardly be found either in primitive Christian or in Catholic teaching. It is the one point in which we can hardly help admitting that Christian ethics are seriously defective. The omission is the more remarkable when we remember that hope filled a larger place in Jewish than in Greek thought. For the Jews God manifests Himself in history. It is true that there was nothing evolutionary in this conception. The action of God was conceived as catastrophic and arbitrary. As the political fortunes of the nation became more hopeless, the " good time coming " was envisaged more and more apocalyptically, and sometimes flew away from this earth altogether The earliest Christians were Messianists, and expected a " day of the Lord " in the near future. But it was to be prepared for only by repentance and humble waiting upon God. The Hebrew tradition was strong enough to destroy the belief in recurring cycles ; the Incarnation at any rate was a unique event, introducing a new order.[1] But the escape from fatalistic acquiescence secured by this rejection of the idea of recurrence was dearly purchased by the new expectation of an early end of the

[1] See the striking passage from Origen quoted by Christopher Dawson (*Progress and Religion*, p. 156).

world, introduced by Christianity. Even after the practical disappearance of Messianism, which had never been
intelligible to Gentile Christians, the belief that "the
time is short" remained. Nor did it cause any regrets.
If the universe were to be dissolved in ruin to-morrow,
that, for the thought of early and medieval Christianity,
would be a quite acceptable end to a sorry business. We
must remember that for about six hundred years, from
about 500 to about 1100, civilisation was in very truth in
a dismal backwater. The only really civilised city was
Constantinople; and though we have at last learned to
do justice to the Byzantines, their culture produced very
little of permanent value except in architecture. A man
would need to be a very robust optimist to take a cheerful
view of the world in the Dark Ages. War, poverty,
ignorance and violence sum up the salient features of life
at that period.

Roger Bacon lived in the thirteenth century, an age
of brilliant promise and awakening life, if he could have
read the signs of the times. But from the first the Middle
Ages looked back, not forward. After a scathing denun-
ciation of the state of the Church in his day—" the whole
of the clergy (he says) are intent upon pride, debauchery,
and avarice "; " none of the religious Orders can be
excluded from this indictment," he goes on: " With
all our Christian privileges, how do we compare with
the ancients? Their lives were beyond all comparison
better than ours, both in decent living and contempt of
the world, its pomps and vanities, as all may read in
the lives of Aristotle, Seneca, Cicero, Avicenna, Alfarabi,
Plato, Socrates, and others. We Christians have discovered

nothing worthy of these philosophers, nor can we even understand their wisdom." Many, he says (and the thought is often with him), believe that the coming of Anti-Christ must be very near.[1] This attitude is typical of the thirteenth century writers.

The Renaissance thinkers, absorbed in the task of recovering what could be recovered of the lost treasures of antiquity, still looked back rather than forward. A typical example is Machiavelli, whose position was rather like that of Spengler. Human nature does not change ; the same passions have the same results ; but societies have their periods of advance and decay. A nation which has reached the top never stays there, and those which have fallen into ruin may expect to revive.

In the generations which followed the Renaissance we find a different tone. For Englishmen the best-known voice is that of Francis Bacon. He does not seem to have thought much about the distant future ; the modern notion that humanity is still in its childhood was quite foreign to him. The ancients were children ; his contemporaries had arrived at the wisdom of old age. But the recent discoveries—he specifies printing, gunpowder, and ocean-sailing—made it impossible for him to think that the ancients were more advanced than the moderns ; and he has a definite conviction that time, instead of being the enemy, is the friend of man. He rejects with indignation the theory of recurring cycles.

This was the age of Utopias—More's Utopia, the New Atlantis, Campanella's City of the Sun, and others less

---

[1] Coulton, *From St. Francis to Dante*, p. 57 ; B. Russell, *The Conquest of Happiness*, p. 56 ; Bury, *The Idea of Progress*, pp. 24-29.

well known. It is significant that while modern Utopias
are placed in the future, most of the early romances were
laid in distant parts of the earth.

The modern movement began with the literary culture
of the Renaissance, which especially in France took
the form of a one-sided classicism. Molière regarded
"Gothic" civilisation as merely barbarous. He speaks of

> Le fade goût des monuments gothiques
> Ces monstres odieux des siècles ignorants.[1]

For Voltaire, the Grand Siècle in France ranked with the
ages of Alexander, Augustus, and the Italian Renaissance
as the only four centuries worthy of serious study.

The influence of Descartes, which was lasting, led to a
purely intellectualist conception of progress. Reason was
the progressive factor in human life, ethics were static,
and religion retrograde. The precursors of the Revolution looked forward to the Age of Reason, when, as
Condorcet said, "the human race, freed from its fetters,
withdrawn from the empire of chance and from that of
the enemies of progress, will walk with firm and assured
step in the way of truth, virtue, and happiness." [2]
Fontenelle emphasised that each generation may start
where the preceding one left off, and was convinced that
"men will never degenerate." But it is only in knowledge
that this continuous improvement can be predicted. The
unbelieving Abbé de St. Pierre, humanitarian and pacifist
before his time, was also one of the first to look forward
to a long future for the human race. We are now "only

[1] Quoted by Dawson, *Progress and Religion*, p. 9.
[2] Dawson, p. 13.

in the infancy of human reason." [1]   Thus he was led to think of a progress in social order as well as in reason.   He represents, as Bury says, a transition from Descartes to the social reformers of the Revolution period.

The Encyclopædists were full of the notion that man is what his institutions make him.   Reform the constitution and the laws, and man will at once move forward. They believed in progress, but their attitude was sober and cautious.   Nearly all writers of this period—the generation before 1789—have great hopes that " Liberty " will bring about an era of happiness and increasing well-being.   Gibbon, for example, though he reasonably believed that the period of the Antonines was much happier than the Dark Ages, lets us " acquiesce in the pleasing conclusion that every age of the world has increased, and still increases, the real wealth, the happiness, the knowledge and perhaps the virtues of the human race."

There were, however, many voices raised in protest. Rousseau idealised the noble savage ; others wished to fly, at least in imagination, to the Middle Ages, or to China, or to some imaginary Utopia.   Goethe had no faith in the apocalyptic dreams then popular in France ; he anticipated a slow but certain advance in cleverness and discernment.   " The world," he said to Eckermann, " will not reach its goal so quickly as we think and wish. The retarding demons are always there, intervening and resisting at every point, so that though there is an advance on the whole it is very slow."   " The development of

---

[1] Bury, p. 156.

humanity," said Eckermann, " appears to be a matter of thousands of years." " Who knows ? " replied Goethe, " perhaps of millions. But let humanity last as long as it will, there will always be hindrances in the way, and all kinds of distress, to make it develop its powers. Men will become more clever and discerning, but not better nor happier nor more energetic, at least except for limited periods. I can see the time coming when God will take no more pleasure in the race, and must proceed again to a rejuvenated creation. . . . But that time is certainly a long way off, and we can still for thousands and thousands of years enjoy ourselves on this dear old playing-ground, such as it is." [1]

The Italian Vico, whose work, written a hundred years before, was translated by Michelet and so made known to French readers, was a Spenglerian before Spengler. He thought that civilisations pass through much the same evolutions, under aristocracy, democracy, and monarchy, after which there is a period of barbarism followed by a new cycle. In reality, history resembles itself but never repeats itself, and analogies drawn from ancient civilisations are of very little help to us in forecasting our own future.

Hegel, followed by Cousin, whose thought had more influence in the United States than in England, uses the idea of evolutionary progress in interpreting the past, but strangely enough seems to have regarded the process as already completed. Guizot dissociated the idea of progress from Hegelian metaphysics, and was content to

[1] Quoted by Bury, p. 259.

prove that the European nations are becoming more and more civilised. Saint-Simon (who died in 1825) maintained that periods of construction and of criticism alternate. A new epoch of construction, on Socialist lines, was, as he believed, approaching. Under this régime men of science would be the high priests. Democracy and liberty were played out, and would give way to rigid governmental control. We seem here to listen to a precursor of Marx and Lenin.

For Comte progress was the ultimate fact of social science. He regarded the study of metaphysics, and also of natural science, as waste of time, and wished mankind to concentrate on the service of humanity. His law of the three stages—theological, metaphysical, and positive, does not fit even European history well, and breaks down completely if it is applied to the civilisations of Asia. But the idea of reorganising society by the help of scientific sociology was acceptable to many of Comte's contemporaries, who ignored the fact that he was no more an admirer of liberty than Saint-Simon. Proudhon, on the contrary, described progress as the railway of liberty. He was theoretically an anarchist, and in spite of his famous dictum that private property is theft, had no sympathy with State Socialism. The Vatican by this time had begun to take alarm, and in 1864 the celebrated *Syllabus Errorum* ends by condemning the proposition that "the Roman pontiff can and ought to reconcile himself with progress, liberalism, and modern civilisation." It was a bold anti-modernist manifesto, and it is probable that many Catholics have been embarrassed by the uncompromising terms of the condemnation, which nevertheless ought to be judged in relation to the controversies of the time.

It is strange to contrast the optimism of Herbert Spencer and his school, described in the earlier part of this chapter, with the pessimism of his contemporary von Hartmann, who thought that civilisation has only made mankind more miserable. Hartmann says: " I know of no study which is so saddening as that of the evolution of humanity as it is set forth in the annals of history. Man is a brute, only more intelligent than other brutes, and even the best of modern civilisations appears to me to exhibit a condition of mankind which neither embodies any worthy ideal nor even possesses the merit of stability."

The doctrine of progress as a cosmic principle is now seldom heard in this country. It is so manifestly a product of crude anthropomorphism that even apart from the Law of Entropy one might suppose that it could hardly be defended by an intelligent man. But it has been revived in a truly amazing fashion by the Italian school of New Idealists. They can claim no support from the older idealists. I have quoted in my chapter on the Problem of Time the fine protest of F. H. Bradley against historicism in philosophy, with its repudiation of the eternal values. The Modernist school protest against this, as depriving history of all reality and value, and perhaps Bradley's language sometimes lays him open to this charge. But Croce is surely fantastically wrong when he says, " From the cosmic point of view reality displays itself as a continual growing upon itself; nor can a real regress be conceived, because evil, being that which is not, is unreal, and that which is, is always and exclusively good. Cosmic progress then is itself an object of affirmation, not problematic but apodeictic." "The Spirit, an infinite possibility overflowing into infinite actuality, has drawn and is drawing at every moment the cosmos out of chaos . . . and is creating modes of life ever more lofty. The work of the Spirit is not completed, and never will be so. Our aspiration to something superior is not vain. The Infinity of our desire is a proof of the infinity of that progress. The plant dreams of the animal, the animal of man, and man of superman. . . . A time will come in which the great exploits and achievements which are now our memory and our pride will be forgotten, as we have forgotten the exploits of those beings of genius who created human life." Bosanquet, to whom I owe this last quotation, complains of the " narrow humanism " of Croce. I confess I can see nothing in his hymn to progress except delirious nonsense.

Spengler's much discussed book is not, I think, destined to long life, though it will be read as a curiosity in illustration of the rather unreasonable pessimism which invaded Germany after what, from the military point of view, was a glorious defeat. Spengler's philosophy, to put it briefly, has no room for progress, except as the temporary flowering of a " culture " before it declines into a " civilisation." His culture-cycles are isolated from each other ; each is a self-contained whole, which follows a pre-ordained course of growth and decay. This theory fits historical reality no better than the schemes of Hegel and Comte. It recalls the philosophies of classical antiquity in its conviction that at present civilisation is on the down-grade. Whether this is so I will discuss presently.

If we want to form an intelligent opinion on the whole question, we shall be wise to dismiss the notion that subjective idealism can alter the physical facts. Croce seems to wish to be as independent of fact as Fichte, with whom he possibly has something in common. Bosanquet has said (my readers may complain that I am too fond of these two quotations) that to throw our ideals into the future is the death of all sane idealism, and Anatole France that the future is a convenient place in which to store our dreams. Such sayings would be cynical and faithless if they were applied to reasonable hopes and efforts for the improvement of society; Bosanquet at any rate was far from wishing to quench such aspirations; but they are true of the universe as a whole, for there can be no progress of the whole. We must, I think, be realists when we look at the picture of the universe which science draws for us. No juggling with the almost incomprehensible idea of Time as a fourth dimension can make much difference to the facts and figures of the new astronomy, nor to the law of entropy. I have already dealt with the " biologism " of some modern thinkers; I do not see how the life-processes of animal organisms can be so extended as to form the basis of a cosmic law.

Aristotle says that nature is superhuman and marvellous (δαιμονία) but not divine. This is our general impression when we think of the universe of astronomy. It is difficult to believe that the stars were created in order to be the abode of life. Life is a very rare and sporadic phenomenon. Jeans and Eddington suggest that life as we know it is the result of a pure accident which happened to the sun about two thousand million years ago, after he had existed undisturbed for seven or eight billion years. The narrow limits of temperature within which life is possible must be a very rare exception in the whole of space and time.

It is always right to remember that our senses, on the reports of which our knowledge must be based, are very imperfect. Our world perhaps resembles an impression of a tune played on a piano in which most of the notes are dumb. We hear a few vibrations towards the bass end, and see a few towards the treble end. It is said that we know of sixty " octaves," and see only one. Our minds do the rest, synthesising from a few scraps of knowledge. But we shall not make things better by discrediting what we do know. We have nothing else to go upon.

If we are asked why God made the earth, sun, and stars, it is best to say simply that we do not know. Disinterested curiosity is a noble passion, but nature has not seen fit to gratify it. We have enough light to walk by, and not much more.

Let us then consider the problem of progress as it concerns one species only—our own—on the minor planet on which our lot is cast. We have finally dismissed the notion that progress is or can be a law of the macrocosm. It remains to discuss whether it is even a local and temporary fact in our microcosm. More than a local fact it cannot be, for it does not affect even our nearest neighbour in space, the moon, not to speak of the other planets in the solar system. A temporary fact we must call it,

for the ultimate extinction of life on our earth is absolutely certain. A million years ago the ancestors of *homo
sapiens* must have been living on the earth somewhere ;
but we do not know what they were like. Most anthro-
pologists think that the early skulls, including those of
the Neanderthalers or Mousterians, belonged to races
which are now extinct. A small number of skulls found
in France, perhaps about twenty thousand years old, are
assigned to ancestors of the modern man. The Cro-
Magnons, as they are called from the place where their
bones were found (or the Neanthropic race, as it is now
proposed to call them), were quite equal to the modern
European in stature, strength, and brain-capacity. They
were savages, no doubt, but in natural endowments they
were our equals. Since that time progress has taken the
form of accumulated knowledge and experience, the use
of tools, and the customs and traditions which make life
in society possible. The evolution of the individual has
practically ceased ; the physical changes which are still
going on are mainly degenerative. *Homo sapiens* must
have slowly developed from a simian stock ; it would be impossible to decide which of our ancestors first deserved the
name of man, even if we had his remains. We may take our
choice of any date between half a million and a million
years ago. I am disposed to favour the longer period.
It is worth while to remember this time-scale, that we
may realise how very recent civilisation is. Some of the
most important discoveries, such as the domestication of
the wheat-plant, and making fire by rubbing sticks, were
made very early ; but if we allow even as much as ten
thousand years since the beginning of civilisation, that is

a very small fraction of the time when our ancestors remained savages.

Ten thousand years for the past of civilisation ; and how much for its future ? Science sees no reason why the earth should not remain habitable by men for a million years more. Many of the dreams of scientific discoverers will be realised, and perhaps stranger dreams than they have ever imagined. Man will be even more completely master of nature's secrets than he is now. For practical purposes we may say that the possibilities of progress in this sense are almost but not quite infinite. They are, however, only possibilities ; we have seen that Time is not always a friend to be relied on.

Undoubtedly there will be serious setbacks. If we re-visited England fifty thousand years hence, we might well find the low-lying parts, including London, under the sea, or, if the present subsidence is followed by elevation, we might find our country covered with glaciers. The only inhabitants might conceivably be a few Esquimaux with their reindeer. But no Ice Age covers the whole earth. The same date may find Antarctica, which seems to be slowly sinking, again habitable.

Nor can we be absolutely confident about the future of our species. It is not likely that a new microbe will exterminate us, but there may be wars of extermination which will destroy civilisation. Russia, for example, when she has recovered from her revolutionary fever, may emulate the fame of Jenghiz Khan and Timour. We remember the old saying that if you scratch a Russian you find a Tartar. There is also the possibility that progress, which is only a method of adaptation to new conditions, may come to an end, when the conditions cease to demand further adaptation. We may pass into a condition of stable equilibrium, like the social insects; and then perhaps survival value will belong to unconscious instinct, and not to intelligence. A completely mechanised civilisation, such as the present rulers of Russia are trying to establish, might end in this way. Further, dysgenic selection, such as is now in progress almost everywhere, may so much enfeeble the bodies and minds of the population that it will be unable to bear the ever-increasing burden of preserving and augmenting the treasures of civilisation. There may, and probably will be, periods of exhaustion followed by chaos and destruction, like the Dark Ages. Whitehead[1] says very truly that the social history of mankind exhibits great organisations in their alternating functions of conditions for progress, and of contrivances for stunting humanity. The history of the Mediterranean lands and of Western Europe is the history of the blessing and the curse of political and religious organisations. The moment of dominance marks the turning-point when the blessing passes into the curse. I think it would be true to say that every institution ends by strangling the ideas which it was formed to protect.

These possibilities cannot be neglected. But the chances seem decidedly in favour of a further growth of what we generally mean by progress, in which first one nation and then another will take the lead. The present unparalleled speed in invention and discovery is not likely

---

[1] *Process and Reality*, p. 479.

to be kept up ; but so far there is no visible slackening in applied science.

We shall therefore have the most ample opportunities, if we like to take advantage of them. But what do we mean by progress ? What is the direction in which we should like to think of mankind and its environment as moving ? Many persons have argued for or against the reality of progress without asking themselves this question or attempting to give a clear answer to it. They are content to say that progress means movement in a desirable direction.

If we take as our standard the net surplus of pleasure over pain, or the maximum of enjoyable sensations, it is hardly possible to decide whether civilisation has been a gain or a loss. The savage may be happier than the cultivated European or American, as the rough or the imbecile may be happier than the scholar ; but this is not the standard which we really use. It is, however, legitimate to ask whether the necessity for hard and monotonous work, the nervous tension, the anxieties and disappointments inseparable from civilisation, are or are not too high a price to pay for the advantages of living in a highly artificial society. Edward Carpenter wrote a book called *Civilisation, its Cause and Cure ;* and many others have cast wistful eyes upon the simpler conditions of barbarism. Mr. Austin Freeman is one of the best-informed of those who have compared the handiness and skill of the African tribes, who can make with their own hands everything that they need, with the European artisan, who can make nothing, and is almost a parasite upon his machine. It would take too long to discuss the question whether machinery may not in time destroy the inventiveness and ingenuity of the race which discovered it, and whether all the devices to dispense with muscular exertion may not impair the physical development of those who use them. Probably few things would surprise a savage more in a white man's home than to find there a pair of dumb-bells or a physical exerciser.

These questions might be argued, not very profitably, for hundreds of pages. We might bring in the question of the division of labour, and the relative advantages of socialism and individualism, the former aiming at the organic efficiency of a political group, the latter at the free development of personality. It is indeed by no means easy to decide what changes we should regard as really progressive. But on the general question whether civilisation is better than barbarism it seems to me unreasonable to hesitate. As Lotze says : [1] "Every man who is a member—though only in a subordinate and unfavourable position—of a civilised society, has, unless hindered by his own fault, not only participation in an infinitely richer mental life than would have been accessible to him as a result of his own isolated strength, but also possesses greater possibilities of material well-being." This is indeed almost too obvious to need saying ; and we may add that the supposed freedom from restraints in the savage life is illusory. The civilised man is usually the freer of the two. I hold therefore that by any reasonable standard the development of our race from something like the pithecanthropus of Java to *homo sapiens*, and

[1] *Microcosmus*, Vol. II., p. 98.

from the man of the Flint and Bronze Ages to the man of to-day, may be called progress. Man in society has been, and still is, on the up-grade. But progress has always been local, temporary, and sporadic; there have been many retrogressions—one of them, after the fall of the ancient civilisation, very severe and protracted. Another Dark Age is possible, and if the insane militarism and nationalism of the pre-war period continue to turn Europe into a mutual suicide club, it is even probable.

When we turn to spiritual progress, the picture is not very different. We need not go back further than ancient Egypt. There we find a close connexion between religion and the cultivator's year. Religious rites were a symbolical enactment of the processes of nature. In Babylonia, at the same period, the country belonged to the god, and irrigation works were carried out at his command. But within the thousand or twelve hundred years which ended with the rise of Islam, all the world-religions had their birth. There was a great wave of thought and belief, which passed over Asia and eastern Europe. Very shortly, it may be described as idealism—as belief in an unseen and unchanging world behind the changing temporal scene. We find it in India, where the greatest name is Buddha; in the Orphism of the Greek lands, in Persia and Asia Minor, and even in China, though there the positivist and common-sense traditions of the race soon asserted themselves. In Platonism and Christianity this type of thought reached its full stature. Here then we find a profound spiritual revelation which has permanently enriched humanity. In the Christian revelation the religion of the Spirit found its fullest expression. We may add that in the coalescence of Jewish and Greek ideas in the early Church we may note an illustration of a law which seems to be of great importance—that advances in culture, whether secular or religious, result from the fusion of two races, or of two types of thought and civilisation. It happens sometimes that after a war of conquest the traditions of the vanquished people are for a time submerged, and their country partially barbarised. After a time they lift up their heads again, and the blend of the two cultures produces something of higher worth than either could have produced alone. This seems to have been the origin of Hellenic civilisation, after the northern invasions of the " Pelasgian " homelands. It was certainly the condition of the rise of the Christian Church. Thus, if we choose the name of Plato to represent the first permanent enrichment of human nature on the spiritual side, we may take the name of the Founder of Christianity, who placed Himself in the succession of the great Jewish prophets, as representing the second. When Christianity passed over into Europe, these two affluents combined to make a mighty river. The contributions of the Renaissance and Reformation are not quite on the same grand scale, though in art this period ranks with the great age of Greece, and the Reformation was the condition of the characteristic contribution of the northern races to Christendom.

The era in which we live is difficult to appraise, because it is still in the making. It is undoubtedly an exceptional age, probably the most extraordinary that the world has seen. It is a phase of civilisation which, as many think, has now produced the fruits which it is capable of bearing, and no one knows what will follow it. The idea of progress has itself changed, because even the man in the street knows that the vista of possible developments in the future, for better or for worse, has been immeasurably enlarged. The masses think of further progress mainly as an increase of comfort and amusement, and of leisure in which to enjoy them. In detail, these aspirations are for the most part innocent enough, though not heroic ; we shall not be censorious when we remember how much the poorer classes were excluded from the benefits of civilisation a hundred years ago. We are in the middle of a great experiment, which aims at establishing at least a fair measure of comfort and culture embracing the entire nation. It is a question whether such a nation would have as great a survival-value as one organised on a hierarchical scale, with less individual liberty ; but the experiment appeals to the generous instincts of almost everybody, and we must all hope that it will succeed.

But the new revelation which has come to mankind in modern times, a revelation which will make our age rank in importance with the creative ages of Hellenism and of Christianity, is the amazing progress of the natural sciences, and the application of them to social life. How completely these new inventions have transformed our civilisation is known to all. The scientific attitude of mind would be equally important if it had permeated the uneducated and half-educated masses to the same extent as applied science has done. But it is doubtful whether crude superstition has declined much in the last two generations. The higher achievements of science are

intelligible only to a few; and the dysgenic trend of our
civilisation is probably making first-class brains fewer in
each generation. The succession of great discoveries will
not go on for ever. But we can hardly doubt that the
future of civilisation will be determined mainly by science.
In philosophy and religion, this will discredit dualism and
supernaturalism; what forms of belief will be favoured
by it is not very easy to say. The dangers of over-
mechanisation and excessive standardising of life may be
increased; some are afraid that new engines of destruction
may be discovered which will obliterate civilisation itself.
In any case, progress has entered upon a new and dangerous phase, and the danger comes precisely from what
ought to be the main instrument of progress. Nevertheless, I believe that few who are well acquainted with
the conditions of life in the ages before modern science
would wish to go back to any of those ages.

In my opinion, a dispassionate survey of the course of
history gives ground for a reasonable and tempered hopefulness for the future. But this reasoned and dispassionate
meliorism, tempered by serious misgivings, is very different
from the unreasoned and often extravagant optimism
which in the last century was a kind of religion, and which
some even held to be sanctioned by Christianity. Can
we find clear traces of teleology—of a divine purpose
leading towards perfection—in history as a whole?

It is often said that Hope is the gift of Hebraism to
mankind, and that Hope projected on the world of
becoming is belief in progress. This opinion must be
examined. The old Hebrew belief was that Jehovah
was the champion of His people, the unseen commander

of their armies, the dweller upon their holy hill. He
tolerated no rival within His own domain, but Chemosh
held much the same position as champion of his own
people, the Moabites. The political misfortunes of the
Hebrews were regarded by the prophets as a punishment
either for disloyalty to Jehovah, or for moral offences,
which were even more hateful to Him. In the same way
individual transgressions were visited by temporal penal-
ties. The conflict of this crude theodicy with the facts
of experience may be said to be the main subject of the
Old Testament. Every possible expedient was tried to
justify the ways of God to men. Assyria was an instrument in God's hands. A remnant of Israel would be
saved, and reserved for future glories. In the lives of
individuals, the apparently virtuous sufferer was being
punished for secret sins. The righteous is never really
forsaken ; his troubles are only temporary. Or the
family, not the individual, is the unit ; in the next
generation the name of the wicked is clean put out.
Later, it is suggested that the sufferings of the good man
have a redemptive value for the nation ; and finally, a
new world is brought into existence to redress the balance
of the old. In one way or another, Abraham's question,
" Shall not the judge of all the earth do right ? " must be
answered in the words of Job, " Yea, verily ; though He
slay me, yet will I trust in Him."

This is not much like the modern idea of progress.
It is a stubborn belief in the justice of God, which must
be manifested on a large scale, in the fate of nations, as
well as in the fortunes of individuals. As a matter of
fact, the Jews have stood by the graves of all their

oppressors in turn. The nation which against hope believed in hope has been justified by its faith, though it may be doubtful whether hopefulness is specially characteristic of modern Judaism.

Thus, for the Jews, the idea of God was firmly embedded in the historical process. Even when, perhaps partly under the influence of Greek thought, the process was transferred from the historical to the supramundane, Jewish apocalyptism was quite unlike the Greek theory of cycles. Apocalyptism was still " trust in the arm of the Lord," who was to vindicate His unique purpose for His people by some stupendous miracle.

The Gospel entered into the inheritance of these vague apocalyptic dreams. But Messianism meant nothing to the Gentile Church, and the Kingdom of God almost at once took wings and flew away into Plato's " intelligible world." Millenarianism, in which the old apocalyptism survived feebly and fitfully, had nothing to do with the idea of progress. Nevertheless, there remained the conviction that with the coming of Christ a new principle of higher life had entered the natural order ; and the Fourth Gospel clearly teaches that the gift of the Spirit is a progressive revelation of the divine purpose for man. Moreover, the conflict against Gnosticism, which was radically unhistorical, drove the Church Fathers into assertions of the value of the historical process. Irenæus, in a remarkable and hardly typical passage which has a modern sound, says : " God arranged everything from the first with a view to the perfection of man, in order to deify Him and reveal His own dispensations, so that goodness may be made manifest, justice made perfect, and the Church fashioned after the image of His Son. Thus man may eventually reach maturity, and being ripened by such privileges may see and comprehend God." [1]

It would further be true to say that the Christian heaven contained a doctrine of perfectionism, and that when in modern times, in consequence of growing disbelief in a future life, the apocalyptic vision returned again to earth, it joined with revolutionary optimism in proclaiming, as a quasi-religious dogma, the perfectibility of the species.

It is also true that Hope as a moral quality is characteristic of Christianity. St. Paul places it between Faith and Love as one of the three great Christian virtues. This was, I think, a new thing. When the later Neoplatonists used the same triad, adding Truth as a fourth, I believe they were borrowing from the Christians. To the Pagans Hope had been a gift of doubtful value, an illusion which helps us to endure life, and a valuable spur to action; but on the whole, an *ignis fatuus*. As in the philosophy of Schopenhauer, Hope is the bait by which Nature catches us, not for our own advantage.

St. Paul condemns Paganism partly on the ground that the heathen " have no hope, and are without God in the world." His epistles are full of exhortations to hope. But is hope for him purely otherworldly, or is it perhaps connected with the slowly fading expectation of the second coming of Christ ? Mainly it must be otherworldly ; " if in this life only we have hope in Christ, we are of all men most miserable." But his life " in Christ "

---

[1] *Adv. Haer*, V. 36. Quoted by Dawson.

had already begun, and this was a life of Hope. There is the isolated passage in Romans when he has " hope that the creation also may be delivered from the bondage of corruption into the glorious liberty of the children of God." I doubt if anything more was in his mind in this verse than the " new heavens and new earth " of prophecy. It would be an anachronism to read into the words anything like nineteenth-century evolutionary optimism. In the Epistle to the Hebrews we have the outline of a philosophy of history. Hope is an anchor of the soul; but earthly hopes are doomed to disappointment, and even the heroes of the Old Testament never received what they believed that God had promised them. Hope must die to live many times ; but only because " God hath provided some better thing."

Hope, then, in some sense, is a Christian virtue, the sister-virtue of Faith and Love. We must not explain it as merely a temper of hopefulness, a habit or faculty of looking at the bright side of things ; nor yet at what is called trusting to Providence, which in practice generally means trusting to improvidence. The pragmatic value of hopefulness is of course notorious, and is emphasised in the proverbs of many nations. " He that regardeth the clouds shall not reap." " Lose heart, lose all." In medical practice the importance of encouraging the patient is well known. It is the foundation of the strange modern cult which calls itself Christian Science. Hopefulness means happiness, and happiness tends to health and efficiency.[1]

[1] In these paragraphs I have borrowed from a pamphlet of mine called *The Call to Hope*, published by the S.P.C.K. about ten years ago.

But Christianity does not bid us to play tricks with our souls in order to produce any results, external or internal. Christianity does not wish us to believe anything except because it is true. And when Christianity says that a thing is true, it does not mean merely that it works, nor that we should be happier and better for believing it. It means that what it tells us to believe is objectively true, part of the constitution of the world in which we live, part of the laws of God's creation. St. Thomas Aquinas defines Hope as " a divinely infused quality of the soul, whereby with certain trust we expect those good things of the life eternal which are to be attained by the grace of God." " If we are hopeful in the Christian sense of the word," says Bishop Francis Paget, " we shall live and think and work with the resolute conviction that the goal and aim of human life, for ourselves and for others, is that which the Bible declares it to be." This is unquestionably the traditional idea of the meaning of Christian hope. It is the temper natural to immortal spirits under temporal probation, who know that their heavenly Father loves them, that their Lord has redeemed them, and that the Holy Spirit is ever with them to help their infirmities.

I do not think that any other meaning of Hope can be found in the New Testament. But our generation is not content with it. The question is asked, and must be faced, whether Christianity is optimistic about the world in which we have to live, or only about that other world which we cannot see, and which often seems to us " the land which is very far off." The cry of world-weariness, " O that I had wings as a dove, for then would I fly away and be at rest," now sounds almost like treason. "See that thou make all things according to the pattern showed thee in the mount," is a command which appeals to us much more strongly. Our religion, I know, has been grievously secularised; but we are not willing to banish Hope altogether from this earth. If we turn our backs on this world, and contemplate eternity merely as the negation of time and change, as our deliverance from " the sorrowful weary wheel " of earthly existence, our minds will dwell in an empty heaven; we shall grasp at infinity and find only zero.

The answer seems to lie in a revaluation of temporal experience in the light of eternity. The defects of Hebrew religion were partly the neglect of that wide range of intellectual and spiritual values, the understanding of which was the imperishable glory of Athens. But partly also they over-estimated those external and instrumental values which constitute what the world calls success. The man whose " mind to him a kingdom is " does not complain much of the injustices of life. Still less does the Christian complain, or call the world which he has found full of love and beauty and wisdom an evil place. The chastisements of God fall on low ideals and on selfishness. Disraeli in his detached way said once : " The European talks of progress because by the aid of a few scientific discoveries he has established a society which has mistaken comfort for civilisation." That is exactly what we have been doing. It would be ungrateful and unreasonable to speak evil of the pleasant, kindly, orderly nineteenth century; it may be long before Europe sees so happy a time again. But we have mistaken comfort for civilisation. Our main wish has been to have " a good time " ourselves, and to give others a good time. And now the shadow of the Cross has fallen, stark and grim, across our sunny fields. We lament our lost prosperity, but we have not yet learned that those higher gifts which to some extent we began to prize during the acute perils of the Great War will never be given to those who seek them for any ulterior end, even the greatness of their country. They are to be won only through the firm acceptance of the Christian standard of values, which is the basis of Christian hope. Our Lord's words : " Seek ye first the Kingdom of God and His righteousness, and all these things shall be added unto you," are universally true. " The things that are seen are temporal, but the things that are not seen are eternal." So St. Paul makes his own, and our own, the fundamental doctrine of Plato.

But I have not answered the question, Can we discern any divine purpose in history as a whole ? We cannot with any confidence trace the hand of God in the development of merely material civilisation ; and it might be difficult to prove that in the realisation of the higher values we are superior to the first Christians, or to the contemporaries of Socrates. So far as I can see, the purposes of God in history are finite, local, temporal, and for the most part individual. They all seem to point beyond themselves to the " intelligible world," beyond this bourne of time and place. I cannot think that St. Paul's words, " If in this life only we have hope in Christ, we are of all men most miserable," are without a meaning and a warning for ourselves. In so far as the modern doctrine of the predestined progress of the species is only a spectral residuum of traditional eschatology, I think we must be prepared to surrender it. If we are unwilling to do so, our reluctance may prove that we have secularised our religion in an illegitimate manner. If, however, we cherish the belief that the purpose of the Incarnation can only be achieved by a Christophany in redeemed humanity itself, a Kingdom of God on earth, that is an inspiring hope which very many Christians have thought warranted by the new type of spiritual life which our Lord left us as His legacy when His bodily presence was withdrawn from earth. But it does not seem to me to follow necessarily from belief in the Incarnation, nor to receive much support from the course of history in the last two thousand years. There is nothing in the Gospels to encourage such a belief. "When the Son of Man cometh, shall He find faith on the earth?"

5

THE WORLD OF VALUES

THE idea of Value is beginning to dominate all philosophy. As Windelband says: "We do not now so much expect from philosophy that which it was formerly supposed to give, a theoretic scheme of the world, a synthesis of the results of the separate sciences, or transcending them on lines of its own, a scheme harmoniously complete in itself. What we expect from philosophy to-day is reflexion on those permanent values which have their foundation in a higher spiritual reality, above the changing interests of the times." Many have found in the idea of Value the key which, as they hope, will unlock the innermost shrine in which the most intractable dualisms and contradictions in human experience may find an explanation. Like all key-words—like evolution, relativity, emergence, and the like, it is very liable to abuse, and without careful definition it may easily cover up the difficulties which it offers to solve. In this book I shall argue, or express my conviction, that the appreciation of value is as integral a part of our experience as the judgments which are based on sense-perception, and that in consequence it must be accepted among the data upon which our view of reality must be founded. I shall even maintain, here following the Platonists and Lotze,[1] that value and reality are ultimately identical, and that value, which implies existence, covers a wider field than existence conceived of as apart from value. Existence apart from value is an abstraction. If we distinguish truth from reality, a thing which I am loth to do, we may say that a relative truth only becomes absolute when it is the expression of an absolute value.

Speaking as a theist, I regard religion as an affirmation and apprehension of absolute values, and I believe that our absolute values are the content of divine revelation, which necessarily speaks to us in our own language, but conveys to us the conviction that certain things are not merely instrumental to life, but of a higher order and importance than life itself. This I shall hope to explain presently.

Value is not, as is sometimes supposed, a new term in philosophy, and the ideas which it expresses are far from being purely modern. We have only to remember the ancient controversies about the Form of the Good, about the scope of the Beautiful (τὸ καλόν), and about the *summum bonum*, all of which terms belong to the philosophy of Value, in order to dispel the notion that the problems which are now discussed under the general names of value and valuation were unfamiliar to earlier thinkers. The whole of the *philosophia perennis* is based on the belief in the capacity of the Intelligence (νοῦς), or, as I have translated it in my book on Plotinus, the Spirit, to

---

[1] Lotze says : " In its feeling for the value of things and their relations, our reason possesses as genuine a revelation as, in the principles of logical investigation, it has an indispensable instrument of experience.

apprehend supra-sensual and supra-personal truth. The spiritual world which is the objectivity of νοῦς would be called in modern language the kingdom of values. I have argued in my exposition of Plotinus that that philosopher would have expressed his meaning more clearly if, when dealing with the intelligible or spiritual world, he had abandoned the Aristotelian categories, and substituted for them the absolute values, Truth, Goodness, and Beauty, these being in fact the attributes of the divine nature as knowable by Spirit. I gave my reasons for what might seem temerity in differing from Plotinus on so important a point.[1] I was fortified in my opinion by finding that Proclus, the ablest of the later Neoplatonists, had anticipated me in my criticism. " There are three attributes (he says) which make up the essence of divine things, and are constitutive of all the higher categories—Goodness, Wisdom, Beauty (ἀγαθότης, σοφία, κάλλος), and there are three auxiliary principles, second in importance to these, but extending through all the divine orders—Faith, Truth, and Love (πίστις, ἀλήθεια, ἔρως). In another place [2] he explains the relationship between these two triads. Goodness, Wisdom, and Beauty are not only the attributes of the divine nature as such ; they are also active causes. When they are exercising their activity, they take respectively the forms of Faith, Truth, and Love. " Faith gives all things a solid foundation in the Good. Truth reveals Knowledge in all real existences. Love leads all things to the nature of the Beautiful."

[1] See my *Philosophy of Plotinus*, Vol. II., p. 76.
[2] See references in my book, *loc. cit.*

It is hardly necessary to insist that this doctrine of the Intelligence or Spirit, and of the knowledge proper to it, is an integral part of traditional Christian philosophy, from St. Paul downwards. Nicholas of Cusa, in calling God *Valor valorum*, anticipates the modern terminology, which, however, has become current coin in philosophy only in recent times. In its modern form the emphasis on Value is probably derived in part from Lotze, in part from the theological writings of Ritschl, which for many years had a great vogue in Germany, and in part from a more vulgar source, the prominence of the utilitarian and economic calculus in the nineteenth century. Lotze's theory of value will help us; the others will not. Ritschl, under the influence of Kantian dualism, distinguishes sharply between judgments of fact and judgments of value. The purpose of Kant's first *Critique* is to separate value completely from fact by denying that the ideals of speculative reason have any relation to genuine knowledge.[1] This separation, which cuts at the root of the *philosophia perennis*, is also the foundation of Catholic Modernism, as represented by men like Loisy and Tyrrell, with its fatal divorce between truths of faith and truths of fact. It was not entirely without justification that the Curia condemned this modernism as " a compendium of all heresies." For us, on the contrary, a value which has no existence is no value, and an existence which has no value is no existence. It is a matter of faith for us that whatever *is* is in its nature intelligible, and there are no concepts which do not involve valuation. It is the felt inadequacy

---

[1] A. E. Taylor, *The Faith of a Moralist*, Vol. I., p. 33.

of concepts based on mere sense-perception, and on mere psychic activities, which leads us on to the recognition of those absolute values which are the revealed attributes of God.   In the case of moral values there is also the contrast between the *is* and the *ought to be*, which impels us not merely to apprehend the higher values but to actualise them.   We are told—and the distinction is true—that the judgments of morality are not existential, while the judgments of religion are always so.   Religion is the apprehension of a higher reality, eternal and perfect ; morality always speaks in the imperative mood, and prescribes creative action.   But those who make this distinction sometimes forget that the higher values, as known to us, are themselves essentially creative activities. Perfect and complete in their own sphere, the spiritual world, they energise unceasingly on the lower planes of reality.   Thus when we are occupied with moral action in the world of time and place we are right to substitute for " the eternal values " the more familiar phrase " the will of God."   Even the two other absolute values, in which the conative element is less apparent than in the striving after moral goodness, are not inert.   Truth or Wisdom is always for us a goal, not a present possession ; and Beauty, in our present experience, ever freshly produced, is a copy of the perfect Beauty of the divine nature.   The quest of the divine is always creative of value, not least in the very strenuous inner life of the mystic, in which external activity is reduced to a minimum In all spiritual effort the reward is a progressive resolution of the discord between fact and value.   The world of our surface consciousness becomes irradiated by the spiritual values, and this is what the mystic means by the beatific vision. For the mystic, says Hocking, the world is an almost untouched reservoir of significance and value. " Living is reaching out to the reality of things as a region in which the discovery of value need never end." [1]

The use of the word value in economics will not be any help to us, though it has been discussed at perhaps unnecessary length by some recent writers on the idea of value. We should have escaped this confusion if like the Italians we had two words—*valore* for value in the philosophical sense and *valuta* for value in the economic sense. [2] Hobbes, it is true, says that " the value or worth of a man is, as of all other things, his price " ; but we do not equate the cynical saying that every man has his price with our assertion of the value of human personality, nor agree with Sir Hudibras that " What is worth in anything But so much money as 'twill bring ? " Even in economics this meaning of " worth " is quite obsolete. It is recognised by modern economists that their science cannot be carried on in abstraction from ethical and other values, and in consequence of this realisation the idea of value in economics has been much expanded, so as to cover a wider field than it did a hundred years ago. But for our present purpose it is not necessary to enter into the distinction of utility values, exchange values, and the like. Such a discussion would be irrelevant.

The distinction between fact and value is real, according to our view, in the psychical world, that is, in the world which is our normal environment, but not in the

---

[1] *Types of Philosophy*, p. 438.
[2] So Kant distinguishes *Würde* and *Preis*.

higher world of Spirit, where value reigns supreme, apprehending facts in their ultimate significance. We cannot accept any dualistic theory which assumes a final contradiction between fact and value. Nor can we, with Kant, give the primacy to the practical over the speculative reason without denying the cardinal postulate of Platonism, that the perfectly real must be perfectly knowable. The Great Tradition gives the primacy to the theoretical reason or intelligence, the objects of which are the absolute values, universal truths. The faculty which perceives these is not the discursive reason, which the Greeks called διάνοια, but a higher faculty which, as Plotinus says, all possess but few use. This is the Intelligence or Spirit, which the Greeks called νοῦς, and St. Paul, followed by Christian thinkers generally, called πνεῦμα. This is a superhuman faculty, which apprehends a range of realities above our normal experience ; but we " participate " in it, as the Greeks said ; even while we live here we may have " our citizenship in heaven." It is pure ignorance to call this philosophy " intellectualism " in a disparaging sense. The mistake arises from sheer confusion between νοῦς and διάνοια, which are quite distinct in Greek, though our words " intellect," " reason," " intelligence " make the confusion easy in English. This fundamental error infects very much of modernist philosophy, and makes Platonism quite unintelligible.

The modern tendency to find the meaning and explanation of everything in its roots rather than its fruits, in its origin instead of in its completed development, has led to numerous attempts to derive value from beginnings which have no value. Sorley, in his excellent book on *Moral Values and the Idea of God*, has shown how impossible it is to explain our idea of the Good in this way. But his book professedly deals with only one of the absolute values, namely, ethical value. His allusions to the other values are slight, and it seems to me that in his pre-occupation with morals he has not quite adequately elucidated the nature of value generally. For him, the difference between fact and value is almost identified with the difference between " is " and " ought to be." This is no doubt the difference as it appears to a moralist ; but it is unsatisfactory in dealing with the value of truth, and also with the æsthetic values, where conation is either absent or very subordinate. Or, to put it more accurately, the will, when it aims at the apprehension of the true and the beautiful, desires to *change* nothing except the imperfection of our own minds.[1]

Descartes, speaking for the rationalist school generally, says : " All knowledge is of the same nature throughout, and consists solely in combining what is self-evident." He wishes to build all knowledge on mathematics, with the axiom of causality. His fundamental position is that a man must start with the certainty of his own existence as a thinking subject. This is the argument by which he is best known, but many think that it contains a *petitio principii*, since the pronoun in " *I* think " assumes the very thing which he wishes to prove. But the axioms of mathematics and of causality are also treated as

---

[1] Lotze in his earlier writings seems to follow Kant in identifying value with moral good. In his later books I think he ranks Truth and Beauty also as ultimates.

self-evident. When he passes ethical value-judgments, as of course he does, he is bound to attempt to deduce them from non-ethical premises, an attempt which always fails. Or if he regards value-judgments also as " self-evident," he is abandoning his canon that " all knowledge is of the same nature throughout "; for the validity of the value-judgment is independent of mathematics.

We are trying to establish a certain view of the reality of values, as one of the facts upon which any philosophy must be built. Our position is that of Pringle-Pattison, when he says, " the presence of the ideal in human experience is as much a fact as any other. It is indeed the fundamental characteristic of that experience. The presence of the Ideal is the reality of God within us." [1] But since on the ordinary levels of thought there is a kind of opposition between value and existence or fact, we must also enquire what we mean by existence. Some have accepted John Stuart Mill's definition of existence as a permanent possibility of sensation. Others take it to mean position in time and space, or in one or other of these two ; others would say that it involves permanence, either in an objective world or in the mind. But position in an order of time and space does not prove existence, until we have made up our minds as to the status of the framework in which particular things and events are set. This framework is not given to us ; it is a conceptual construction. We first apprehend things merely as existing, and then test these apprehensions by placing them, or failing

[1] *The Idea of God*, p. 244.

to place them, in our spatial and temporal scheme. A hallucination is condemned as unreal because it has no spatial or temporal relations to anything outside the mind.

Are existences independent of mind ? When Plotinus said, οὐκ ἔξω νοῦ τὰ νοητά, he was not enunciating what Sidgwick was the first to call mentalism, but only insisting that the Intelligence and the Intelligible World are inseparable from each other, so that neither can exist without the other. My position is that real existence and value are inseparable ; it is the differentia of "mere appearance" that it has no value. But there are degrees of value, and therefore there are degrees of reality ; many things appear otherwise than as they are. I do not identify relations with values, for value is universal and prior to particular existence, while relations are between existents as existent ; nor do I, with Sorley, hold that while relations are found in *things*, values are always manifested in *persons*.[1] This distinction belongs, I should say, to moral values only.

The evolutionary philosophy of the last century assumed, as we have seen, that in the process of evolution new values are created, and it tried to make this transition easier by adopting a hedonistic calculus of value. Behind this logically inadmissible jump there was an act of faith that "the universe is friendly," which I also believe, though without supposing that progress is a cosmic principle.

Hegel, I cannot help thinking, wavers between the

---

[1] Sorley, *loc. cit.*, p. 233.

idea of the growth of mind into spirit (Plotinus' νοῦς ἐν ψυχῇ), in the course of which the real hierarchy of existence becomes plain to the " spirit in love " (νοῦς ἐρῶν) —this is a mystical philosophy like that of Plotinus and Eckhart—and the earlier doctrine of evolution, in which the course of time itself creates values which were only potentially existent before. " It is only ideally," he says, " that the earlier stage virtually implies the later." But has the process of spiritual illumination no result in the outer world ? Is there no sense in which Spirit or Soul creates its own environment ? Perhaps the best answer is that Spirit does create after its own likeness in the world of space and time, and that what seem to us new and higher forms of life must be derived by us not from mathematical or mechanistic first-beginnings, but from a higher principle imparting itself to the world of nature. Whenever we are dealing with values this explanation is more helpful than the other, since values are not amenable to treatment by the quantitative sciences. But, since values are closely attached to facts, which are the subject-matter of these sciences, this recourse to the direct causality of a higher spiritual principle may easily lead us into the quagmire of supernaturalistic dualism, in which no natural science can live. The question in fact has not been answered. Is the real world a more adequate picture of the half real world of our surface-consciousness, or is there an objective actualisation of values apart from our perception of them ? It seems to me that both are true ; and this allows us to affirm degrees of truth and reality, a conception which seems to me to be true, but full of difficulty. Idealism, says Pringle-Pattison, means essentially the interpretation of the world according to a scale of value.

It is an interesting question, which I raised in my book on Plotinus, whether the scale of existence can be brought into harmony with the scale of value. I have maintained that value and existence cannot be separated, and I would add that we cannot understand existence without arranging our experience of things in an order which is frankly valuational or axiological, to use a word which the philosophy of our time really requires. But the idea of " degrees of reality " is certainly difficult ; and since it is a fundamental principle of modernist thought that value and reality must be separated, contrary to the equally fundamental conviction of the Great Tradition, something must be said about it here.

Modernists do not reject the words higher and lower, in speaking of existential levels ; but the words in their mouths are misleading. They conceive of a unilateral relation between existents. If A involves B, whereas B does not involve A, A may be called higher than B. Sometimes the superiority seems to consist merely in greater complexity, a notion which we criticised in Herbert Spencer. Alexander says that life is not more real than matter, but is a fuller kind of reality, a distinction to which I confess that I can attach no meaning. Even in dealing with valuation he says, " there are no degrees of good," an amazing statement, since " better " and " worse " are inseparable from all judgments of value when applied to existents.

There are, however, real difficulties which an adherent of the Great Tradition must face. For the subjective idealist or mentalist there is not much trouble about degrees of reality. The lower degrees of reality are imperfect or premature constructions of the one real world, which is the creation of mind. But the Great Tradition, like natural science, begins with the world of common sense. Science is ontological from the start ; it assumes the reality of the external world. It soon leaves behind the world of naïve realism, to substitute for it a world of objects which are not perceived directly—atoms, electrons, and so forth. (For a long time it was possible to hold that the atom was merely hypothetical.)   Then these objects are illegitimately turned into mathematical symbols. Finally, the ultimate doom of all that exists is said to be annihilation, and we are left with the unthinkable idea of empty time, after the irreversible process of dissolution has ended in self-destruction. I have argued that mentalism is no refuge from this impasse. The Great Tradition transcends the world of common sense in a different way, by making it a reflection or copy of the stable and perfect world of Spirit. But it does not deny the reality of the phenomenal world, and it does not explain very clearly how there can be degrees of reality within that world, apart from the inadequacy of our constructions of it.

One special difficulty, to which I called attention in my *Plotinus*, is that the scale of values registers negative values, which I compared to temperatures below freezing-point, whereas the lowest degree in the existential scale must be the point which is nearest to non-existence. There seem to be only two ways of meeting this difficulty. One is by investing " matter " (in the Platonic sense of the hypothetical subject of " forms ") with negative characteristics, so that it becomes the seat of the evil principle. This is metaphysical dualism. The other is by forcing our judgments of value to conform to a monistic scheme set by the existential scale. Then evil will be only a defect of goodness ; all values will be positive. That is not at all how moral evil appears to us ; the moralist will never be content with a theory which whittles away the fact of sin and the possibility of rebellion against God.

I can get no further than this which follows. I do not submit it as an adequate solution. In the mind of God—in heaven, we may say—there is no battle between good and evil. The antithesis which makes some kind of dualism necessary for all who take the moral choice seriously, belongs to the stage of our probation. It is real, terribly real, for us while we live here, and it is closely bound up with the existential aspect of the world as we know it. There is no great difficulty about the negative signs as such ; it is a matter of choice whether we use a thermometer in which zero stands for freezing-point, or one in which freezing-point is $+$ 32 degrees. We shall, on the whole, choose a monistic scale both for existence and value, but at the lower end of both scales in the world as known to ordinary consciousness, are things which " ought not so to be." We may leave it to Bradley and other philosophers to explain, if they can, how evil is "somehow" transmuted and neutralised in a higher sphere. We cannot really solve the problem, because we are living on a plane where the conflict between good and evil is real. We are not cut off from a vision of the sphere where the elect form a church " without spot or wrinkle or any such thing "; but we cannot describe the conditions of such a life as if we knew all about it, or as if it were already our home.

Is anything valuable in itself? The fashionable philosophical creed says No ; we are told that absolute unchanging values, which are not merely valuable for this or that person, are an illusion. Many, however, are getting weary of this disintegrating scepticism and relativism, which seem to endanger the meaning of life. When we are not trying to philosophise, it seems plain that the religious man who counts the world well lost for the love of God, the moral man who " lives ever in his great Taskmaster's eye," the patriot who dies for his country, the artist who lives for his art, the scientist whose interests are entirely absorbed in the discovery of nature's secrets, and indeed any person who devotes himself to a worthy cause, serve absolute values. Disinterestedness is a fact which the pragmatists seek in vain to explain away ; and disinterestedness implies that life itself is not the highest value.

We have seen that the ideal of physical science is a closed system of logical sequences, often miscalled cause and effect. Whether this ideal scheme is invulnerable within the limits of physical science is much disputed. In any case, it is an abstract scheme, since it leaves out much which a philosophy is bound to include. Not only does it neglect most of our values, but it attempts to describe the totality of things as independent of any subject. This is an abstraction, but it does not necessarily follow, though it has been often asserted, that all valuation is excluded from this view. I have argued that it is not true to say that all values are values for a person,[1] nor that it is only when our business is with the individual, and not when our interest centres in the universal, that the consideration of value arises at all.[2] Sorley is sound, from our point of view, in rejecting the theory of values as merely subjective; but the highest values are, as we hold, super-individual and absolute. The difference between the two points of view may be lessened if we say (with Sorley himself) that " there is no such thing as a pure ego," and that the " person " is capable of infinite expansion, till it can apprehend and express pure values. " When he *came to himself*, he said, I will arise and go to my father." But in opposition to the statement that all values are personal, we must assert that in the appreciation of æsthetic values and of the values of truth there is usually no reference to a person; the values are recognised as super-personal and universal. Even in morals the will does not aim at a good determined by personal motives. In the mathematical and mechani-cal sciences the only value sought is that of truth; but truth is one of the absolute values. It is a serious philo-sophical error to say that science excludes, or tries to exclude, all valuation.

Psychology is an abstract study, like natural science. The word should be confined to the science which *describes* inner experience. For it, desire and rejection are part of the neutral content of consciousness. We are still,

---

[1] The rejected view is held by Meinong, and by T. H. Green, *Prolegomena to Ethics*, paragraph 84; also by Sorley.

[2] Sorley, p. 110.

in psychology, outside any valuation except the scientific value of truth.

When we come to the world of Will, in the consciousness of individuals, we have of course valuation. But the world of personal desires has no unconditional values. If there is nothing super-personal, there are no absolute values.[1]

Our difference from some good authorities as to the existence of super-personal values depends partly on different theories of what constitutes personality. I find the ancient distinction between spirit and soul illuminating. The two words indicate two phases or stages of life, stages which are traversed by the human personality in its normal progress, and which also correspond to a less and a more adequate knowledge of the real world. Life on the psychic plane (there is no intention of dividing the two stages sharply from each other) gives us a dualism of subjective and objective, and an unresolved disparity of existence and value. Valuation is present all through. The *psyche* observes its own states from outside. It contemplates its own inner states, and an outside world ; it cannot unify them. Spirit, when fully master of itself,

---

[1] So Münsterberg, who, however, says, " If there is no super-personal *Will*, there are no absolute values " This misuse of the word *Will* vitiates, in my opinion, parts of his admirable book on *The Eternal Values*. " The true experience," he says, " is always of Will directed to a goal." This is true only of moral effort; "Spirit," as George Meredith says, "raves not for a goal." The apprehension of value is an appreciation, not a conation. In fact, in contemplating existences we try to get rid of the subjective bias, that which Münsterberg strangely calls " the judgment of the Will." It was Pasteur, a devout Christian, who said, " It is the greatest disorder of the mind to allow the Will to direct belief."

is the self-consciousness of the completely real. For it existence and value are one. From this higher state comes the irradiation of absolute value imperfectly perceived by the Soul.

To the pragmatist who will have no dealings with the Absolute, even in valuation, Münsterberg replies, I think, cogently, that " every doubt of absolute values destroys itself. As thought it contradicts itself, as denial it denies itself, as belief it despairs of itself." The arguments of the pragmatist have no force when we acknowledge beforehand the independent value of truth. If the proof of the merely individual significance of truth has itself only individual significance, it cannot claim any general meaning. If, on the other hand, it demands to be taken as generally valid, the possibility of general truth is acknowledged from the start. As Münsterberg says again, " to deny every thought which is more than relative is to deprive every thought, even sceptical thought itself, of its own presuppositions." If I want to be a logical sceptic, my own " I " crumbles.

Our moral consciousness affirms emphatically that the moral Will does not aim at a good determined by personal motives. The *ought* is fundamental in morals, and cannot be explained as a means to anything else. The same absoluteness belongs to beauty and truth. It is a common error to say that values must be subjective because they are appreciated by us. We might as well say that facts are subjective because they are apprehended by us. It is of course possible to hold this, but only if with Hume we argue that there is no objective connexion between our experiences of the outer world. A science of nature then becomes as impossible as objectively valid value-judgments.[1]

What are the absolute values, those which are valued not as instruments to anything else, but which stand in their own right, guaranteed by the testimony of our whole personality as being ultimately real? I have already indicated that I accept the usual triad of absolute values—Goodness, Beauty, and Truth. But what are the criteria? There are, I think, three. First, they are not means to anything else, nor even to each other, though they are not sundered from each other, but united as a threefold cord not quickly broken. Next, they have a universal quality. They take us out of ourselves, out of the small circle of our private personal interests. In a sense, they are essentially impersonal. Lastly, they satisfy, delight, and elevate us, so that when we have been in contact with them we feel that we have found our highest or deepest selves. In asserting their absoluteness we assert that a relation exists between ourselves and the universe which is a relation not of use, but of love, and that the relation of love is more real than the relation of use.[2]

The famous three—Truth, Goodness, and Beauty (the order in which we name them matters not at all, since we may call them co-eternal and co-equal)—all have these necessary marks of real or spiritual being. The love of *Truth* has these marks. No matter in what field we are seeking truth, that is, the correspondence of our thoughts with the nature of things, we feel when we have found it

[1] Sorley, pp. 134-136.
[2] Clutton Brock, *Studies in Christianity*, p. 10.

that here is something which exists in its own right, which
stands proudly aloof from our little personal schemes, and
which we are permanently the better for having found.[1]
Lord Balfour points out how little we are interested in a
story if we find that it is not true. This proves that the
work of the student and investigator is a branch of the
larger priesthood. Bishop Berkeley declares this in noble
words: " Truth is the cry of all, but the game of a few.
Certainly, when it is the chief passion, it doth not give
way to vulgar cares and views ; nor is it connected with
a little ardour in the early time of life, active perhaps to
pursue, but not so fit to weigh and revise. He that
would make a real progress in knowledge must dedicate
his age as well as youth, the later growth as well as the
first fruits, at the altar of Truth." I will also quote the
late Professor Carveth Read, who paraphrases what
Aristotle says in praise of his own vocation ; the quotation
may be useful as illustrating what I mean by absolute
value: " All that Aristotle says of the philosophic life is
true, namely, that it is the exercise of that which is highest
in our nature, and concerned with the highest things—
the being and laws of the universe ; that for those who
are capable of it, it is a more enduring activity than any
other ; that it gives the purest enjoyment to those who
sufficiently practise it ; that it is less dependent than any
other pursuit upon external condition. . . . Philosophy
more than anything else is its own end and reward. It is
above the level of human nature, but so much the more

---

[1] I cannot agree with Laird, who argues that Truth is not an Intrinsic
Value. But sometimes " Wisdom " seems a better word than " Truth."

should we aspire to it." [1]   The consideration of Truth as an object of pursuit raises the rather interesting question why it is that all the higher Values are ours only as the prize of effort.   The fatal mistake of authoritarian dogmatism in religion is to suppose that religious conviction can be had ready made.   We cannot make spiritual truths our own by merely saying, " I believe whatever the Bible says," or "what Holy Church teaches," and by anathematising those who think differently.   Clement of Alexandria and Lessing both aver that the search for truth is better than the possession of it, meaning of course that without the effort the possession is illusory.   So Emerson says :   " God offers to every man the choice between truth and repose.   Take which you please ; you can never have both."

I am defending the *intuitive* theory of divine knowledge.   It is imparted to us from above.   This has been held by all the Platonists, and is expressed in religious language by Cudworth :   " All the knowledge and wisdom that is in creatures, whether angels or men, is nothing else but a participation of that one, eternal, and increated wisdom of God."   If I were writing a treatise on epistemology, it would be necessary to investigate this general theory of Truth much more in detail.   What kind of truths can thus be revealed intuitively ?   When Spinoza says that " just as light manifests itself and darkness, so truth is the norm of itself and falsehood," he gives us no criterion by which we may distinguish true intuition from false opinion.   Plato and Aristotle both assume that

---

[1] Carveth Read, *Natural and Social Morals*, p. 42.

Truth is attainable, and this is what they are most concerned to assert. Plato mentions what logicians call the
principle of contradiction, infallibility, and distinctness as
tests of true knowledge in contrast with opinion. Aristotle
admits chance among the principles of things; in other
words, he renounces the claim to bring all Truth under
the laws of cause and effect.[1] The Stoics found the test
of Truth in the irresistible conviction which accompanies
some impressions; the Epicureans in distinct sense-
impressions, especially of touch; this last is of course only
a criterion of empirical reality. Cicero turns the criterion
of "common conceptions" (common to all men) into
a doctrine of innate ideas, especially in morals (*semina
innata virtutum*). Descartes emphasised clearness of conception as the test of truth, without distinguishing perception and conception; "*sentire, imaginari, et pure
intellegere, sunt tantum diversi modi percipiendi.*" This is
more like intuitivism than the rationalism which determines much of his thought.

The Catholic philosophers have continued to work out
the *philosophia perennis* on their own lines. Quite recently
there has been a vigorous revival of Thomism in the hands
of men like Maritain and Bloy in France, Sheen at Louvain,
D'Arcy, and Christopher Dawson in England. The
English apologists of this school are, I think, more balanced,
less rhetorical, and therefore more cogent than the French.
The chief fault that I venture to find in some of them is
that they undervalue religious experience as an organ for
the apprehension of truth. It is probable that they shrink

---

[1] Carveth Read, *Natural and Social Morals*, p. 39.

from assigning much weight to a faculty which is certainly not confined to Roman Catholics.[1] The mystical experience is clearly independent of denominational loyalties. They also fall back upon the authority of revelation in matters where no external revelation is conceivable, such as the question whether the universe was or was not created in time; and they pin their faith too unflinchingly upon the old scholastic arguments, which, even if they are logically without flaw, seem to many modern thinkers to substitute rigid concepts for the complex problems of the real world. The intelligence, which they rightly desire to place again upon its throne, is an organ of truth which does not operate only by logic; in its own domain it "*sees* the invisible." We do not fall into what these writers condemn as " ontologism " when we assert that the knowledge of God can be attained only by the activity of the entire personality, using its own prerogative on a higher plane than that of mere rationalism. The new Thomists are far too good Platonists to deny this, but I think they rationalise revelation rather too much.

Plotinus says, " Are not Spirit, the Spiritual World, and Truth all one ? " [2] Truth, for him, is subjectively a complete understanding of the laws and conditions of actual existence, a true interpretation of the world of sense as knowable by Soul when illuminated by Spirit.

---

[1] See especially D'Arcy, *The Nature of Belief*, pp. 235 and 245. But I am reluctant to criticise an author who has taken upon himself, *proprio motu*, to *canonise* my master Plotinus (p. 232) !

[2] *Enn.*, 5. 5. 3. Strictly, Truth is the correspondence between θεωρία. contemplation, and its object, τὸ θεωρητόν. It requires the *activity* of the perceiving Spirit. Sense perception (αἴσθησις) only conveys δόξα, opinion, because it is passive (5. 5. 1).

Objectively, it is an ordered harmony or system of cosmic life, interpreted in terms of vital law.[1] This is substantially my own view. Do we believe in disinterested curiosity, in the pure desire to know ? The pragmatists do not, and therefore Truth for them is merely relative and instrumental. Their scepticism about the existence, or at any rate about the knowableness, of absolute Truth is based on what I think we might call metaphysical solipsism. But I cannot help suspecting that the popularity of this philosophy with Americans is due partly to their experience of commercial methods. The old way of doing business, said Mr. Ponderevo in Mr. Wells' *Tono-Bungay*, was to tote commodities. The new way is to create values (by advertisement) ; "no need to tote." The Americans are so much used to bluff each other that they think they can bluff nature and God. For most of us, the pure love of Truth is so precious and so precarious an acquisition that we are jealous at any attempt to deprive us of it. It is as devotees of Truth that men of science have conferred such signal benefits upon civilisation.

We will consider next moral *Goodness*, as the second of the absolute values. So far as we are brought close to goodness, and especially to goodness in the form of disinterestedness, sympathy, or love, we feel that we have reached the heart of life, that we are lifted out of ourselves, and that we are enjoying a happiness which, come what may, will be a permanent enlargement of our experience. If we mentally compare human affection with the other good things of life, we shall recognise, I think,

---

[1] See my *Philosophy of Plotinus*, Vol. II., p. 77.

that it has this absolute character which distinguishes it from most of them. It is an end in itself. It brings us, so far as it is really pure and disinterested, into harmony with the mind of God, Who is love. And it " never faileth." " It is better," we are told, " to have loved and lost than never to have loved at all," because love's labour is never really lost.

Kant, it is well known, held that there is nothing purely good except the good will. For us, what we call morality is the time-form of a goodness or perfection which is not itself in time. The good will strives to actualise in time an absolute value which in itself is above the clash of good and evil. Morality as we know it belongs to the psychic, not to the spiritual plane. The will, in realising its object, must lose its property as conation.

I have noted the abuse of the word " Will " by Münsterberg; I think that Kantians generally tend to make the scope of this faculty too extensive. If a man wants to know what his real religion is, he should ask himself this question, " What are the things which I would die rather than do ? " With many men, the list would consist mainly of things dishonourable rather than sinful; cruelty and base ingratitude would appear on almost every list. But whatever the unpardonable sin for us is—even if it is merely to act like a cad—if there are any things which we would die rather than do, we have acknowledged Goodness as an absolute value. Professor Taylor, in his contribution to *Essays Catholic and Critical*, gives examples of things which must on no account be done, and adds that, if we admit this absolute obligation,

" the greatest good, to which I must at need be prepared to sacrifice everything else, must be something which cannot even be appraised in the terms of a secular arithmetic, something incommensurable with the 'welfare' even of the whole human race." If it is to be had in fruition at all, it must be had where the secular environment has finally and for ever fallen away.

The third strand in our threefold cord is *Beauty*, which is more obviously an end in itself than the other two, since it subserves very few practical uses in human life. It, too, has the three marks of spiritual reality which I have mentioned. It claims to exist in its own right. It takes us out of ourselves. And it is a permanent enrichment of experience. So we may say with Augustine, Platonising as he so often does, " All that is beautiful comes from the highest Beauty which is God."

It may seem strange that there has been an old quarrel between art and philosophy, and sometimes between art and religion. Plato, the greatest artist among philosophers, led the indictment against art. He regarded it as two degrees removed from reality, and distrusted its moral tendency. At the same time, no thinker has given more importance to the cult of the beautiful as a path to the knowledge of the good. Between Plato and Plotinus (Philostratus deserves special credit here) it came to be recognised that art is no mere " imitation " of visible reality, but a work of the " imagination," now first given its true value—imagination, which, as Philostratus says, is a more cunning craftsman than imitation, since imitation copies things which it has seen, but imagination things which it has not seen. He instances the idealised representations of the human form in great sculpture.

We may hesitate to say with Eucken that "Jesus effected an artistic transformation of human existence." But He loved nature as few others have loved it between His own time and Wordsworth, and His parables show a creative imagination which is full of poetry.

The Greek idea of beauty gained influence in the Church. Augustine, following Plotinus, taught that through the beautiful an ascent to an all-embracing unity can be made. The whole universe is an ethical work of art, an order reconciling justice and love.[1] In the Middle Ages we all know with what splendid success art was employed in the service of religion. This alliance was dissolved, or partially dissolved, before the Reformation ; the revived Paganism of the later Renaissance was less wholesome and less religious than the models which it sought to imitate. In the Reformed Churches there was a curious recrudescence of Jewish antagonism to plastic and pictorial art. In the Eastern Church iconoclasm, as Christopher Dawson has lately shown, was part of the Semitic revolt against the Hellenisation of the East. In the West there can be no question of direct Semitic influence, except through the reading of the Old Testament, which no doubt had a considerable effect. But the Jewish hatred of " idolatry " provided Scriptural support for the new type of asceticism, which was at once the strength of Calvinism and the foundation of its harshness. Kant, in spite of his austere moralism, recognised the independence of the concept of beauty, and its fountain-

---

[1] Eucken, *Main Currents of Modern Thought*, p. 375.

head in the soul itself. It has been said of Schiller that
" the unique quality of his mode of thought consisted in
a high purity of moral standpoint combined with the
fullest recognition of the independence of artistic life."
But the old quarrel is continually breaking out again, and
is sure to break out as soon as men begin either to subordinate morality to art or art to morality, or to deny
any close connexion between the two. The absolute
values are autonomous but never really antagonistic to
each other. The great creative artists have never been
" æsthetes," and the great moralists have never been sour
Cynics.

In our own age there is probably as much conscious
appreciation of natural beauty as at any earlier period,
and certainly more appreciation of the beauty of the
human form than in the early Middle Ages, though
industrialism, with its unnatural conditions, produces
ugly types of humanity. In music the northern Euro-
peans have, I suppose, produced greater masterpieces than
ever came from the south. But at present there is not
much creative art of the highest quality in literature,
painting, or sculpture, and the almost instinctive gracious-
ness of the old architecture, in humble buildings as well
as in those which aimed at splendour or dignity, has,
since the industrial revolution, given place to an un-
sightliness never before seen in the dwellings of civilised
men. The recovery from the age of bad taste is in
progress, but it is painful and somewhat artificial. Our
civilisation seems no longer to express itself naturally in
beautiful forms. As for the deliberate ugliness of much
modernist sculpture and painting, I can only regard it as

a disease, and hope that the evil fashion will soon pass away. It aims, we are told, at "expressiveness," disregarding all accepted standards of beauty. Unfortunately, what it expresses is barbarous and repulsive. There may also be some idea of a geometrical art, as Spinoza gave us a geometrical ethics. But the whole movement is absurd, or would be if it were not connected with the horrors of Bolshevist materialism.

The greatest gifts of art, it has been lately said, are peace and reconciliation. " In those rare moments when we are moved by some beautiful poem or a great work of art, we are not only absorbed by it, but our mind is raised to a higher altitude when it beholds the vision of things far above sense-knowledge or discursive reasoning."[1] So Vaughan speaks of times

> When on some gilded cloud or flower
> My gazing soul would dwell an hour,
> And in those weaker glories spy
> Some shadows of eternity.

The man that is not an artist, said Blake, is not a Christian. This sounds rather severe for the worthy Philistine ; but the sense of beauty finds queer bypaths. Poincaré assures us that the higher mathematics are full of beauties, "which all true mathematicians recognise." And even the most inartistic of Christians may "make their lives a true poem," as Milton exhorts us to do.

Are these three—Truth, Goodness, and Beauty—the only absolute values ? Claims have been made to place *happiness*, *life* itself, and *holiness* by the side of the famous three. Let us take these three candidates in turn.

[1] Radhakrishnan, *An Idealist View of Life*, p. 194.

We shall almost all admit that what contributes to happiness is valuable. But happiness is a mere form into which almost any view of the worth of life may be fitted.[1] A word which is easier to handle, as having a more definite meaning than happiness, is *pleasure*. Hedonism gives a standard which most people habitually accept, though few avow it. The calculus of pleasure and pain is in fact the one most commonly applied to all problems of social ethics. Its attraction for thinkers—under the name utilitarianism—is that it offers to make ethics a quantitative science, as when we are bidden to aim at the greatest happiness of the greatest number. It is now almost universally admitted that Bentham's attempt to weigh the imponderable was a failure, since pleasures differ in kind and are not commensurable. Pleasure, as distinguished from happiness or well-being, is also discredited as an unworthy aim, and few would venture to avow that it is their highest good. Indeed, we all frequently give up pleasure for the sake of something that we value more. When a soldier (for example) gives his life for his country, can he reasonably be said to be promoting his own pleasure? This disposes of the claim of pleasurable sensation to be an absolute value. In its higher forms happiness is the subjective feeling which arises when we are in contact with any one of the three absolute values, but to aim directly at it is to miss it.

But, it may be asked, Does not the happiness of heaven, as imagined by Christians, belong to this class? Is not the consummation of bliss an absolute value? I should answer that the hope of heaven belongs not to the

[1] Sorley, p. 28.

calculus of pleasure and pain, but to the ideal of *perfection*, which some would substitute for the word *goodness* as the name of the absolute value which we considered second. The essence of immortal life is not pleasure or enjoyment, but the fulfilment of all that we have it in us to become. It is life in and with God, in the knowledge of whom, and not in any dream of endless progress, still less in the curious arts of the necromancers, we find our immortality. That is the only proof of the future life which Christ gave —in speaking to the Sadducees, who disbelieved in it. " God is not the God of the dead but of the living, for all live unto him." *Quod Deo non perit, sibi non perit*, as Augustine says, in an unforgettable sentence. As for pleasure, here or hereafter, we may say with Seneca, " Non dux sed comes voluptas, nec quia delectat placet sed quia placet delectat."

In the same way *holiness*, the sense of the " numinous," which Otto has lately brought into prominence, is not another value, distinct from Truth, Goodness, and Beauty, but the feeling of awe and reverence which attaches itself to all absolute values, most commonly perhaps to mani- festations of eminent moral goodness. When God is the object of the sense of the " numinous," the thought of His revealed attributes, regarded as unified in His nature, inspires the emotion of *worship*, a very important part of prayer. The religious man, as Radhakrishnan says, traces the values of truth, goodness, and beauty to a common background, God, the holy, Who is both without and within us. He lives in a new world which fills his mind with light, his heart with joy and his soul with love. God is seen as light, life, and love.

Others have said, Is not *Life*, or the preservation of life, an absolute value ? To this I answer that the mere desire for survival is not a value, or only an instrumental value. This is true, whether our desire is for individual or for racial survival. By valuing life in and for itself, we are in danger, as our Lord warns us, of losing it. Life only becomes an absolute value when it is used, as in the Fourth Gospel, as a synonym of eternal life. And this timeless existence in the spiritual world is not a separate value, but the mode of existence proper to all the absolute values, which are themselves timeless. It cannot therefore be added to the other three. The question remains whether duration is in itself valuable, and if so, what kind or degree of value should be ascribed to it. This is part of the problem of Time, which I have already discussed. Some degree of duration is apparently necessary for the manifestation or realisation of all values. It is the necessary frame of values in the psychic sphere, where all activity takes place under the forms of space and time. But the philosophy which I am upholding in this book forbids us to include duration among the absolute values. Strictly, it is a polarisation of eternal life, which is above time.

We must beware of vagueness in our use of terms, though this is difficult to avoid when we are contemplating, as it were, a triple star, the light of which is blended. Mackenzie (in *Contemporary British Philosophy*, Vol. I, p. 243) wishes to make Beauty the supreme value. But his Beauty is τὸ καλόν, which is as much Goodness as Beauty. So τὸ ἀγαθόν in Plotinus is rather *perfection* than moral goodness. We naturally wish, when we are studying one of the higher values, to exclude nothing from it which we feel to be valuable. This is quite legitimate, though it leads to a want of precision in the use of words.

If we try to form a hierarchy of values, we are brought back to the old question of the *summum bonum*, which is the attempt to determine the supreme value for a human subject. Here we find important differences among social groups, more perhaps geographical than temporal. In the West, the commonest answer would probably be that the highest good is either happiness or perfection. Indian thinkers would say, almost unanimously, that the highest good is peace, or deliverance. Since, as they say, the ideal consummation cannot be attained under the conditions of life in this world, and since unrest and unhappiness are inseparably bound up with the whirl of events in which the life of this world consists, salvation must be a deliverance from the sphere of becoming, of living, working, suffering, and dying. The highest good is a dreamless sleep in the bosom of the Eternal. Sometimes the otherworldliness of Christian thought has approximated to this type, which, however, is not congenial to the western modern man.

I have already deprecated any attempt to reduce any of the absolute values to any of the others, or to subordinate one to another. They shine, as I have said, like a triple star, their light blended, but not confused. In the eternal world none of them can be quite as we see them ; they are unified only in their source, the mind of God Himself, and it is in religious worship that they appear to us most completely harmonised.

It is, in my opinion, an illegitimate use of the principle of value to assume that all the failures of time will be made good in eternity. This optimistic theory bears some resemblance to Bradley's view that imperfect appearances need only to be " supplemented " in order to take their place in reality. But whereas in Bradley this view arises from regarding all problems as soluble by logic,[1] and by depriving Time of nearly all its significance, the optimism of the popular religious teaching of our day seems to arise from a good-natured idea that no one really deserves to be punished. " Dieu me pardonnera ; c'est son métier." There is also the pantheistic notion that the failure of a human being to reach an attainable standard is a partial failure of God Himself, Who willeth not the death of a sinner. For the theist, the loss of a human soul does not affect the *being* of God at all ; whether it affects His happiness is rather more than we can say. Christianity has consistently taught from the first that a man can finally lose his soul, though not the soul which would have been his if he had not been a bad man. Within our experience, evil is *not* made good, either on a large scale or on a small. Injustice and failure are facts, and the supreme heroism is to suffer irreparable wrong for the sake of others. Universalism " heals the hurt " of the problem of evil " too slightly." The Christian doctrine of resurrection was not meant to assert so much the permanence of positive values, or their augmentation, as the irrevocable significance of the moral choice here and now, and the law of retribution. How different the

[1] Bradley's argument is criticised by Pringle-Pattison, *The Idea of God*, pp. 234-235.

conception of theodicy was in earlier times from that
which is popular now may be gathered from Aquinas.[1]
To almost all Catholic theologians the awful fate of the
wicked seemed to follow from the conservation of the
highest value—the satisfaction of divine justice. Augustine regards it as not only ethically, but æsthetically
necessary ; " the contrast may increase the beauty of the
whole."

It is clear that, in our view, man does not make values
any more than he makes reality. But perhaps we have
not sufficiently explained the nature of the assurance
which we have that our apprehension of values is not
illusory. I answer that it is the supreme postulate
of reason, or, if we will, an act of faith similar to that
which we make when we assume that our senses are not
in a conspiracy to deceive us. But are we to agree that
" when a judgment of value is asserted to be ultimately
true, it is useless to seek for a proof or to demand one ? "[2]
We have no wish to assign infallibility to the unenlight-
ened conscience, to the taste of the vulgar, or to the dogmatism of the ignorant or the bigot. Infallibility is a
category which man cannot use. But values are not states
of conscious minds ;   they are, in Bosanquet's phrase,
" spiritual worlds, at once objective and subjective."

---

[1] " Cum contraria iuxta se posita magis elucescant, beati in regno
coelesti videbunt poenas damnatorum, ut beatitudo illis magis complaceat "
(*Summa Theol.*, III., Suppl., 94, 1).   " Homo habet totam plenitudinam
suae perfectionis in Deo.   Perfectio caritatis est essentialis beatitudini
quantum ad dilectionem Dei, non quantum ad dilectionem proximi.
Unde si esset una anima fruens Deo, beata esset, non habens proximum
quem diligeret " (*Summa*, Pars II., Quaestio 4, Art. 8).

[2] McTaggart, quoted by Bosanquet.

We cannot be sure that *our* ideas about the ultimate values are right ; insight into reality must be earned by intellectual, moral, and æsthetic discipline. Nevertheless, with all due humility, we know sometimes that we have touched bedrock—that a fact is certainly true, an action certainly right, an object certainly beautiful. Nor do we deny that a true valuation may be taught. We do not start with a highly developed intuitive perception of the right, the true, and the beautiful. There is a tradition which we have to learn, and a training through which we have to pass. For example, the standard of values revealed in the Gospels is a permanent enrichment of humanity, and the same may be said with an almost equal degree of confidence of other notable flowering-times of the spirit of man. In short, we do not claim that we ourselves, or anyone else, is in possession of final truth, goodness, or beauty. We only claim that these attributes of God exist in their own right, that we know them in part, and that they are the ultimate standards by which, as an eternal background, all our lower, instrumental values must be measured.

I have said that morality is concerned not so much with the apprehension of values, as with their production and increase. The presence of the ideal in human experience is a fact ; but the ideal is essentially something desired and reached after. It is through this striving that our nature fulfils itself in self-transcendence. Our ideals —the awakening of the ultimate values within us—are the creative forces which enable the soul to grow to its full stature. In religious language, the ideal is the Spirit of God within man. Thus we find that at least in one part

14

of the universe there is a purposive production of values. The human Will introduces final causes into the processes of nature. Nor is this creativeness confined to the moral Will. The artist also creates after an eternal pattern, not merely imitating the given, but imparting visible form to the ideas which come to him from a higher sphere. The man of Science, too, creates values in the sensible world by interpreting eternal ideas under the form of vital law.

Höffding, in his *Philosophy of Religion*, makes faith in the *conservation* of value the essential part of religion. He compares the conservation of value in religion to the conservation of energy in physics. The analogy, in view of recent developments in natural science, is unfortunate as a support of his thesis. And on other grounds the word conservation is not well chosen. He should have been content with maintaining the objectivity and eternity of the highest values. Human values will certainly not be conserved through all time. Our doom is fixed. We are no more certain that the sun will rise to-morrow than that a time will come when he will rise no more, or will rise unseen by any living being on this earth. If the eternal existence of values is what Höffding meant to assert (I do not think it is), conservation, which belongs to the time series, is not the best word to express his meaning. I am not quite clear about his meaning when he says, " there are no definite empirical values in the conservation of which we can believe." What, then, is conserved except the bare form of value, an empty husk ? He says that " value can only maintain itself by change." But the eternal cannot change, and the forms in which it may successively clothe itself are not themselves the values, in our sense. But Höffding is not consistent. He not only admits (p. 262 of his *Philosophy of Religion*) that the conservation of values must be a matter of faith, but (p. 272) he says that value is not dependent on its own conservation. "Were the good or the beautiful to perish, would they be the less good and beautiful ? " Is not this to abandon his main thesis ? The objectivity of value is not the same as its conservation. Varisco (*The Great Problems*, p. 270) is right when he says, " value will or will not be permanent according as the divine personality does or does not exist." He says (p. 278) that he himself believes in the permanence of values ; and yet he is not quite a theist in the Christian sense. He believes only (p. 363) in " a personal consciousness of which all the sensible world is the content."

Meyerson (*De l'Explication dans les Sciences*, p. 567) warns us that theories of conservation have had an unfortunate history. Descartes formulated the principle of the conservation of movement, which in the form which he gave it soon had to be abandoned. Black's theory of the conservation of heat had no better fate. The theory of " phlogiston "—the theory of the conservation of combustibility, was ruined by the demonstrations of Lavoisier. The conservation of energy is not incompatible with the belief that a time will come when it will no longer be utilisable. However that may be, we cannot substitute mere duration (conservation) for eternal life.

Christians may justly claim that in our religion the three ultimate values have been gathered up and unified as they never had been before. Our Lord's whole life was full of the purest affection, of the most dauntless intellectual sincerity, and of simple love for all things bright and beautiful, green fields, flowers, mountains and lakes, and the one thing in nature which is more beautiful than these—little children.

Taken together, these three values are a very full revelation of the nature of God. We need not discuss their relative importance, for all are essential. But St. Paul, if we had asked him the question, would probably have repeated, with a slight change, the last words of 1 Corinthians xiii : " Now abideth Truth, Beauty, Love, these three, but the greatest of these is Love."

6

GOD AND THE WORLD

CHRISTIANITY is a definite religion, the product of a great revelation or world-experience. If it be objected that the experience is only that of the Mediterranean races, which in a plastic age of their development were moulded by two traditions, that of Græco-Roman civilisation and that of the later Hebrew monotheism, we may answer that this has in fact been the main stream of civilisation, with which the religions and philosophies of Further Asia cannot compare in importance. If it be further objected that this legacy from an earlier culture has now been exhausted, and that the modern world remains nominally Christian only from a kind of inertia, the charge may just now be difficult to meet. It could not be discussed without considering at length what the essentials of Christianity are. This is not the subject of my present book, which deals mainly with cosmological theory—the relations of God and the world, of time and eternity, of existence and value. But it is my contention that on all these aspects of one supreme problem the Christian religion has an answer which, though far from claiming to solve all mysteries, is satisfying to the human mind, though it excludes certain attempted solutions of the problem which have been accepted by many thinkers of repute.

The history of Christianity shows that it is essentially
inhospitable to some other religions and philosophies,
which were at first and have often been since its rivals.
It encountered polytheism in the Hellenistic world,
though this was already sublimated into a kind of monotheism in educated circles. Catholicism was to reintro-
duce a subordinate polytheism in its cult of saints, but it
refused to come to terms with the tolerant *theocrasia* of
the later paganism, which treated the gods of the nations
as various names of the same Beings. It encountered
Deism in the writings of Aristotle, Scepticism in those of
Pyrrho and (at one time) in the Academy, Theosophy in
the Gnostics, metaphysical dualism in Manicheism, and
rejected them all. If it did not directly encounter the
Acosmism of Indian thought, there can be no doubt
what its answer would have been. On the other hand,
it accepted on the whole the eclectic Platonism which was
the dominant philosophy of religion under the later
Western Empire, only stiffening the definitely theistic
element in it by its acceptance of the teaching of the Old
and New Testaments, which affirm a personal God.
Christianity has always been a religion seeking a philosophy,
not a philosophy creating a religion, and in consequence
there always have been and still are some ragged edges in
its intellectual presentation ; its eschatology, for example,
is a mass of contradictions, as perhaps every eschatology
must be. But both as a religion and a philosophy it
belongs to an easily recognisable type. It rejects, besides
those theories which I have just mentioned, the pantheism which identifies God with the world, whether this
takes the form of pancosmism and denies the transcen-

dence of God, or of the opposite extreme, in which the world is swallowed up in God. It rejects materialism, whether naked or disguised, and as a child of Platonism it, rejects positivism and sceptical relativism. Many attempts have been made to introduce these views, or some of them, into the coherent structure of Christian philosophy; but in every case the effect has been disruptive. This is why I have attached so much importance to the *philosophia perennis* or Great Tradition. We are not, of course, obliged to be either Christians or Platonists, still less Thomists; but those philosophers who have tried to build up a Neo-Christianity on the basis of the new philosophies which I discussed in an earlier chapter have, in my opinion, failed in their attempt.

This Great Tradition is a river supplied by two main affluents, the Hellenistic philosophy of religion, which, be it remembered, was no mere intellectual speculation, but an attempt to find a reasonable basis for good and holy living, and the contribution made by Judaism. The element furnished by the historical Jesus of Nazareth may perhaps be described as a pure ethical and spiritual monotheism—the noblest teaching of the Hebrew prophets raised to a still higher level. But from the very first the Person of " the Lord " became the centre of the Church's faith, distinguishing it from all rival cults. This core of Christianity was readily transplanted into European soil; its appeal indeed is universal; it is religion itself in its sublimest form. Even in Hellenised Christianity there was a Hebraic residuum, composed not only of a dwindling apocalyptic Messianism and of the inspired authority attributed to the Old Testament Scriptures, but of a consciousness of sin and of the need for forgiveness which was, at least by comparison, alien to Greek thought. The bleak monotheism of the desert, which had a curious revival at the Reformation, was strong enough to counteract, to some extent, the paganising and pantheistic tendencies which soon manifested themselves.

I pointed out in my book on Plotinus that the education given to our students both in classics and in theology has tended to obscure the continuity of the Christian Church with the classical civilisation. Comparatively little attention has been given to Greek philosophy after the Stoics; an " interval of silence " has been wrongly assumed between the last of the Old Testament prophets and the Christian revelation; and the Christian Church has been treated as the legitimate successor of the Jewish covenant. Recent scholarship has sometimes gone to the opposite extreme, regarding the Catholic Church as merely the last chapter in Hellenistic civilisation. This is an obvious exaggeration, when we remember that Paganism was definitely defeated by ideas which came from the East. The two streams had blended before the Christian missions, as we see from the Wisdom-literature and Philo. The great difference between the Judaism of the Dispersion and that of Palestine has not always been recognised. It is no part of my plan in this book to discuss, for example, the origin of the Johannine conception of the Logos. I shall assume that Catholic Christianity was from the first a European religion—those who speak Greek think in Greek—but that the Jewish doctrine of God and of His relation to the world remained authoritative, and caused divergences in Christian cosmology from the prevailing teaching of the later Greek philosophy. Of these differences the ablest of the Christian Fathers, Augustine, for instance, were well aware.

Christianity is theistic without any compromise; Greek philosophy never emphasised the personality of God. We may define theism as the doctrine that the ultimate ground of the universe is a single supreme Being who is perfect or complete in Himself. This definition excludes not only the "gods many" of paganism, but every form of ultimate dualism or pluralism, such, for example, as those very modern philosophies which make God a kind of President in a society of independently real spirits. It is also incompatible with the theory of a limited, non-omnipotent God, which has been advanced from time to time to account for the evil of the world, from which it is desired to exonerate the Creator. We may think of the part played by *Fate* in Greek theology. This doctrine has been advocated by John Stuart Mill, and in our own generation by Rashdall and H. G. Wells. It is, however, inconsistent with theism as Christianity understands it. For if God is limited by anything outside Himself, He is not the source of all reality, and therefore not God, but a spirit among other spirits. To say that He has voluntarily limited Himself is an illusory escape; for if the limitation is a defect, it cannot, as we have seen, be the Will of a perfect Being. If it is not a defect, there is no meaning in calling it a limitation. When we speak of the omnipotence of God, we do not mean that He can do anything absurd or self-contradictory, or contrary to His own nature. It may even be questioned whether He could do anything contrary to the laws of nature, if those laws include the whole constitution of the universe. A miracle, if established, would be not an exception to, but a refutation of a law which claimed to be universal.

The question whether it is correct to call God the Absolute is not an easy one. The God of religion is not the Godhead in an absolute sense, but the self-revelation of the Godhead. It is a pity that Eckhart's distinction between the Godhead and God has not been more generally adopted by Christian thinkers. The " Godhead " is much the same as the " One beyond existence " of the later Platonists, the God whom " no man hath seen at any time," who " dwelleth in the light that no man can approach unto." Parenthetically, I must say that great confusion has been introduced into Platonic studies by the habit of English scholars of translating " the One " or the " First Principle " in Plotinus by the word " God." The results of this mistake are both to make Neoplatonism more unequivocally theistic than it really is, and, a still worse blunder, to suggest that mystical ecstasy, " the flight of the alone to the Alone," is what Plotinus means by religion. The whole rich content of the Neoplatonic heaven, the world " Yonder," the realm of the eternal values, thus falls out.

The word Absolute as a synonym for God is best avoided, because the use of it makes it difficult to assign any independence to created spirits, who are not God nor parts of God, but creatures " made in His image." In " heaven," if we follow the best philosophers, spirits retain their individuality, though not their separateness, since in the spiritual world there are no separations except those which arise from differences of nature.   Beatified spirits know each other perfectly in God. But in the world of our experience, which we may call the psychic as distinguished from the spiritual world, created spirits are real in their separation from each other. In this world God is neither entirely immanent nor entirely transcendent. He is both; but on the psychic plane neither His immanence nor His transcendence is fully known. In the spiritual world He is fully known as the supreme Reality; but this Reality, in order to be knowable, must contain some inner differentiations. In perfect knowledge, subject and object correspond perfectly to each other; they do not annihilate each other. It is precisely this recognition of a unity in duality as the condition of all existence which has led metaphysicians to postulate an absolute unity beyond existence. This Plotinus calls the One, Eckhart the Godhead. In considering cosmological problems I do not think we need speculate on the nature of this ineffable Being, of whom nothing positive can be predicated without contradiction. Orthodox theologians have often found in the doctrine of the Trinity a revelation of differentiations within the divine nature, by which reciprocal interchange of thought may take place in God Himself, without the medium of any created consciousness. It is no part of my plan in this book to discuss this idea. Hegel also thought that he had found a speculative foundation for Trinitarianism; but whereas in Catholic Christianity the three Persons are co-eternal and co-equal, in the Platonists the third hypostasis, the universal Soul, is inferior in dignity to the first and second, in Hegel the Holy Spirit seems to be the supreme deity. Bernard Shaw has said that the Holy Ghost is " the only survivor " of the Christian Trinity. There are some Liberal theologians for whom this gibe does not entirely miss the mark.

The doctrine which underlies these reflections is that our mental pictures both of God and of the world are necessarily constructions built up from imperfect data. We know in part, but we are obliged to frame coherent systems as if we knew everything. Hence if we find that we cannot frame completely closed systems of reality, that may be a sign that we have partial and occasional access to a higher order, which if we knew it completely would give us a different system from the working hypotheses which suffice for the ordering of our habitual conduct. The psychic world is not a closed system, because it is not ultimate reality. I have no doubt whatever that this is the fact. We do not breathe easily in the world " Yonder," but we are by no means cut off from it. In so far as we are in touch with the intrinsic or ultimate values, we are what St. Paul calls pneumatic or spiritual persons ; we are citizens of the heavenly city, " whose builder and maker is God." It follows that we are, though very imperfectly, " partakers of the divine nature," which accordingly is really immanent in the creation, though it is a great error to obliterate the vast difference between the Creator and created spirits.

The legacy of Judaism has been purely theistic. The legacy of Plato has worked on the whole potently in the same direction. Other Greek thinkers have been precursors of non-theistic or imperfectly theistic systems. Aristotle's influence tends towards deism ; Parmenides is the father of those who have denied all change ; Hera-

cleitus has revived in Bergson and his followers ; Demo-
critus is the founder of materialistic atomism ; Protagoras
of American pragmatism. But the influence of Platonism,
modified no doubt by Aristotle and the Stoa, has probably been stronger than that of all these put together.

And yet Plato, for whom God is " the perfectly good
Soul," moving all things according to regular law, is not
a complete theist. Not only does he by preference (by
no means always) speak of " Gods " in the plural—this
is not of very great importance—but the " patterns "
according to which God creates are metaphysically prior
to the Deity. He uses nothing like the later ontological
argument for the existence of God ; the existence of an
intelligent designer, for him, is a valid inference from the
intelligible causality which we find in the world of
phenomena.

The God of Aristotle is so far removed from participation in events, of which he is not even conscious, that
the transition to pure naturalism among some of his
followers was easy. A very interesting development of
Aristotelianism was the *impersonal* " intellectus agens " of
Averroes.

The Stoics, who even before the admixture of Platonism partially altered the character of their system, taught
that the world is governed by an intelligent but material
force which they identified with fire. They laid great
stress on the *consensus gentium* as their main argument
for the existence of God. This was not " ontologism " ;
their doctrine was that the unwarped operations of the
human mind vindicate a natural theology—belief in
a God Whose providence governs the world. But they

narrowed the belief in universal providence to the assertion that man alone has any value in God's sight; the
lower animals are merely " made for our use," a doctrine
which unhappily is still the prevailing view in the Mediterranean countries.

In Neoplatonism the doctrine that " God is Spirit,"
i.e. immaterial reality, is for the first time (though we
must not forget the Fourth Gospel) quite fully understood and clearly enunciated. The last vestiges of
materialism, which the Stoics never got rid of, and which
are apparent in the Christianised Stoic Tertullian, were
now eradicated. Plotinus and his disciples give us a
hierarchy of existence which is also a hierarchy of value,
and they teach that each level in the hierarchy is in a
condition of one-sided dependence on the order immediately above it. The creation of lower levels in the scale
is not a temporal process; the world is everlasting, as
its Creator is eternal. Creativity is necessary to all the
higher orders, not at all because any of them would not
be complete without it, but because the production of
existences down to the lowest grade above indeterminate
and all-but entirely unreal " matter," is the " nature " of
the higher ranks in the hierarchy. There is an opposite
tendency, a *nisus* of all things to rise to the level of the
order next above them, which is the explanation of the
longing of the human soul to become spirit.[1] All things,

---

[1] I have been blamed, even by friendly critics like Professor Dodds,
for translating νοῦς by " spirit " instead of " intelligence." Lossky
prefers " spirit "; and several German scholars render the word by
" Geist." English philosophers no doubt understand " intelligence "
rightly; but the ordinary reader takes it in an " intellectualist " sense.

Plotinus thought, strive upwards towards the law of their being; or, as Proclus puts it, " all things pray, except the First Principle " (the One). This fine conception, whatever we may think of it as an explanation of organic or inorganic evolution, brings what we may call the return-journey of the soul into clear light; the stages of the ascent are lovingly traced. But the process of creation is not explained, nor is any consistent reason given for it except that it is the nature of heavenly beings so to act. My own opinion is that no rational explanation of the existence of the world is possible; it is a given fact, which we must accept as an ultimate.

I wish especially to emphasise the doctrine of *one-sided* dependence. It belongs to Christian philosophy, and is the denial of pantheism. Hebrew thought, it is hardly necessary to say, never dreamed of denying it. Philosophers of the Hegelian school, and many others, not only deny the possibility of one-sided dependence, but treat it as manifestly absurd. In my opinion, there is nothing absurd or irrational in it, unless we begin by assuming that God is merely the soul or life of the world.

It would take too much of my space to add one more to the innumerable discussions of the four famous "proofs" of God's existence. Catholic theologians still find the cosmological, teleological, and moral arguments valid and useful; the ontological argument is plainly distrusted by Aquinas, and is not used by his modern disciples. It may, I think, be restated in a form much less liable to

I have shown elsewhere what prejudice has been created against the *philosophia perennis* by this mistake. The necessity of rendering ὕλη by " matter " has led to an equally luxuriant crop of errors.

objection than that in which it appears in Anselm.[1] Kant's
" refutation " seems to be directed against the argument
as revived by Descartes. I need not go further into this
controversy, because almost all sound theologians would
now admit that no *a priori* proof of the existence of God
is possible. The real proof is of the nature of a valid
inference, and it falls short of demonstration. Nevertheless, I agree with Lotze that the real cogency of the
ontological argument is only disguised by its awkward
scholastic form. It rests on a deep conviction—the immediate apprehension of the intrinsic values of goodness
and truth. Is it conceivable that all that is good, wise,
and beautiful in our experience can be homeless in the
universe or void of actuality ? We infer from what we
know of these values that there is a Supreme Being in
whom these values live as attributes of His own mind.

Kant's treatment of the " moral argument " seems to
me to stand quite apart from his critical objections to the
other three. It in fact assumes that morality or goodness
is an absolute value, and argues quite rightly that unless
this value is realised in a Supreme Being, our homage to
it is based on a delusion. His insistence that no act is
really moral unless it is done from reverence to the universal law as such, without regard to consequences, is a

[1] Lotze (*Philosophy of Religion*, p. 10), says : " This is obviously
a case where an altogether immediate conviction breaks through into
consciousness ; to wit, the conviction that the totality of all that has
value—all that is perfect, fair, and good—cannot possibly be homeless in
the world or in the realm of actuality, but has the very best claim to be
regarded by us as imperishable reality. This assurance, which properly
has no need of proof, has sought to formulate itself after a scholastic
fashion in the above-mentioned awkward argument."

somewhat harsh way of saying that moral values are intrinsic or absolute, not merely instrumental. The defence of the moral argument may be valid for many who do not accept Kant's philosophy as a whole, though it has been objected that his " categorical imperative " is too much of a bare form, without clearly defined content.

The cosmological argument, which is sometimes called the argument *a contingentia mundi*, asserts that since the existence of the world is contingent, it presupposes a necessary Being. The word contingency in philosophy has a different meaning from that which it usually bears in common speech. Everything is said to be contingent when its non-existence would be thinkable without contradiction. It therefore does not contain the cause of its existence in itself. By somewhat doubtful reasoning, this is opposed to the " necessary," which exists because it exists. It is rather difficult to distinguish things which " have their ground in themselves " from things for which we have only failed to find a ground outside themselves. Further, the argument cannot prove that the unconditioned must be a single real Being, nor does it explain how the unconditioned can condition anything else.

The teleological argument is of more importance for the subject of this book. We find in the world numerous signs of apparent adaptation to an end ; and from these signs we are invited to infer a single creative and designing Reason as the cause of the universe. We think naturally of our own Wills, which form purposes and use means to fulfil them. These means are merely instrumental ; they are not in themselves directed to any end ; the design is solely in our minds. But the argument must not be

15

pushed too far. If causality is interpreted as meaning that the contingent implies the necessary, that begs the whole question. It is also conceivable that there may be no external world at all, and therefore it is conceivable that there may be no God. There is no way of proving that all things in the world are guided by a beneficent design, or by any design at all. Nature, it has been said, is like a sportsman who should fire off a hundred thousand guns in all directions in order to kill one hare. Nature is full of waste, of maladjustment, of suffering, and of failure ending in extinction. Can we turn the edge of this objection by the facile optimism of Pope : " all dis-cord harmony not understood, all partial evil universal good " ? This can neither be proved nor disproved, but very little evidence can be produced in its support. It is often assumed that individual organisms, which seem to be thrown away recklessly, are subordinate parts of one great organism, the universe, of which God is the soul. Thus all events in the world may be subsumed as parts of " one increasing purpose," the hardly intelligible phrase of Tennyson which theologians are too fond of quoting. But a universal purpose is not very different from no purpose at all. It is like the fallacy that all matter may be moving in one direction.

If God were only the *anima mundi*, and a living and intelligent Being, we might be perhaps disposed to hold that His life has a single dominant purpose, like the careers of the great men in history. If He is much more than this, and strictly independent of the creation, there is no reason at all why He should have one purpose rather than many, and why the many purposes should not be independent of each other. It would not be easy to suggest any common purpose for the existence of our planet and for that of another abode of life a million light-years away. The argument from the appearance of design in nature is therefore valid as far as it goes, but it does not carry us very far.

The argument from design is also used against the Epicurean theory that the world was formed by a fortuitous concourse of atoms. This theory is by no means out of date. It has been lately revived in connexion with the law of entropy. The process of increasing entropy must, it is said, have begun with a state of matter when entropy was at a minimum. Such a condition is not impossible, but it is almost infinitely improbable. Nevertheless, if the atoms are shuffled from infinity, the most improbable combinations must occur sooner or later. Thus it is attempted to preserve the Second Law of Thermodynamics without postulating creation in time. This argument seems to me a very poor one. The theory of an automatic blind origin to the universe would never have been thought of until the Deity had been thoroughly banished. It is not logically impossible; but it is so wildly improbable that it is quite safe to disregard it. Does anyone really think that printer's pie might be shaken up till *Hamlet* emerged complete?

Before leaving the teleological argument, we may add that it by no means necessarily points to a single Will. Our surface experience harmonises better with polydæmonism than with monotheism, and this conclusion has been accepted in many religions. It is necessary also to enter a caution against the anthropologism which

15 *

underlies the argument as usually conducted. Even if we could satisfy ourselves that the world seems to have been designed to promote the happiness or success or progress of our own species, there are other living creatures, and probably many other worlds, which must engage the attention of an intelligent Creator. It remains to be proved, in order to validate this argument, that the interest of the " inferior animals " has been consulted even in the one world of which we know something. The Creator can hardly be thought to have consulted their wishes when He made man.

In calling attention to the defects in these time-honoured arguments, I am far from wishing to under-mine the theistic position. They point, I think, in the direction of theism. Roman Catholic apologists, as we know, go much further, and claim that the existence of God, and His main attributes, may be demonstrated "apart from revelation." I have already explained that they do not maintain that the existence of God is given to us directly as a self-evident fact ; it is, they say, a valid inference from facts as known or experienced. I could concur with this judgment if it were conceded that besides the knowledge of nature as a body of existential fact we must, if we are to form a coherent philosophy, take into account the intrinsic values which are just as much part of our knowledge as the evidence of our senses. This, I think, many Catholic theologians would readily allow. But even the apprehension of the ultimate values united in a single supreme Mind does not quite bring us to the God of religion and devotion. It seems to me that we must place more reliance on the *testimonium Spiritus*

Sancti than the new Thomist school is quite willing to admit. These writers have external revelation to fall back upon, and the authority of a Church supposed to be infallible. These aids to faith are not so readily available to us. But the " inner light," which means little more than the experience of prayer, can supply the certainty which we crave for. It is only necessary to say that this certainty must be *earned*—that it is given to no one to start with, and that it is not always present to our consciousness. To say that it is not transferable is in one sense obvious, in another sense untrue. The mystics tell us what they have seen; their witness agrees together. If they describe in faltering words what language was not made to express, that does not invalidate their testimony, which remains the one clear proof that God is immanent in the spirit of man, though man is not yet capable of pure spiritual life. Even the supreme mystical experience, even the rapture in which a man cannot tell " whether he is in the body or out of the body," falls within the range of facts of which philosophy must take cognisance. It cannot really be explained away; it is most reasonably taken to be what those who experience it believe it to be—a direct apprehension by the " spirit in love " of the divine nature, so far as this can be known by finite intelligence. I need not here expatiate further upon mysticism. I only assert that if this experience is what it claims to be, it is the best of all " proofs " of the existence of God. Those who try to substantiate the truth of theism without it are weakening their own case unnecessarily. " Hereby we know that we abide in Him and He in us, because He hath given us of His Spirit."

The existence of God is affirmed by man as a religious being. Have these religious ideas any objective validity ? This is the fundamental question, on the answer to which our belief in intrinsic values must depend. Or, as Lord Balfour argues in his Gifford Lectures, what makes naturalism ultimately untenable is that the higher values cannot be maintained in a naturalistic setting. " According-ing to naturalism, these beliefs must in the last resort be counted among the purposeless products of physical conditions, which have no leanings towards truth, no aversions from error, no tropisms of any kind to which it would be possible for perfected humanity to appeal." [1] This is the chief constructive argument in Balfour's book, and I think it is valid. " Divine guidance must be pos-tulated if we are to maintain the three great values, knowledge, love, and beauty." [2] Modern psychology confines us to a subjective view of religion. For it, the " idea of God " may have an instrumental value, especi-ally for the uneducated, but this God is only a personifica-tion of human needs and hopes. The " idea of God " is thus studied as one of the ideas of man. Now as long as the psychologist admits that he is a student of an abstract science, the analysis of states of consciousness, no harm is done, for within his self-chosen limits he can go no further. The objective validity of states of consciousness, their relation, if they have any, to absolute reality, is no business of his. But in practice he has a philosophy which is a revival of the old nominalism, and which lends itself easily to a denial of God's existence. Modernist

---

[1] *Theism and Thought*, p. 236.   [2] *Ibid.*, p. 248.

thought repudiates, almost with indignation, the thought
of God as a living Being independent of our ideas about
Him. Sheen [1] quotes from Bertrand Russell that " in
all things it is well to exalt the dignity of man, by freeing
him as far as possible from the tyranny of a non-human
power," and from Leuba that " it would be difficult to
estimate the harm done by the conviction that for its
ethical improvement society is dependent on a personal
God." God, for William James, is " the name of the
ideal tendency of things." This revolt against God
sometimes takes a ludicrous form, as when McGiffert
(quoted by Sheen) says that " as democratic ideals crowded
out the aristocratic and authoritarian ideals of an earlier
day, of course the character of God appeared in a different
perspective. His absoluteness, and His responsibility
only to His own character, gave way to the notion of
relativity and responsibility to men. They too have
rights, and God is bound to respect them." Pringle-
Pattison quotes similar absurdities about " the desire and
determination to have a voice and a vote in the cosmic
councils," and how " society, democratic from end to end,
can brook no such class distinctions " as the effete European distinction between God and man.[2] This profane
nonsense is worth quoting in proof that the Modernists
really claim to have some sort of religion without God ;
for a hypothetical unseen President of a republic, if he is

[1] *Religion Without God*, p. 218. In this paragraph I am much indebted to Sheen.

[2] *The Idea of God*, p. 238. The article from which this last quotation
is taken (*Hibbert Journal*, Jan., 1913) is worth reading for its exquisite
absurdity.

worth retaining at all, should certainly be called by some other name.

We may give Modernist philosophers credit for good intentions in retaining the name of God while sacrificing the thing; but it is very confusing to their readers. If by the name God they mean a "*nisus*," or a "principle of concretion," or "the ideal tendency of things," or a magnified and non-natural President of the United States, it is a mistake to use a name which has such very different associations. But there are other thinkers who are, in intention at least, much nearer to Christianity, and who differ from Christian philosophy mainly on the subject which I am to discuss in this chapter, the relation of God to the world. To them we must now turn.

It is interesting to observe the contempt which so courteous a writer as Pringle-Pattison shows for the hypothesis of a personal Creator. He quotes Hartmann as saying that " contentment with regress to a God-creator or some similar notion is a true mark of speculative indolence." Hartmann is here following other thinkers. Spinoza thought that the traditional idea of creation made the existence of the world a matter of chance, and the nature of God arbitrary. According to him, the universe has no beginning or end, and follows from its infinite cause by mathematical necessity. Fichte says that the idea of creation is "the root error of all false metaphysics and dogmatics." For Hegel, the creation is the eternal self-revelation of God.[1] These are great

---

[1] There has been much controversy whether Hegel conceived of God as personal or as impersonal Spirit. He affirms that the absolute Spirit is personality, and repeatedly repudiates pantheism. But the pantheism

names, but they do not justify Pringle-Pattison in saying that the idea of a transcendent Creator " carries us back to a primitive stage of pictorial thought like that of the Zulus."

That Pringle-Pattison's view of God is essentially pantheistic, not theistic, is plain from several passages in his Gifford Lectures. "God," he says in his book, *The Idea of God*, " is known to us as creator of the world; we have no datum, no justification whatever, for supposing his existence out of that relation." [1] The only transcendence he can admit is a distinction of value or of quality, not ontological separateness. " The popular conception of creation belongs to the same circle of ideas as the waving of a magician's wand; it has no place either in serious thinking or in genuine religion." "We must definitely abandon the idea of God as a changeless and self-sufficient unit."

In considering the reason for this prejudice against the idea of creation, we are led back to the ancient problem of the " First Mover," which does not, as a rule, meet with much opposition from the scientific side. Kelvin did not feel the philosophical objection which weighs so much with many metaphysicians. " There is nothing," he says, " between absolute scientific belief in a creative power, and the acceptance of the theory of a

which he rejects is merely the type of thought which identifies the phenomenal universe with God; he wishes to affirm " the coherence of the phenomenal world in a single being." Further, by the truth of an idea he understands the culmination of a process; God, for him, is not eternally personal Spirit, but achieves personality by becoming incarnate in rational creatures. Cf. W. P. Patterson, *The Nature of Religion*, p. 357.

[1] *The Idea of God*, p. 310.

fortuitous concurrence of atoms. If you think strongly enough you will be forced by science to the belief in God which is the foundation of all religion." [1] The familiar impasse about the infinite regress does not arise for the Christian thinker. We are not obliged to trace back the whole series of events till we come to the " First Mover," and then to meet the question, " Who moved him ? " What we assert is the absolute *dependence* of the creation on the Creator. The very impossibility of an infinite regress forces us to believe in a Mover who is himself outside the series, and distinct from the world. Why we cannot believe this without putting ourselves on the intellectual level of the Zulus (presumed to be a low one) I do not see.

The theory that God is " organic with the world," which is held by the whole Hegelian school, is naturally welcome to the new biologism, which tries to interpret the whole cosmos in accordance with the laws of life. Whether the supporters of this view really escape the fallacies which were fatal to the old vitalism is a question on which Pringle-Pattison has said something, and on which their opponents have said more. When we remember the very small, perhaps even accidental, part which life occupies in the whole universe, it seems rash to make biology the normative science of the cosmos.

Christian theology asserts that God made the world " out of nothing." The account in Genesis is rather ambiguous, but suggests that God first made chaos, and then turned it into a cosmos. In Christian writings, the

---

[1] *Nineteenth Century*, June, 1903.

author of the Epistle to the Hebrews says : " by faith we
perceive that the world was framed by the Word of God,
so that that which is seen (may be known) to have arisen
not from things which appear." This may mean only
that there is a divine power behind material causation.

The Stoical theory seeks rather to explain the world
as it is than to give an account of its origin. It has some
resemblance to those modern theories which make the
world the self-evolution of God, and with Spinoza's idea
of God as *natura naturans*. Stoicism was radically teleological, and emphasised the close relation of the human
soul to the divine Spirit, which is always energising in the
world. Christian thought owed something to Stoicism,
though more in the field of ethics than of metaphysics ;
but the influence was not wholly good, since the Stoical
Pneuma was itself material, and a residue of sublimated
materialism clung to Christian thought for centuries. As
regards creation, the Stoical view was consistent with the
idea of an eternal process of differentiation. The forms
change, but that which is has always been.

The school of Plato always upheld the transcendence
of God, who made the world out of inert, merely potential " matter," which was not " material " in our sense.
The creative energy of God is sometimes half-personified
as the *Demiurge*, who is said to have made the ideal,
intelligible, or spiritual world of which our world is an
imperfect copy. The analogy of an artist and his work
is employed, and may perhaps be the best way in which
we can conceive the relation of the Creator to the universe.
These two drifts of thought, the Stoical and the Platonic,
afterwards approached each other. The idea of the

Logos helped to mediate between them. The Platonic Forms or Ideas, which produced the sensible world after their own likeness, were closely akin to the Stoical Logoi. Philo, who is specially important as a Hellenised Jew, was in no way willing to surrender the transcendent God of his own religion. He follows Plato in saying that God made the world because He was good, and wished to make it as like as possible to Himself. " By goodness he begat the universe, and by power he governs it." He made the world out of formless and characterless matter ; but Philo here follows the Stoics rather than Plato in giving this chaotic matter some kind of substance, so that his theory is to that extent dualistic. The agents in creation are the Forms or Ideas, " since it was not right that the all-knowing and blessed One should touch confused matter." These forms he sometimes calls Logoi, and sometimes angels or dæmons. " The archetypal pattern is the Form of Forms, the Reason of God." God is also spoken of as the Father of the world, Wisdom as its Mother. " Wisdom, receiving the seed of God, with fruitful birth-pangs brought forth the world, his visible, only, and well-beloved son." Although God works through subordinate agents, He is the sole creator of the universe. Irenæus later explains the " hands " by which the Father created as the Son and Spirit. Philo, like the Platonists, makes the heavenly or spiritual world the primary expression of the thought of God ; but whereas in Plotinus the Intelligence or Spirit and the spiritual world are strictly correlatives, neither of them derived from or subordinate to the other, we do not, as far as I know, find this thought in Philo. In a fine figure, which recalls the most famous passage in Goethe's *Faust*, the Logos of God, the eldest born of the "I am," robes himself with the world as with a vesture, the robe of the High Priest, embroidered by the powers of the seen and unseen world.

The Christian Church accepted the words of Genesis, "In the beginning God created the heavens and the earth" as fundamental truth. But thought was soon busy upon this simple statement. Among the Gnostics, who, it must be remembered, were not all outside the Church, a kind of barbaric Platonism defended in mythological form a theory of emanations, intended to account for the origin of the imperfect world which we know. Justin Martyr, following Plato, who, he believes, borrowed the doctrine from Moses, says that God constructed the world out of formless matter. There was still great ambiguity as to whether this matter had any substantial existence. The Greek language could distinguish between τὸ μὴ ὄν, "no thing," and οὐδέν, "nothing."[1] But these niceties were obscured in post-classical Greek. Plutarch says that "before the birth of the cosmos there was disorder," and quite definitely that "the birth of the world was not from nothing, but out of something, the state of which was not good or adequate." The Wisdom of Solomon repeats the words "out of formless matter"; and Athenagoras compares the creation to a potter working on his clay. But if "matter" had a kind of substantiality, was it coeval with God, or did God create the chaos before He turned it into a cosmos? Christian thought

[1] The difference may be illustrated by a line about the dissolution of the body after death: τὸ μηδὲν εἰς οὐδὲν ῥέπει.

soon decided that whatever "matter" might be, God created it. In other words, before the Creator began His work, there was absolutely nothing at all. This being settled, the question whether primordial "matter" was merely potential being or the still disordered elements of the cosmos lost much of its interest. It is more important that Irenæus, stating what was already the orthodox doctrine, says that "through the Logos (the heavenly Christ) the Father made all things without exception, objects of sense and objects of intelligence, things temporal and things eternal." Only the Logos Himself was not "made out of nothing," being coeternal with the Father, though "begotten." Thus the transcendence of God even in the intelligible world was asserted. In Plotinus this unqualified transcendence belongs only to the Absolute "beyond being."

Plotinus teaches that matter was created, though not in time. It was created in order that the will-activities proceeding downwards from the One might be actualised. This creation was "of necessity," which some have taken to deny any voluntary action on the part of the Creator. But, as Proclus says, "Divine necessity corresponds with divine volition."[1] Since he believes that creation had no temporal beginning, the question whether it was "out of nothing" can only mean the question whether the creation is entirely dependent on the Creator, and this Plotinus answers in the affirmative. Although Plotinus never willingly deserts Plato, I think that he discards any possibility of dualistic misinterpretation more decidedly

[1] See my *Philosophy of Plotinus*, Vol I.. pp. 143 *et seq.*

than his master, who was believed by Plutarch and Atticus (probably wrongly) to have supported the view that the universe was created out of chaos and in time. He may have given some ground for this interpretation, since Xenocrates and other early Platonists suggested that though not accurate, it was permissible in popular exposition. The theory in question obviously gives an opening for a weak metaphysical dualism, as if " matter " were an obstructive force impeding the action of the Good. This has been a common feature in popularised Platonism, and has been a ground of objection against Platonism to this day. Plotinus repudiates the idea of a spatial chaos into which the higher principle descends with its forms, but even he finds it difficult to divest " matter " of all positive qualities. He is in the same difficulty with the One above being as with matter below being. Both conceptions are obviously very elusive, since they are not subject to the categories of human reasoning.

Before considering the problem of the creation of the world in time, it may be worth while to summarise the little-known controversy of Joannes Philoponus, a " grammaticus " of Alexandria, against Proclus, the champion of the Platonic tradition. Joannes, a very learned and able man, was the leader of the " Tritheists," a heresy which is the creed of most Christians to-day, who would be shocked if their orthodoxy were impugned. His arguments against Proclus throw light on the state of the controversy when he wrote (in 529, the very year when Justinian closed the philosophical schools at Athens). Proclus, in the preceding century, had argued that the Christian theory of creation in time would prove an impotence to create; otherwise why was the world not created earlier? Philoponus replies that from the nature of the time-process past events cannot be without limit. If God could create a finite world in space, why not also in time? For Proclus, Creator and created are necessary correlatives. If the created is not " in act," neither is the Creator. (As we have seen, this correlation, in Neoplatonism, applies only to the intelligible world.) Philoponus replies, " No, creation is an act of will, not a necessary emanation. The Creator may be already Creator 'in act,' though not as Creator of this particular thing." Proclus says, " The unmoved Mover must create always or not at all." Answer: " To the eternally self-contemplating life of God the change in changing things makes no difference. It is in virtue of fore-knowledge that God is eternally perfect. Eternity was when time was not, and will be when time shall be no longer." Proclus: " The Universe must be perpetual, as its model is eternal." Philoponus: " No, the nature of things that come to be in time does not permit of their existence without limit in the past. The resemblance is as great as possible if the universe endures throughout all future time." This last sentence raises a question of great interest, in view of the surprising statement of Sir James Jeans in *Philosophy* (January, 1932) that " Time has a beginning in the past, but no end in the future." Philoponus, arguing for the Christian tradition, says that a product of time may be made imperishable by the omnipotent will of the Creator. Galen [1] strangely takes the same view.

[1] 17. 5: εἰ μὲν ἀγένητόν τι, πάντως καὶ ἄφθαρτον, εἰ δὲ ἄφθαρτον, οὐκ ἐξ ἀνάγκης ἀγένητον.

Aquinas defines creation as " a production of a thing according to its whole substance, nothing being pre-supposed, whether created or not created." The last clause is intended to exclude both pantheism and dualism.

The objections to the idea of creation are purely meta-physical, not scientific. I have already quoted Kelvin, and we may add that Huxley says, " It appears to me that the scientific investigator is wholly incompetent to say anything at all about the first origin of the material universe. The whole power of his organon vanishes when he has to step beyond the chain of natural causes and effects. No form of nebular hypothesis that I know of is necessarily connected with any view of the origination of the nebular substance." [1] If, however, the world was created in time, the origin and existence of the world are entirely outside any physical or mathematical explanation ; and if this element of the irreducible or irrational is admitted, we must not forget it when an attempt is made to put together the universe out of mathematical symbols

The controversy about the creation of the world in time is of permanent importance, though few are now interested in the properties of the hypothetical " matter." That creation is in one sense a continuous process would be admitted by almost all ; but when we speak of creation we usually mean the origination of the cosmic process. Must we, in accordance with Christian tradition, believe that the universe began to exist at a point of time which we could date if we knew it, as Archbishop Ussher did when he assigned the date of creation as 4004 B.C. ? The

[1] *Nineteenth Century*, Feb., 1886.

argument for a First Cause is independent of the eternity of the world. Urban quotes from Leibnitz : " Even by supposing the eternity of the world, we cannot escape the ultimate extramundane reason of things, that is to say, God. For in eternal things, even if there be no cause there must be a reason, which for permanent things is necessity itself, or essence."

Origen was not satisfied with the beginning of the world in time, and taught that there is a series of worlds without either beginning or end. Augustine in a famous argument holds that time and the world were created together. This is not unlike the view of Plotinus that the Soul " entimed itself," and caused things which came into being to be " slaves to time." Erigena and Eckhart both disbelieved in creation in time.

The attitude of St. Thomas Aquinas towards this question has already been mentioned in an earlier chapter. We need not suppose that he really disbelieved what he was obliged to accept on authority—the beginning of the world in time ; but it is plain that it was unwelcome to him. The modern Thomists follow him ; they give " speculative " reasons for believing that the world had no beginning in time, and do not argue for the other view, which has been " revealed." But although we may ask how such a fact could be the subject of external revelation, the Thomists do not feel this difficulty.

We may pass now to the manner in which modern astronomers deal with the problem of the beginning of the universe. I have shown in an earlier chapter that the half-hearted recourse to mentalism is no remedy. In the first place, the antinomy of finite and infinite is *in* the mind, and cannot be escaped from by subjective idealism. The acceptance of the law of entropy introduces, as I have said, a fatal contradiction into a mechanical or mathematical universe, and our astronomers, in dealing with its implications, betray not only perplexity, which is most intelligible, but, as I cannot help thinking, some confusion of thought. Eddington (*The Nature of the Physical World*, p. 83), says : "We have been studying the running down of the universe ; if our views are right, somewhere between the beginning of time and the present day we must place the winding up of the universe." And yet this winding up is a reversal of the law of entropy, which is assumed to be of universal significance. If we use the criterion of "probability," which is much in favour with present-day physicists, we may say that the progress towards maximum entropy is so probable as to be certain, while a supposed condition of minimum entropy is almost infinitely improbable. Eddington proceeds : "Scientists and theologians must regard as somewhat crude the naïve theological doctrine which (suitably disguised) is found in every textbook of thermodynamics, namely, that some billions of years ago God wound up the material universe and has left it to chance ever since. This should be regarded as a working hypothesis rather than its declaration of faith. It is one of those conclusions from which we can see no logical escape—only it suffers from the drawback that it is incredible. As a scientist I simply do not believe that the present order of things started off with a bang ; unscientifically I feel equally unwilling to accept the implied discontinuity in the divine nature. But I can make no suggestion to evade the

16 *

deadlock." This is very honest; but we can hardly acquiesce in a theory which "suffers from the drawback that it is incredible." The hypothesis that the order of things "started off with a bang" is not incredible; nor does it imply discontinuity in the divine nature, any more than it implies discontinuity in the nature of an artist when he begins a new picture, even if it is his first. But it is so unlike what we observe of the divine working that most of us would be unwilling to accept it, unless we were obliged to do so. However, Eddington does offer a suggestion (p. 95): "Entropy is frankly of a much more subjective nature than most of the ordinary physical qualities. It is a mind-spinning of the statistician. It has about as much objectivity as a batting average." Now this must mean one of two things: either that a statistical average does not compel a batsman to make exactly so many runs in his next innings (which no one disputes), and that consequently statistics are of no value in predicting how he is likely to play (which is not true); or secondly, that mathematical calculations are out of all relation with the real universe. I have refused to admit that natural science, which began—as all must begin— with naive realism and a philosophy of common sense, can logically end with sheer mentalism, since (as we are reminded) mathematical problems may be worked out quite independently of the question whether their symbols correspond to anything *in rerum natura*. But this strange avenue of escape is really barred to the scientist, who from first to last is tied to observed phenomena, however far his calculations may carry him from objects which we can see or touch. There is not the slightest reason for saying that entropy is " more subjective than other physical theories " ;[1] it merely contradicts them on their own ground. Lucretius, it seems to me, is right :—

> Corpus enim per se communis dedicat esse
> sensus ; cui nisi prima fides fundata valebit,
> haut erit occultis de rebus quo referentes
> confirmare animi quicquam ratione queamus.[2]

So Taylor (*The Faith of a Moralist*, Vol. II., p. 215) says : " If there are undeniable facts recorded on the testimony of sense which refuse to square with the best assured analyses and deductions of the intellect, it is the intellect which has to submit."

There is no doubt that the Christian tradition has always upheld the view which I quoted from Philoponus a few pages back, that human souls have a beginning in time, and exist, whether for weal or woe, in perpetuity. Popular thought cannot conceive of eternal life except strictly in the form of duration. But the philosophical difficulties in the way of this belief are very great. Among them is the obvious one that no habitation in space can be found for these deathless beings. We are lost at once in the impenetrable jungle of traditional eschatology. The " conferred immortality " of which Philoponus speaks (and there is something like it in Plato's *Timæus*), is rather the redemption of the human soul from the sphere

---

[1] Meyerson, *De l'Explication dans les Sciences*, p. 38, says : " La thermodynamique n'est pas moins ontologique en son essence que n'importe quelle autre partie de la physique, et la conviction contraire est une illusion."

[2] *Lucretius*, I., 423-426.

of time altogether, whether with the Orphics and Indians we dream of the " sorrowful weary wheel " of successive incarnations, or whether we imagine the discarnate soul subsisting in time in some other place. Shall we even, perhaps, like our misguided necromancers, pry into the occult, in the hope of discovering the habitat of the surviving soul—

> quo cursu deserta petiverit, et quibus ante
> infelix sua tecta supervolitaverit alis ?

My own belief is that whatever is born in time must perish for time, and this must be true of world-systems no less than of individual lives. Time and space are not part of the framework of the real or spiritual world ; they are as real as the lives of those who live in them, while they live in them, but they are not—neither of them, nor the two rolled into one—the stuff of which reality is made. If the present world-order had a beginning, " with time, not in time," as Augustine says, it will have an end, " not in time but with time," that is to say, with its own time-framework. We are not obliged to believe that ours is the only world-order. It is more natural to suppose that as God is eternal, so His creative activity is perpetual. The different world-orders may be entirely independent of each other. But here we are guessing about what we neither know nor can ever hope to know.

It has been necessary to argue at length against the prevalent pantheistic theory that the world is as necessary to God as God is to the world. This error, as we regard it, comes from metaphysics, not from natural science. But though Christianity asserts the transcendence of God, it is equally emphatic in maintaining His immanence. On this subject a little more must be said.

However we regard matter and mind, and the relation between them, they are as a fact given to us in combination. We do not perceive matter by itself, but as it affects our minds through the senses. Colours and musical sounds come, as we know, from vibrations which have no sound and no colour. To this extent we may claim that the immanence of mind in matter is given to us in experience. External nature has always had a religious influence upon mankind; we think we can find in the external world traces of divine working. Of course the interpretations differ widely. One man finds evidence for a good God; another for two warring principles; another for polytheism; another for pantheism. But the belief that there is a spiritual reality behind phenomena is itself, by its general prevalence, a very impressive phenomenon. I have emphasised in an earlier chapter the great importance for philosophy of this apprehension of values, which though they are immanent in visible things plainly belong to a higher order. It is also worth saying that this spiritual vision is neither simply emotional nor moral nor intellectual; it is an affirmation of the undivided personality. If we may trust our own impressions, we are equally sure that we are in touch with the divine in our contact with these values, and that our knowledge of the divine mind is fitful and incomplete. From this we infer that though we live and move and have our being in God, He is immeasurably above us while we live here.

The Christian doctrine of the Logos, the indwelling

light and life of the world, who is fully divine but distinct
from the Father, has been helpful to many in holding the
balance true between deism and pantheism. And we
must remember that Christianity teaches that once in
actual history this divine principle was fully incarnated in
man; " the Word became flesh and tabernacled among
us." The closely allied doctrine of the immanence in
man of the Holy Spirit of God, the Spirit of Christ, or,
as some express it now, of the Christ of experience, shows
that the Incarnation is not to be regarded as an isolated
portent, but rather as the inauguration of a new era in
human history, a conception which asserts nothing irrational or incredible, since there have been other permanent enrichments of humanity to which an approximate
date may be assigned. These doctrines, when rightly
understood, are so decisive in favour of belief in an actual
divine presence energising in the world that if we take
pantheism and deism as the two poles, the former over-
emphasising immanence, the latter transcendence, we may
say that Christianity is more alien to deism than to the
opposite error.

It is often assumed that the production of man must
have been the sole or chief end of creation. This seems
to me unjustifiable anthropolatry. Of course bulk has
nothing to do with value; I do not wish to return to the
old idea that the heavenly bodies must have souls propor-
tioned in dignity to the circumference of their material
envelope. But from the astronomical point of view we
are only creatures of a day; and even if the other globes
in our system are permanently unfit to be the abode of
life, it is wildly improbable that among thousands of

millions of stars there is only one planet capable of being the abode of "living souls." If the inhabitants of these other worlds needed redemption, no doubt God visited them as He has visited us. This thought came to Alice Meynell, in her poem, "Christ in the Universe":—

> Nor, in our little day,
> May His devices with the heavens be guessed,
> His pilgrimage to thread the Milky Way
> Or His bestowals there be manifest.
>   But in the eternities,
> Doubtless we shall compare together, hear
> A million alien gospels, in what guise
> He trod the Pleiades, the Lyre, the Bear.

The thought is to my mind an inspiring one. There is, I think, something derogatory to the Deity in supposing that He made this vast universe for so paltry an end as the production of ourselves and our friends.

This, however, is a comparatively unimportant question, except indeed when it affects our moral duties towards other sentient creatures in the world, and towards the protection of natural beauties, which, I think we may assume, are part of the pleasure with which the Creator regards His work. Most of us, when we think of the relation between God and the world, are asking the question, Is there any intelligent and beneficent purpose in the stream of events, or are they determined by blind mechanism? The question is extraordinarily difficult; and it is partly for this reason that I propose, as briefly as possible, to summarise the opinions of some great philosophers who have dealt with the subject.

But first, it may be asked, Are causality and teleology mutually exclusive conceptions? Causality is generally understood to mean a law of merely mechanical movements, teleology an arrangement of particular things by a will external to them. In the first place, this is a misuse of the word causality. We do not say that night is the cause of day, or summer of winter. Invariable sequence is not the same as causation; it rather denies it. Events cannot be causes of other events; it would be better to dismiss the word cause, in the sense of a transaction between two events, altogether from natural science. If the whole scheme of nature, obeying, as we say, invariable laws, is the work of an intelligent designer, there is certainly no contradiction between design and mechanical regularity. We should expect regularity, rather than unpredictable and capricious interruptions of orderly sequence, in the work of an all-wise Creator. I have already quoted Lichtenberg's suggestion that mechanism may be the teleology of the inorganic; and there is no reason why this should not be true. The quarrel is not between causality and teleology; it is between a monistic theory of the cosmic order and one which points to a dual control. The former view is on the whole that of the philosophers whom I am about to quote.

Kant declares that the mechanical and the teleological interpretations of nature are equally legitimate. "To exclude the teleological principle in favour of the mechanical, is to condemn reason to flit about fantastically among shadowy semblances of powers of nature which thought refuses to entertain. A merely teleological explanation which pays no regard to the mechanism of nature reduces reason to a visionary." Although he at first says that both principles are " merely regulative," he later sees that both point to an objective principle which justifies both interpretations, "a supersensuous real ground." Schelling says that " with all its mechanism nature is full of purpose." Hegel makes the world itself " an organic life, a living system," " the organs of the one subject." Fechner goes further, and believes that every planet has its own world-soul. Schopenhauer says that " every sound head must be brought by a contemplation of nature to a teleological position " ; Hartmann that " logical necessity is the one principle which appears, when looked at from one side, as the causality of mechanical law, from the other side as teleology."

These thinkers all reject the idea of an external architect, and still more decidedly that of occasional interference. Their arguments point to an *organic* view of nature, in which the unity of the whole determines the character of the parts. On this conception something more must be said. The word " dynamical " is used, like the word " organic," as a rival interpretation to the " mechanical."

Boyle, the philosopher and chemist, called nature *mechanismus universalis*, and Leibnitz called the soul *automaton spirituale*. Herbart aims at " splitting up the organism of reason into chains of ideas, whose formation can be explained only by the mechanism of mind." The word " organic " comes from Aristotle ; but for him ὄργανον means an instrument, whether animate or inanimate ; a slave is an animated instrument, ἔμψυχον ὄργανον

It is only in modern thought that " mechanism " and
" organism " are sharply opposed to each other. The
idea of the State as an organism was familiar to the
Greeks, and that of the Church as an organism to the
Middle Ages. An organism is conceived as a unit, with
a life of its own, which according to the old modes of
thought was to realise a definite form or idea, its
" nature," as Aristotle said. Teleology was thus everywhere present—in the realisation of the organic idea.
The beginning of the modern period saw a reversion to
atomism and individualism, which in denying any inner
connexion between events destroyed teleology. But
Descartes, Berkeley, and Leibnitz all believed that
behind the mechanism of nature there is the purposeful
control of Providence. An obvious expedient was to
deny that living beings are under the control of mechanism. So Cudworth, for example, argued.

Now, partly under the influence of historicism, the
idea of organism, which is a principle of becoming rather
than of being, has come again into favour. The young
science of biology is wedded to the organic, not to the
mechanical theory. Whitehead and others have quite
recently laid great stress upon the idea of organism.

What is the bearing of this dispute between organism
and mechanism upon teleology ? Strictly, like evolution,
it is only a question about the method of God's working.
God does use both animate and inanimate instruments;
He does use corporate groups as well as individuals. To
all appearance, both individuals and groups carry out
purposes of which they are only partly conscious. To say
that God is not carrying out any plan or purpose except

through the medium of conscious agents is obviously untrue. The consciousness of God, if we believe that there is a God, must be quite distinct from that of His agents, some of whom may partly know what they are doing, while others certainly do not.

But although teleology seems to fit in fairly well with biology,[1] doubt comes over us when we turn to astronomy and physics. The very existence of our planet and its inhabitants was, we are told, due to a pure accident, and such an unlikely accident that its extreme improbability seems to some a reason for suspecting the now accepted theory. And what rational purpose can be found in the contraction of nebulæ into groups of stars, the jamming together of some of the stars into " white dwarfs," and the final dissolution of stars into radiation ? It is not merely that the purpose of these stupendous operations is " mysterious " ; it seems plain, to our finite comprehensions, that there is nothing rational in them at all. At any rate, the contemplation of the heavens makes what I have called biologism—the attempt to erect the laws of conscious life into a cosmic principle—a very difficult theory to hold.

My subject in this book is cosmology, and I have approached it from the side of the phenomenal world and the concepts of science, based ultimately on the observation of phenomena. But I have insisted that the absolute values, and the mystical experience which is the core of religion, are among the facts which philosophy, even a

[1] Meyerson says, " L'idée d'une fin semble s'imposer impérieusement à l'esprit du biologiste." Perhaps *finalism* would be a better word than vitalism for this attitude.

philosophy of science, must take into account. Nature taken in abstraction from these imponderables is great and marvellous, but not divine; so we have found Aristotle saying. Religion does not claim to be directly deducible from a study of nature. It is a strange notion that God reveals Himself more clearly and directly in inanimate nature than in the human mind and heart. Rather we may say with Macarius, "the throne of the Deity is our mind." Our minds are made in the image of God, who created the universe; they are therefore, we may say, of one piece with other created beings and with the laws which they obey. Hence in studying nature, which after all we know very imperfectly, we are learning something of the workings and methods of the divine mind. It is in virtue of our God-given spiritual faculty that we are able to contemplate nature, as it were, from outside, and to know it in a way which we could never do if we were ourselves caught in the flux of events. If naturalism were the truth, we could never know it. As Otto says, "if naturalism is in the right, thought is not free; and if thought is not free there can be no such thing as truth, for there can be no establishing of what truth is." This is not said to discredit natural science, but to insist, as I have done before, that the disinterested love of truth is a homage to one of the absolute values, and that the scientist who fancies that he disregards all valuation is guilty of mental confusion. There is no " naturalism " which does not contradict itself.

I have quite definitely defended theism against rival theories of ultimate reality. God is both in us and out of us; He is both immanent and transcendent. There can be no fundamental contradiction between God as known to philosophic thought and God as known to personal devotion. In philosophy we seek to know God and to honour Him through our intelligence; in devotion we approach Him through love and adoration. We have ample warrant for confidence that neither quest is in vain.

Much has been written about the "personality" of God, a word for which I have no great affection. We may suppose that in comparing God with the highest thing that we know we are likely to be nearer the truth than in comparing Him with anything lower. Personality, when attributed to God, is a symbol, and a very inadequate one. We do not know how far we ourselves can call ourselves "persons"; the soul is the wanderer of the spiritual world, not really quite at home anywhere. It is in the life of devotion that the "personality" of God appeals to us most strongly. "Speak to Him thou, for He hears, and spirit with spirit can meet." We know that in prayer we are not merely soliloquising.

For the religious mind, the world is primarily a "vale of soul-making," to borrow a phrase of Keats, or, as Origen is reported to have said, a *schola animarum* (probably ψυχῶν διδασκαλεῖον in Greek). If it is asked, "for what are we being trained ?" we are tempted to answer with Pindar, γένοιο οἷος ἐσσί μαθών—learn what you are and "make it so." We are to become what God meant us to be, partakers of the divine nature, which is immortal. A well-lived life is the sacrament of the thought of God which He meant us to express in this manner.

My conclusion is that the fate of the material universe is not a vital question for religion.   In philosophy it does matter, because if entropy is true, some philosophies are in ruins.

7

THE ETERNAL WORLD

" Thou art a God that hidest thyself." Hooker repeats
the warning so often given before his time by the speculative mystics. " Dangerous it were for the feeble brain
of man to wade far into the doings of the Most High ;
Whom although to know be life, and joy to make mention
of His name, yet our soundest knowledge is to know that
we know Him not indeed as He is, neither can know Him,
and our safest eloquence concerning Him is our silence,
when we confess without confession that His glory is inexplicable, His greatness above our capacity and reach.
He is above and we upon earth ; therefore it behoveth
our words to be wary and few." In our attempts to work
out a philosophy of theism we sometimes forget that " un
Dieu défini est un Dieu fini." No one but God can know
God as He is. The creation, which includes the spirit of
man, reveals some of God's attributes, which we attribute
per eminentiam to Himself. In studying these copies of
the original in a wholly inadequate medium, we are
obliged to isolate them, as when in an earlier chapter we
studied Truth, Goodness, and Beauty as distinct from
each other. This we had to do, since otherwise we should
have found ourselves subordinating one of the supreme
values to another, or interpreting one in terms of another.

Again, we can hardly avoid classing the objects of our apprehension as percepts and concepts, or, with St. Paul and the Platonists, as the visible things which are temporal and the invisible things which are eternal. These bisections of a single experience are necessary, as an artist draws outlines. It is difficult to rise to the meaning of Plotinus, when he says that " all things which are Yonder are also Here," or of St. John's identification of the knowledge of God with eternal life. In this chapter we shall have to note how one unreconciled dualism after another has marked the failure of thinkers to find the unity in duality to which we are irresistibly impelled by the demands of our nature. The main obstacle has been the extreme difficulty of grasping the idea of a spiritual reality which is not spatial or temporal. No sooner has a vision of such reality dawned upon us than we begin to set it in a spatial and temporal framework, changing the eternal into " somewhere else, not here," or " some day, not now," or creating a new mythology by metamorphosing our moral and social ideals into forces at work in the historical order. It is one of my main contentions in this book that idealists as well as realists have not been willing to " take timelessness seriously " (as Alexander says that Bergson taught us to take time seriously), and that in consequence speculations as to the future, which belong only to the temporal order, are constantly obtruded into discussions about the eternal Values or Ideas. Many of our leading thinkers in consequence present us with an apocalyptic eschatology which metaphysics and modern science alike condemn.

Philosophers who have realised how completely the

inner nature of God is hidden from us, and at the same time how much of His design for His creation is revealed to us in various ways, have often, like the great mystics both in Europe and in India, refused to make any positive statements about God. *Neti, neti,* as the Indian sages have said; He is not this, and He is not that. This is the famous *via negativa,* which has been unsympathetically compared to peeling an onion. One attribute after another is removed, till nothing is left; and Western mystics have not shrunk from saying that " Deus propter excellentiam non immerito Nihil vocatur." The Absolute is above all differentiation; He is said by the school of Plato to be " Beyond Being " (ἐπέκεινα τῆς οὐσίας); but those who use such language are obviously not thinking of the God of religion. Nor should we suppose that the imperfect images which we can make of Him have no positive value in showing us what He is. Exclusive mysticism has sometimes fallen into this error, which is due less to a speculative fallacy than to the desire to purify the vision of God from all taint of human self-interest. The truer mysticism is sacramental. Every symbol of the divine, in being what it is, points to something beyond itself.

We are almost compelled, as I said in the preceding chapter, to follow Eckhart, and to distinguish between the Godhead and God. Not that they are two Beings, though Eckhart can hardly escape from thinking of them as actually different. But the God who is knowable to man through His works is not and cannot be the metaphysical Absolute *in propria persona.* In placing " the One " beyond Being, Plotinus indicates that the highest reality with which we have to do, except in rare moments of ecstasy, is the perfectly harmonious but richly complex world of spiritual knowledge and existence, not " the light that no man can approach unto," a blinding light which cannot be distinguished from darkness.

Our citizenship is in heaven, that is to say, in a space-less and timeless world in which all the intrinsic or absolute values are both actual and active. In this higher world we find God and our own eternity. It is the only completely real world. I do not think that any later philosopher has equalled Plotinus in his exposition of what we mean by the eternal world, and therefore I must take leave to summarise what I have already written on the subject in my Gifford Lectures of 1918.

We must first ask, Is this philosophy of Spirit a form of idealism ? It is, but it is not a form of mentalism. Things are not created by thoughts about them. Reality consists in a trinity in unity of Spirit ($\nu o\hat{\upsilon}\varsigma$), Spiritual Perception ($\nu \acute{o}\eta\sigma\iota\varsigma$), and the Spiritual World ($\nu o\eta\tau\acute{a}$). I will not quote the numerous passages in which I have proved conclusively that this is the doctrine of Plotinus. I hope that I have made misunderstanding on this im-portant point impossible. But I will transcribe a very remarkable passage of Maimonides, translated by Bouillet, which summarises the Neoplatonic doctrine with admir-able clearness: " Tu connais cette célèbre proposition que les philosophes ont énoncée à l'égard de Dieu, savoir qu'il est l'intellecte, l'intelligent, et l'intelligible, et que ces trois choses, dans Dieu, ne font qu'une seule et même chose, dans laquelle il n'y a pas multiplicité. Comme il est démontré que Dieu (qu'il soit glorifié !) est intellecte en acte, et comme il n'y a en lui absolument rien qui soit en puissance, de sorte qu'il ne se peut pas que tantôt il perçoive et tantôt il ne perçoive pas, et qu'au contraire il est toujours intellecte en acte, il s'ensuit que lui et la chose perçue sont une seule et même chose, qui est son essence ; et que cette action de percevoir, pour laquelle il est appelé intelligent, et l'intellecte même qui est son essence. Par conséquent, il est perpetuellement intellecte, l'intelligent, et l'intelligible. Il est clair aussi que si l'on dit que l'intellecte, l'intelligent, et l'intelligible ne forment qu'un en nombre, cela ne s'applique pas seulement au Créateur, mais à tout intellecte. Dans nous aussi l'intellecte, l'intelligent, et l'intelligible sont une et même chose." Reality, as this medieval philosopher perceived, is neither thought nor thing, but the indissoluble unity of thought and thing, which reciprocally imply each other. The relation between them is one of essential identity actualised under the form of essential reciprocity.

"Reality is that which is seen, not the act of seeing." Thus Plotinus disposes of mentalism. But "the knowledge of immaterial things is identical with the things known. Thus Spirit and the real world are one." This doctrine is emphasised again and again in the Enneads. Plotinus is able to preserve the complete unity in duality of Spirit and its objects, the "intelligible world," without subordinating either of them to the other, because they both derive their being directly from the One, the Absolute. He sometimes makes them flow over into each other, asserting something like what Christian theologians, in discussing the attributes of the Deity, called περιχώρησις. In the relations of spirit and the spiritual world

(I have said) we have a complete reconciliation of the One and the Many, of Sameness and Otherness; and if this is so, it is manifestly impossible to give distinct characters to Spirit on the one side and to the Spiritual World on the other. Reality is not to be identified either with Thought or with a kind of transcendental physical world which is the object of thought; nor can we arrive at it by forming clean-cut ideas of these two, and saying, in Bradleyan fashion, that they are "somehow" joined together. Reality is eternal life; it is a never-failing spiritual activity; it is the continual self-expression of a God Who "speaks and it is done, Who commands and it stands fast." [1]

What is the relation of the archetypal world which is spaceless, timeless, immaterial, and eternal, to the world of phenomena? The philosophy which I am trying to explain is a kind of panpsychism; but very different from the modern pluralistic idealism which is often only a thinly disguised materialism grown sentimental. The phenomenal world contains, Plotinus says, all that there is in the eternal world ($\pi\acute{a}\nu\tau a$ $\grave{\epsilon}\nu\tau a\hat{v}\theta a$ $\mathring{o}\sigma a$ $\kappa a\grave{\iota}$ $\grave{\epsilon}\kappa\epsilon\hat{\iota}$); but in the world of space and time the absolute Values (we may, I think, substitute this modern word for the Platonic Forms) are split up and partly disintegrated by the conditions of existence here below. We have here externality instead of compenetration, becoming instead of being, a striving Will instead of pure contemplation. And yet, Plotinus asks, what could be more beautiful than the world Here, except the world Yonder?

[1] *The Philosophy of Plotinus*, Vol. II., p. 48.

In comparing the two worlds he adopts a spatial diagram, as we usually adopt a temporal diagram. His perfect world is " Yonder " ; ours is " the future life." We cannot help using these diagrams. If we deny ourselves the use of spatial and temporal symbols, we have no others to put in their place except that of substance and shadow, or reality and appearance. Yet these, too, are symbols—symbols perhaps less misleading than the others, but still symbols only. For we are not dealing with two worlds which can be rightly pictured as existing side by side, or one in succession to the other, or one the shadow of the other. Still less, if there are degrees in error, can we call one the world of facts and the other the world of values. A very old dualism contrasted movement with stability, and we have seen that some modern philosophies have deified movement and change, pouring scorn on stability. They have gone back to the crude controversies of the Ionians, which ended, long before the Neoplatonists arose, in the recognition that change and permanence are complementary ideas which imply each other.

We cannot understand the Platonic cosmology unless we accept the old tripartite psychology which makes man consist of spirit, soul, and body. This, I need not remind my readers, is at the root of St. Paul's religion ; it belongs to Christianity not less than to Greek philosophy. In Plotinus the demarcation is not rigorous. It is one of the merits of this philosopher that he will draw no hard lines anywhere. His map of the world is full of contour-lines, which, as in our charts, represent gradual slopes, not precipices. But the triple nature of man is taken as a fact, and a fact I believe it to be. In any system of objective idealism man is a microcosm, and differences within his nature reflect differences within the macrocosm itself.

Objectively, Body, Soul, and Spirit are respectively the world as perceived by the senses; the world interpreted by the mind as a spatial and temporal order; and the spiritual world. The first of these is apprehended by the five bodily senses; the second by the discursive reason; the third by the spiritual perception which alone conveys real knowledge. This is said by Plotinus to be "a faculty which all possess, but few use." It is not, however, a separate organ, but the Soul, which usually operates in the second sphere, that here enters into its full rights as a denizen of the spiritual world.[1]

The world as apprehended by the senses is, as he says rightly, devoid of reality. It may be doubted whether there is such a thing as perception without conception. "Matter," for the Platonist, is not ponderable stuff, but the all-but nothing which remains when we have stripped phenomena of all that the mind brings to their interpretation. The elementary blunder of supposing that Plato's ὕλη is "material" is responsible for much misleading talk about "dualism" in the Platonists. It will be easier to understand the Neoplatonic view of matter if we realise that it is a relative term. Matter is matter only as the passive recipient of form from above it. The same thing may be form in relation to what is below it, and matter in relation to what is above it. I will not

---

[1] This classification would be open to the criticism brought against the old "faculty-psychology," if we did not remember that (as I said in the preceding paragraph), there are no "hard lines" in Plotinus.

now go into the real difficulty of accounting for " false opinions," which seem to result from the imperfect penetration of the lower principle by the higher, without investing the lower with some positive power of resistance. Plotinus is not entirely consistent (who is ?) in dealing with the problem of evil. When he falls back on " it was necessary " (with which compare the words of Christ, " it must needs be that offences come ") he practically admits that the universe contains a few surds which cannot be rationalised or reduced to anything else. We have seen that some modern thinkers, notably Meyerson, attach great philosophical importance to these " irrational " elements, as they call them.

The real puzzle about the world of appearance is whether it is the real, the spiritual world, seen by an imperfect instrument and through a distorting medium, or an actual but imperfect copy of an existing archetype. Platonism tries to hold both together, though trying hard not to imagine two separate worlds. It is difficult, but the difficulty is diminished if we think away the stubborn residue of materialism which gives substantiality to the data of sensuous perception. Both the form and matter of " sensible reality " are unreal ; it is incorrect to call it reality at all ; we should call it only " that which in the world of sense we miscall reality." Nor should we speak of " knowledge " of it, but only of " opinion," which, as Aristotle says, accompanies or comes from sensation. The Soul does not perceive objects of sensation, but their " forms," which belong to the intelligible world. All this is in the language of long ago ; but it is certain that the world as known to science is a mental construction from very defective data. We have only to think, for example, of the very small range of colours which our eyes can distinguish, and of sounds—about eleven octaves, I believe, which human ears can hear.

The world, according to the school of Plato, is created by the Universal Soul, after the likeness of the Spiritual World, which it ever contemplates. "Nature," "the lowest of the spiritual existences," is its intermediary. Nature is the rational, and therefore unvarying, expression of a perfect intelligence. It follows that, though the material objects which science studies are themselves without real being, the construction built up by human thought and observation upon it belongs to the intelligible or real world. What is real in science is the realm of law which "Soul" both makes and finds there. I have insisted, in opposition to the mentalism of some modern physicists, that science begins with what it *finds*, not with what it makes.

How and why does Spirit, or the Universal Soul, thus project from itself inferior reproductions of its own nature? The question "How?" is not, and cannot be, answered; as for the "Why?" Plotinus says plainly that without the world of becoming the spiritual world would not be "in act"—it would not be actualised. This, if pressed, might suggest that God without the world would not be God—a favourite modern doctrine, neither Platonic nor Christian. The Platonic God does not need the world. But since creative activity is part of His nature, we may say that the creation had to be. The whole hierarchy of existence and value comes ultimately from the One who is also the Good, and he who beholds

the creation with reverent eyes finds it "very good."
Plotinus has no sympathy with the Gnostics who despise
this beautiful world, which is full of the "footprints" of
its Maker.

The Soul (or Life—we must keep both renderings of
it in mind, for neither is really satisfactory) is the wanderer of the metaphysical world, having affinities with
every grade of existence and value. And since we only
see what in a sense we are ourselves, it is no wonder that
our view of reality is blurred. The Soul "binds extremes
together"; but its place is within the confines of real
being. In a remarkable sentence, Plotinus says that
"each of us is an intelligible world," a saying which
has a bearing on the status of personal identity in the
eternal world. But the Third Person in the Neoplatonic Trinity is not a society of individual centres of consciousness, but the Universal Soul. The Universal Soul
has a life of its own; but its main activity is in ordering
and governing the world below it, in accordance with
what it beholds in contemplating the world of Spirit.
We cannot identify the Universal Soul either with the
Johannine Logos or with the Holy Spirit; but the resem-
blances are obvious. The Christian Logos is a cosmic
principle, the agent in creation, the life of the world,
the sustainer in being of all created things. So in
Plotinus the Universal Soul is the creator and sustainer of
the world; "it is never at a loss, in spite of partial opposition; it abides unchanged in one and the same work."
Its energy pervades all living things, and slumbers even
in inorganic nature. Like Spinoza, Plotinus believes that
omnia sunt, quamvis diversis gradibus, tamen animata.

The alternative is to divide nature into persons and things, or into conscious and unconscious beings, or into animate and inanimate objects. Wherever we choose to draw these lines, they will be arbitrary and unscientific.

The Universal Soul is not incarnate in the world, which it directs without being involved in it. It has self-consciousness, but is not conscious *in* its creatures. Plotinus speaks of " an activity of contemplation," " a yearning to create many Forms," as the work of the Universal Soul through the Logoi or creative powers.

This panpsychism raises the question whether there is soul-life in all parts of the universe. I do not think we need follow Fechner in believing that every heavenly body has a soul of its own. But I would rather be a star-worshipper than believe with Hegel (if he was not merely speaking impatiently, which is likely enough) that the starry heavens have no more significance than a rash on the sky, or a swarm of flies. There may be, and no doubt are, an immense number of souls in the universe, and some of them may be nearer to the divine mind than we are.

Far more important, from the religious point of view, is the question whether human individuality belongs to the eternal world, or only to the world of souls on their temporal probation. Mysticism, says Keyserling, always ends in an impersonal immortality. He is thinking of the philosophic mysticism which is built on Platonism ; and there is no doubt that many, holding this view of the ultimate tendency of this mode of thinking, reject it on that ground. I will first summarise the teaching of Plotinus on this subject, and will then consider the question generally. I prefer still to take Plotinus as my text, both on account of my very high estimate of his rank as a thinker, and because he is under no obligation to square his conclusions with any authoritative dogma. It is a further advantage that he has a much clearer and more consistent idea of eternal life as timeless than most of our modern writers, whatever their religious opinions may be.

Souls, being immaterial, cannot be divided quantitatively, nor can one soul be part of another soul. They are not parts of the Universal Soul, but are active powers of Spirits, who are fully real in the world Yonder. Both the Universal Soul and particular souls emanate from this higher world, and they preserve their rights in this higher world. The soul, according to Plotinus, does not "descend" entire into the world of time and place, which means, if we drop the deliberately metaphorical use of the spatial word " descent," that the higher part of the soul, as well as the Spirit from which it proceeds, is impeccable and immutable, like the *funkelein* or *synteresis* of the medieval mystics. The *distinction* of souls " Here " corresponds to distinctions in the world of Spirit ; but their *separation* is an affection ($\pi\acute{a}\theta\eta\mu a$) of bodies, not of Soul itself. In the world Yonder there is distinction without division ; there is complete compenetration of all real existences, so that the whole is present in each part. In the world Here there is separation and discord ; but a system of sympathies, which runs through all nature, testifies to the unity which is realised in the world of Spirit. In my book on Plotinus I have quoted a summary of the teaching of Plotinus by Porphyry, which makes his meaning clear : " We must not believe that the plurality of souls comes

from the plurality of bodies. Particular souls subsist, as
well as the Universal Soul, independently of bodies, without
the unity of the Universal Soul absorbing the multiplicity
of the particular souls, or the multiplicity of particular
souls splitting up the unity of the Universal Soul.   Particular souls are distinct without being separate ; they
are united to each other without being confused, and
without making the Universal Soul a simple aggregate."
Souls differ from each other by inner diversity, not by
local or temporal separation, and they lose nothing of
their individuality by entering into the larger life of the
whole.   A particular is most itself when it is most universal.   The unity of soul-life consists in its being entire in
every part, and since this is realised only in a higher state,
we may no doubt say that Yonder " Soul is undivided."
But this is not the destruction of personality ; it is only
the perfection of sympathy.   In one passage—the thought
is not much emphasised—the distinction of persons Here
consists in the particular work which they are given to do,
the particular goal which they have to reach.   But in this
philosophy the source and the goal of life are always the
same.   Aspiration, activity, life, are what is most real in
the world of becoming.   They are the return journey
which all living beings have to make, in order to realise
their true nature.   It is no doubt almost impossible to
apply this to the humbler forms of life ; but the status of
Soul is determined entirely by the sphere of its activity ;
and the only way of doing our duty where we are is to
" contemplate " a realm higher than our own.   " All
things pray, except the First Principle," as I have quoted
from Proclus.

The abstract ego is not the same as the Soul. On this I have said :[1] "This identification seems to imply three assumptions, all of which are disputable. The first is that there is a sharp line separating subject and object, corresponding to the antithesis of ego and non-ego. The second is that the subject, thus sundered from the object, remains identical through time. The third is that this indiscerptible entity is in some mysterious way both myself and my property. Just as Lucretius says that men fear death because they unconsciously duplicate themselves, and stand by, in imagination, at their own cremation, so we are seriously concerned to know whether that precious part of our possessions, our 'personality,' will survive death." Plotinus holds that even on the psychic plane subject and object flow freely into each other, and that in the spiritual world there are no barriers at all. Secondly, the self is by no means identical throughout, and the "Soul become Spirit" is ours only potentially. St. Paul's doctrine of soul and spirit is much the same. Thirdly, though individuality is a fact, the question whether it is *my* soul which has a distinct place in the eternal world has no meaning at all. Our soul is not a part of our possessions. "It is not *my* soul," says Eckhart, "which is transformed after the image of God."

At this point it may be instructive to compare the doctrine of Spinoza, which has much in common with Neoplatonism. Spinoza distinguishes clearly between eternity and duration. "Eternity is an attribute under which we conceive the infinite existence of God ; duration

[1] *The Philosophy of Plotinus*, Vol. I., 245.

is an attribute under which we conceive the existence of
created things in so far as they persevere in their actuality."
Infinite existence is attributable to God only, not to out-
ward things even if they endure for ever. But here
Spinoza plainly changes his views. In his later work,
the *Ethics*, he assigns eternity to the human mind, which
therefore is in a different category from other created
things. Eternity is itself the divine nature (cf. *Met.*,
II., 1). The crucial question is whether the human mind
has any knowledge of such a mode of existence. If not,
we can say nothing about it ; if it has, it must have
within itself that which belongs to the eternal world.
Experience of duration would not give us this knowledge,
for duration belongs to the temporal order. Spinoza is
confident that we have this power. " We feel and experience that we are eternal." In so doing we do not lay
aside our finitude ; we perceive the finite *sub specie quadam
æternitatis.* So far as we know the temporal we are temporal ; so far as we know the eternal we are eternal.
This higher knowledge, which Plotinus calls νόησις,
he calls *scientia intuitiva.* This is the culmination of
Reason. Like Neoplatonism, Spinozism is a system of
rationalism leading up to mysticism. Like Plotinus,
Spinoza assumes that the hierarchies of reality and value
are parallel or identical ; " by reality and perfection I
mean the same thing." The state of mind which accompanies the apprehension of eternal existence is not " joy,"
which belongs to duration, but " blessedness," or *mentis
acquiescentia in seipso.* This is a reflexion of the divine
love with which God loves Himself. Spinoza quite
clearly denies human immortality in the sense of endless

duration; it is equally clear that he asserts individual, and not merely corporate "eternity." The eternal part of the mind neither was, is, nor ever will be in time; we cannot assert either pre-existence or post-existence for it. "Sempiternity is the account given of the existence of *Natura* from the point of view of one of its parts." [1]

This view of eternity differs from that of the scholastic mystics in its repudiation of *ævum*, on which I shall say more presently, as the surrogate of eternity appropriate to created beings. We are not to call ourselves immortal, but eternal. This philosophy makes eternity purely qualitative—a blend or synthesis of the absolute values. We are severely forbidden to throw our ideals into the future. But can we view the finite *sub specie æternitatis* without making it, in our imagination, durational? Spinoza attributes no great importance to the "imagination," which to Wordsworth and others is the mode in which reason realises ideas beyond the range of logic. It seems better to suppose that there is a real connexion between duration and eternity, so that the *species immortalitatis* is the only way in which we can conceive *æternitas*. If the "soul made Spirit" is above the durational mode of existence, we cannot say as much for the man of our ordinary activities. Our outer life is essentially durational.

Strictly, then, the question, What part of us is eternal or immortal, is meaningless, since the self is neither a fixed entity nor an owner of a fixed entity. The self is the Soul, and the Soul, as I have said, is the wanderer of

[1] Hallett, p. 112.

18

the metaphysical world. We are what we can make of ourselves. There is an idea in the mind of God of what each individual is meant to be. Our actual rank in the scale of existence and value depends on what we are interested in, what we love, what we " make our own." This is the conclusion of the whole matter, in ethics and soteriology, both for Plotinus and Spinoza. The two quotations from Spinoza which follow are very well known, but I admire them so much that I cannot refrain from transcribing them : " When a thing is not loved, no quarrels will arise concerning it—no sadness will be felt if it perishes—no envy if it is possessed by another— no fear, no hatred, no disturbances of the mind. All these arise from the love of what is perishable, such as the objects already mentioned. But love towards a thing eternal and infinite feeds the mind wholly with joy, and is itself unmingled with any sadness ; wherefore it is greatly to be desired and sought for with all our strength." And at the end of the *Ethics :* " Blessedness is not the reward of virtue, but virtue itself ; neither do we rejoice therein because we control our lusts, but because we rejoice therein we are able to control our lusts. . . . If the way which I have pointed out as leading to this result seems exceedingly hard, it may nevertheless be discovered. Needs must it be hard, since it is so seldom found. How would it be possible, if salvation were ready to our hand, and could without great labour be found, that it should be by almost all men neglected ? But all things excellent are as difficult as they are rare." So Plotinus says, " If a man seeks in the good life anything beyond itself, it is not the good life that he is seeking.

Disinterestedness is the root of all virtue ; disinterestedness carried to the pitch of not caring very much whether " our " soul or psyche is gained or not. We Christians have learned, or ought to have learned, this from our Master : " Whoever wishes to gain his soul shall lose it, but whoever is willing to lose it for My sake shall find it."

Next to the question as to the subject, the permanent being, who is to enjoy eternal life, comes the equally difficult problem as to survival in the literal sense. In this problem our whole position in regard to time is involved. The revival of so-called spiritualism, and the cult of necromancy, among masses of the half-educated, show how very crude are the notions of a " future life " among many who do not reject the idea altogether. Priestcraft of the baser sort, and sheer charlatanism, have been quick to exploit the pathetic cravings of the bereaved, the number of whom was so sadly augmented by the destructive war of 1914-1918. As to the nature of these beliefs, I cannot improve on what I wrote several years ago : " What a starveling hope it is that necromancy offers us ! An existence as poor and unsubstantial as that of Homer's Hades, which the shade of Achilles would have been glad to exchange for serfdom to the poorest farmer, and with no guarantee of permanence, even if the power of comforting or terrifying surviving relations is supposed to persist for a few years. Such a prospect would add a new terror to death, and none would desire it for himself." Psychical research is trying to prove that eternal values are temporal facts, which they can never be.

Faith in human immortality (I use this word without forgetting Spinoza's objection to it as a synonym for

18 *

eternal life) stands or falls with the belief in God. Belief in God is central, belief in human immortality is peripheral. This is the key to the whole problem. The absolute values, in which we have access to God, are eternal and indestructible. "Nothing that really *is* can ever perish "; or, as Höffding puts it, " no value perishes out of the world." Time is the frame of the soul-life, and the entire cosmic process is the life-frame of the divine Logos. With this life we are intimately connected, however brief our earthly span.[1] " Nothing that really is can ever perish." But does this mean that our lives here, once finished, take their place irrevocably in the eternal order, present immediately to the mind of God, for whom there is no present, past, or future ; present in their summed up meaning and value ? We mean this, and it is an answer to those who dread Time as the destroyer. But is this all ? Plotinus says that the disembodied soul " is no longer in act, but it is not annihilated." Does it then pass into a state of suspended

---

[1] Von Hugel says : " The soul, *qua* religious, has no interest in just simple unending existence, of no matter what kind. The specifically religious desire of immortality begins not with immortality but with God ; it rests upon God and it ends with God. The religious soul does not seek, find, or assume its own immortality, and thereupon seek, find, or assume God. But it seeks, finds, experiences, and loves God ; and because of these experiences, which lie right within the noblest joys, fears, hopes, necessities, certainties which emerge within any and every field of its life here below, it finds, rather than seeks, immortality of a certain kind." (*Essays and Addresses*, p. 197.)

So Jowett, expounding Plato, says : " If God exists, then the soul exists after death ; and if there is no God, there is no existence of the soul after death. We are more certain of the existence of God than we are of the immortality of the soul, and are led by the belief in the one to the belief in the other."

animation, or into a kind of Nirvana ? Or if we desire some further activity, some relief from what we might be tempted to think might be never-ending boredom, must we have recourse to some theory of reincarnation ? Have we done with Time once for all when we die, and together with Time have we done with the Will, which requires time in which to energise, when we take our last look at the world ? The popular notion of a further probation receives no support from the New Testament, nor from traditional Christian teaching. Purgatory, of course, is not a further probation, though many Protestants misunderstand the Roman teaching on this subject. And if we take eternity seriously, as a state of being " beyond this bourne of time and place," the fear of boredom, the expectation of protracted and monotonous enjoyment, the horror of unending torment, are alike out of place, except as a crude translation into another language of a state of being of which we can form no clear conception. The idea of progress in eternity is a reflexion from the secular idea of unending progress of which I have said so much in this book.

It is indeed remarkable how the idea of eternal life as *fruition* or consummation has faded out of religious thought in Protestant countries. The Catholic teaching is that eternal life, the bliss of communion with God, is the absolute goal in which active life finds its meaning and in which at last it will be swallowed up.[1] Bonaventura speaks of the beatified soul " rejoicing with God in the universe wherein He rejoices, and in His own eternal being." To see the universe as God sees it is to see all

[1] Carpenter and Wicksteed, *Studies in Theology*, p. 11.

the scattered leaves of the universe bound by love into a single volume.[1]   Life eternal is to be won not for what it leads to but for what it is.   There is no loss of consciousness, as in Indian thought ; but self-consciousness is now God-consciousness.   Augustine says that " all human perversity or vice consists in wishing to enjoy what we ought to use, and to use what we ought to enjoy."   There are then good things which are to be enjoyed, not used, and such is the vision of God when fully given.   Do not let us invade heaven with thoughts appropriate only to earth, and think of God's will being done in heaven as it is on earth.   In the Scottish catechism the end of man is rightly said to be to enjoy God for ever.

In theological language the Church triumphant, the whole number of the elect, is *one* in a sense in which we could not use the word of the world which we know.   The redeemed are one by virtue of their communion with God, which involves the promise that they will be, so to speak, transparent to each other.   So much I think we are justified in believing ; but it is honest to admit that we know much less than we should like to know, and very much less than popular religion fancies that it knows.

It is a question of considerable philosophical interest whether the scholastic conception of *ævum* has any value. This is an intermediate category between time and eternity, which is not suggested by Plotinus, but which may owe something to the speculation of Proclus.   For him

[1] Nel suo profondo vidi che s'interna
Legato con amore in un volume,
Cio che per l'universo si squaderna.
      --Dante, *Paradiso*, XXXIII., 85.

perpetuity is a lower form of eternity. There are authentic existents which are not in the full sense eternal. Boëthius, who was treated very respectfully by Aquinas, defines eternity as "a simultaneously full and perfect possession of interminable life." Aquinas says : "Even supposing Time to last for ever, we can still distinguish within it a beginning and an end, by noting various parts of it. Eternity, on the other hand, is all together." "Time has an earlier and a later, *ævum* has no earlier and later in itself, but both can be connected with it ; eternity has neither an earlier nor a later, nor can they be connected with it." "Spiritual creatures, as regards their affections and intellections, in which there is succession, are measured by time; as regards their vision of glory, they participate in eternity; as regards their natural being, they are measured by *ævum*." "*Ævum* is *totum simul*, but it is not eternity, for it may contain within itself an earlier and later."

It is plain that *ævum* is intended to mediate between time and eternity, and that it is the frame of soul life, which holds an intermediate position between spirit and body. It is durational, admitting of earlier and later, though not, it appears from the sentence last quoted, of past and future. The meaning and value of *ævum* are capable of being summed up in a kind of specious present. I do not agree with von Hügel that Aquinas is "groping after" something like Bergson's *durée ;* his only perplexity is that having defined eternity as "having no earlier or later, nor can they be connected with it," he has deprived temporal succession of its status even as a symbol of reality. And yet in the psychic life time and succession certainly cannot be explained away. Some have met the difficulty by saying that though for the mind of God there is no past or future, His vision of events may include their relative position as earlier or later than each other. This seems to me perfectly sound. The degree of reality to be ascribed to duration is a very difficult question. Duration is as real as the life of the Soul as we know it; and though the conception of *ævum* is no more successful than other intercalated middle terms in bridging over the chasm between two incommensurables, it does indicate the attitude towards time and eternity which it is natural for us to take, as beings who participate in both.

Baron von Hügel has argued that *ævum*, durational immortality, is not only our imperfect idea of eternity, but is, actually and finally, the condition of human nature. Eternal life in the fullest sense implies pure acting, non-successiveness, and simultaneity. It precludes not only time as a series of mutually exclusive moments, but duration. In this sense, eternal life is an attribute of God only, not also of the human mind, as Spinoza came to think. There is an impassable gulf between human nature and the divine. Nevertheless, eternal life is attributable to man, though not in the fullest sense. It appears to have its true form in duration, " an ever more or less overlapping succession, capable of being concentrated into semi-simultaneities." Von Hügel has perhaps been over-sensitive to the persuasive charm of Bergson's writing; but the suggestion that *ævum* is the permanent form of human nature, borrowed as it is from St. Thomas, is to be treated respectfully. " This lesser eternal life, though unending, is never boundless ; nor does it (here below at least) ever become entirely actual."

Von Hügel follows the Neoplatonists in saying that this double relation, of likeness and unlikeness, to the Eternal Spirit both makes it possible for us to apprehend eternal life and explains our unquenchable thirst for eternity in its fullest sense, for life in the presence of God. This desire cannot be explained as a merely human projection ; it must be the attraction of a mode of being which is far above us, but in which we, after our measure, are sharers. It is also psychologically certain that what attracts us is not the idea of a perfection being gradually realised, but of a perfection eternally real and complete. The appropriate attitude in approaching such a Being is adoration rather than aspiration, though adoration is itself a yielding to the attraction of the higher principle. Practically, it is important to realise that we do *not* approach God by trying to think away duration. Our knowledge of the Eternal Spirit is communicated to us mainly, if not entirely, through experiences which, though not necessarily successional, are in von Hügel's sense durational. Nor need we wholly distrust the spatial imagery which seems to us rather more remote from spiritual reality than the temporal. The physical and mathematical picture of the universe also has its place in the full life of the soul. It provides that preliminary pantheism which by proclaiming its own limitations makes ultimate pantheism impossible.

Man, in short, as we know ourselves, is " essentially durational and quasi-eternal," as von Hügel says. Such an idea will be rejected by modernist philosophy; but it corresponds with what we seem to know about ourselves. If it is true, it may mitigate the severity with which otherwise we might have to reject the very idea of a "future" life, as if it were merely myth or poetry. But the difficulty remains, how an "essentially durational life" can be thought of in a state when "there shall be time no longer." I am disposed to think that while Space and Time are the necessary framework of our thought even about eternity, we cannot accept the view that the life of blessed spirits is "essentially durational." Von Hügel, I think, has hardly realised that Bergson, in his glorification of *la durée*, has really lifted it out of temporality and treated it, illegitimately, as one of the ultimate values.

Besides the philosophical problem of immortality, which as we have seen was thoroughly discussed by the later Greek philosophers and the early Christian theologians, we have to consider the popular beliefs which helped to mould the orthodox tradition of the Church. The Hebrews were strangely late in developing anything like a real and consistent eschatology. Until after the loss of their national independence they had no doctrine of individual immortality. They combined with the worship of Jehovah, as Archdeacon Charles says, a primitive eschatology, a piece of true Semitic heathenism. Sheol was beyond the jurisdiction of Jehovah; the relation between God and His worshippers ceased at death.[1] At death the dust returns to the earth as it was, and the impersonal breath or spirit returns to God who gave it. It was a short step from belief in this shadowy realm of

[1] Cf. Psalm cxv 17, and many similar passages.

Sheol to a denial of a future life altogether ; this was the avowed creed of the Sadducees in the time of our Lord. The beliefs of the early Romans were not unlike those of the Jews. There was no singular of the word *Manes ;* and till the end of the Republic the *Di Manes* did not represent the individual spirit of the departed. In the official religion of Greece a few great heroes and notorious criminals are promoted to the Isles of the Blest or consigned to Tartarus ; but the rest of mankind, whether good or bad, were herded together in the unsubstantial abode where the " strengthless heads " (ἀμένηνα κάρηνα) of the dead flit about like shadows, and envy the most sordid denizens of the upper world. The soul was a mere ghost, with no place in the psychology of the living man. In Sheol and Hades alike there is no element of value. It is noticeable that among the sepulchral monuments from the Cerameicus at Athens, full of tender feeling as many of them are, hardly any of them touch the life of the after-world. They depict scenes of sorrowful farewell, or they recall the favourite pursuits of the departed, the youth with his hounds, the lady with her box of cosmetics, and the like. Nevertheless, there was a popular cult of ancestors both in Greece and Italy. The last day of the Athenian festival of Anthesteria was a commemoration of the dead.

Real belief in immortality came in with the mystery-cults. Because sacramental worship symbolises and makes actual the union of the soul with God, the soul must share the divine prerogative of immunity from death. This exemplifies a truth which cannot be stated too often —that the belief in immortality in the higher religions is both historically and essentially independent of primitive animism. It had a different source, and it has a very different content.

As soon as immortality came to be conceived as essentially " becoming like unto God " (ὁμοίωσις τῷ θεῷ), the need of purification, in order to fit the soul for its heavenly origin and destiny, began to play an important part. The fallen condition of the soul is clearly not caused by any errors committed in this present life. It must therefore be the result of some defilement contracted in a previous state of existence. The promise of the Orphic religion, with its sacraments, was deliverance from original sin. The body is the tomb of the soul (σῶμα σῆμα) ; our true life can be ours only when we are delivered from " this body of death." The Orphic tablets found not long ago give the soul careful instructions how to act in the world below. " On your left you will find a stream, and near it a white poplar. Go not near this ; but you will find another, cool waters flowing from the lake of Memory, and by it are guards. Say to them, ' I am a child of earth and of starry heaven, but my race is of heaven alone. This ye know well yourselves.' " In other tablets the soul of the initiated addresses Persephone thus : " Out of the pure I come,[1] pure Queen of those below. For I claim that I am of your blessed race. I have flown out of the sorrowful weary wheel ; I have paid the penalty of deeds unjust ; and now I come as a suppliant to holy Persephone, beseeching her to be gracious and to send me to the abodes of the blessed." She hears the answer : " Happy and blessed one, thou shalt be a god instead of

---

[1] Or perhaps the comma should be placed after the second " pure."

a mortal." But ritual purifications are not enough. Sin must be expiated by suffering, and the soul may need further purification in fresh reincarnations.

The imagination quickly runs riot when we think of the scenes of bliss and torment which await the soul after death. But the pains of the sinner in the Orphic eschatology are purgatorial, not vindictive, nor are the authors of these fragments careful to distinguish in their descriptions what in Christian theology would be called paradise and heaven.

On the influence of Orphism upon Greek religion Dr. Farnell says very well : " It familiarised the world with the conception of the divine element in the human soul, with the kinship between man and God. It quickened this sense by means of a mystic sacrament whereby man's life was transcendentally fused with God's. It raised the religious emotion to a pitch of ecstasy and rapture far above the Hellenic scale. Its chief aim and scope was otherworldliness, its mission was the preaching of salvation, of an eschatology based on dogmas of posthumous retribution, purgatory, and of a succession of lives through which the soul is tried ; and it promised immortal bliss through purity and the mysterious magic of a sacrament. It must be reckoned as one of the forces that prepared the way for a new era and a new faith."

In Socrates and Plato we come to the clear conviction that the soul, instead of being a ghost which at the moment of death flies off to Hades, is the real self ; the body, not the soul, is the unsubstantial image. The doctrine is frankly Orphic. We must not suppose that when Plato expresses contempt and indignation against the charlatans who resembled the "pardoners" and indulgence-mongers of the Middle Ages, he means to discredit Orphism itself.   Plato's philosophical arguments for immortality are not very convincing ; but behind them lies a strong religious conviction that the soul of man has its true home among the eternal "Forms" which can never fade.   The philosophy which sets out these ideas in a coherent shape has already been briefly summarised in speaking of Plotinus.   The eternal Forms, or as we should say, the absolute values are underived and irreducible truths ; in our apprehension of them we feel and know that we are eternal.   But our souls are not themselves eternal monads, though they are indestructible.[1] In his deepest passages, where Plato discards the mythical form, he thinks of eternal life as a timeless state into which we can enter here and now.   Neither he nor Aristotle has much to say about the "future" life in its literal sense.   In the *Timæus* he distinguishes between the immortal part of the soul, which is divine and pre-existent as well as sempiternal, and the mortal soul, which is different in nature and subject to various passions. We might easily infer that the rational part of the soul is alone immortal, and that this higher soul is super-personal.   This idea, borrowed from Aristotle, is the most characteristic part of the philosophy of Averroes. But Plato has always been held to be a champion of individual immortality.

His ultimate argument for immortality is that God is good, and could not have wished to destroy His creatures. He accepts the belief in future compensation and retri-

[1] Plato, *Laws*, p. 904.

bution, as the Orphics did ; but he does not use this claim as an argument for immortality.[1]

In broad outline, the Orphic and Platonic eschatology became part of the Christian tradition, with the exception of the doctrine of reincarnation. Origen took the step which to Greek thought generally seemed the corollary of belief in a future life—he taught the pre-existence of souls. The soul being immaterial—in the third century the meaning of " God is Spirit " was at last beginning to be understood—it can have, Origen argues, neither beginning nor end. But even he cannot free himself entirely from the Stoical notion of a " spiritual body," which he seems to think of as an ultra-gaseous envelope of the soul. This conception seems to have no scientific or religious value.

The theories of pre-existence and of reincarnation may be considered together. Empedocles professed to remember his previous incarnations. "I was once a boy, a maiden, a plant, a bird, and a fish in the sea." This doctrine was naturally caricatured and ridiculed, but it survived even as late as Plotinus, who, however, does not, in my opinion, take it very seriously. Porphyry and Iamblichus deny that the human soul ever inhabits the body of a beast or bird.

[1] I have found help here from Pringle-Pattison's *Idea of Immortality*. But when, on page 56, he says that the existence of God and the immortality of the soul are not treated by Plato as part of a scientific theory of the unseen world, but primarily as " regulative ideas " for the direction of our life here below, I disagree. The phrase seems to be taken from Stewart's book on the Myths of Plato, which takes a view of the Platonic Ideas which is not mine, nor (I should have thought) Pringle-Pattison's own.

The belief in reincarnation is especially associated with India. The theory of Karma, which is said to mean "action," is older than Buddha, though I am told that it does not appear in the old Vedic hymns. Karma, as preached both by Hindus and Buddhists, is the inexorable law of moral causation. "Whatsoever a man soweth, that shall he reap." In the absence of belief in retribution in another world, justice can be done only in successive lives in this world, each person born into the world inheriting, not the memory of his former life, but the bare continuity of existence, with its liabilities. But Buddhism does not believe in permanent individuality. Educated Buddhists certainly do not believe that a congenital idiot is a man who has misused his intellect in a former incarnation. In fact, the idea of individual retribution belongs to that illusion of the ego which this philosophy seeks to eradicate. But the popular belief of Buddhism resembles that of Hinduism. Plato, as is well known, holds that "memory," unconscious or half conscious, may connect successive lives. Leibnitz thought that "immortality without recollection would be ethically valueless," which I think is untrue. We may be keenly interested in the welfare of our descendants, and of a posterity who are not our descendants, and this interest, being (as we say) "disinterested," has a high ethical value. In India, however, the attractiveness of the doctrine is less in providing for the future than in explaining apparent injustices in the present. "Shall not the judge of all the earth do right?" If the answer is in the affirmative, and if it is the deed and not the doer which should be rewarded or punished, the attractiveness of Karma, which has satisfied many millions of persons for more than 2000 years, is explained.[1]

Some writers, like Pringle-Pattison, reject the doctrine for two reasons : first, that such punishment must be vindictive and not remedial, and second, that the hypothesis of an unchanging soul-substance underlying the series is a figment. But in my opinion punishment is essentially retributive ; remedial measures which are incidentally unpleasant to the subject of them are not punishment at all. It might even be argued that to inflict unnecessary pain on anyone for any other reason than because his actions deserve it—e.g. to deter others from doing the like—is immoral. And the doctrine of a soul-substance—i.e. of a distinct and imperishable entity in the spiritual world, not belonging to the time-series, has the authority of a great philosophical tradition, not to be lightly surrendered to a mere fashion of thinking. When Pringle-Pattison goes on to accuse the doctrine of denying the expiatory value of vicarious suffering, he seems to me to do injustice to the fine unselfishness of Buddhism at its best. "The process," he says, "is an endless one, and can never effect a release from the weary wheel of endless becoming." But Buddhism does promise a very complete release, in Nirvana, or everlasting rest. Perhaps there are few who shall be so saved ; perhaps sin and its consequences will continue while the world lasts. Does any rival system, except the exploded superstition of inevitable progress to perfection, promise anything

[1] For Buddhism as it is now taught to educated persons see David, *Le Modernisme Bouddhiste*, Paris, 1911, and other sympathetic accounts of this religion by European scholars.

different ?   He even accuses Buddhism of a hedonistic calculus—"always the righteous act brings happiness, the wicked act unhappiness," and contrasts with it the Platonic and Christian doctrines that the penalty of unrighteousness is to be "unrighteous still," the very thing which Karma asserts.   Pringle-Pattison seems to have taken the vulgar perversion of Buddhism as the norm for the religion in general, a method which might be applied with deadly results to Christianity.

The doctrine of reincarnation has had a long history in Europe and Western Asia.   Not only was it held by Pythagoras, Empedocles, and Plato, but there are traces of it in Philo,[1] and it was definitely adopted in the Kabbala.   The Sufi writers accept it.   In Palestine, Herod thought that Jesus might be John the Baptist, whom Herod had lately beheaded, and others suggested that He might be " one of the old prophets risen from the dead."   In the Fourth Gospel, the disciples ask Jesus whether the man born blind had sinned in a previous life. The doctrine is definitely accepted in the Wisdom of Solomon.[2]   Julius Cæsar found the belief among the Druids.   In later times it was advocated by Giordano Bruno and van Helmont ;   by Swedenborg, Goethe, Lichtenberg, Lessing, Herder, Hume and Schopenhauer (as a reasonable hypothesis), Lavater, Ibsen, Maeterlinck, and McTaggart.

The real objection to a belief which in many ways is so attractive is rather to the Brahminic than to the Buddhist form of the doctrine.   If we believe in personality—and we can hardly dismiss it as mere illusion—

[1] Radhakrishnan, p. 286.   [2] Wisdom viii. 19, 20.

there is not the slightest reason to identify incarnation B with incarnation A, since there is no link between them except the liabilities of A, which are arbitrarily laid upon the shoulders of B. The hypothesis is a pure assumption. The objection does not hold if it is the deed and not the doer which is to meet with its deserts. But in this case there is no personal theodicy at all, and the consequences of the deed are not the natural and traceable consequences, but are transmitted by some incomprehensible law of transcendental genetics.

It has been argued on the other side that the alternative is to suppose that every individual soul is a new creation, and that this is palpably untrue, since it is impossible to hold that " we brought nothing into the world." We inherit almost everything from our parents. But this hardly justifies us in believing that we inherit our very selves from some one who was not our father or grandfather.

Nirvana is not annihilation, but it is the eternal slumber of the Will. Is this after all a worthy goal of human endeavour ? Of course, the same difficulty arises about the Christian heaven as often imagined. Modernist Christianity echoes the prayer of Tennyson about the soul —" Give her the wages of going on and not to die," and assumes with Robert Browning that the saved soul will be able to say :

> And I shall thereupon
> Take rest, ere I be gone
> Once more on my adventure brave and new.

This means either progress in heaven, for which there is no warrant either in the New Testament or in traditional Christian theology, or it means reincarnation.

Do we want final " release," or do we not ?   It is interesting that some of the later Neoplatonists, such as Sallustius and Proclus, recognised this problem.   Proclus says that every soul must " descend " once at least in every cosmic cycle.   Without being so definite as this, I confess that I find the doctrine both credible and attractive.   The beatified spirit has its citizenship secure in the eternal world ; but must it not, even by virtue of its assimilation to the Father of spirits, share in His activity in the world of space and time ?   May it not do in little what we believe the Eternal Word to have done when He became incarnate, and what in fact He never ceases to do as the divine Spirit immanent in the world ?   These are questions which we are so manifestly unable to answer that it is futile even to put them ; but I think that when we have rejected the idea of a progressing universe, with which God is literally organic, some such thoughts as those which I have suggested may once more be acceptable to many.

In the eastern religions, survival in time, so far as it is accepted, is a necessary law or a postulate of theodicy. It is not " the blessed hope of everlasting life."   The wheel of becoming is a fate from which the Oriental would be glad to escape.   It has often been said that here we have a remarkable contrast between the sanguine and energetic Western mind and the world-weariness of the East.   But it is easy to exaggerate this contrast.   The notion of progress, and even of further probation, in a future state is foreign to traditional Christianity, as I have already said.   Heaven, in traditional Christianity, is a state of static fruition, hell of static punishment.   In our own day, though the idea of progress beyond the grave is often welcomed, the more popular hope is secular, temporal, and impersonal; we identify ourselves in imagination with the future advance of humanity. Since this is not enough to satisfy human hopes, there has been a revival of necromancy and spiritualism, of which it is only necessary to say that if these phenomena were proved they would belong exclusively to the physical or psychical world, and would have very little interest for religion. Spiritualism is often the spurious mysticism of the materialist. Moreover, the questionnaires issued by American psychologists make it doubtful whether the desire for survival is so general as is often assumed. It would be an interesting question whether it was more universal in some earlier periods than it is to-day. Pringle-Pattison quotes from Plutarch : " The hope of eternity and the yearning for life is the oldest and strongest of human desires. I might almost say that all men and women would readily submit themselves to the teeth of Cerberus, and to the punishment of carrying water in a sieve, if only they might remain in existence and escape the doom of annihilation." He refers also to Claudio's ignoble dread of extinction,[1] or of something worse than extinction; to Milton's archangels contemplating the possibility of annihilation at the hands of an enraged Deity; and Heine's terror at the prospect of being released by death from his bed of suffering. The following lines of Maecenas have been rescued from oblivion by their craven sentiment :—

---

[1] In Shakespeare's *Measure for Measure.*

Debilem facito manu, Debilem pede, coxa ;
Tuber adstrue gibberum, Lubricos quate dentes ;
Vita dum superest, bene est ;
Hanc mihi vel acuta Si sedeam cruce, sustine.

But it is not likely that there has been much difference
between one age and another. Fear of death is mainly
a matter of temperament. Some good and brave men,
like Samuel Johnson, have suffered greatly from it. Many
others, whose lives are outwardly and probably inwardly
happier than his, are able to face the prospect with
complete equanimity. Those who have seen the young
dying are often amazed by the tranquil courage with
which they put down the cup of life which they have
hardly tasted. Most of us, I think, are not afraid of
being dead ; but " pour être mort, malheureusement il
faut mourir." Survival, in the strict sense, which is
necessarily subject to temporal and possibly even spatial
conditions, must, if we reject any kind of reincarnation,
with continued or renewed activity on earth, offer the
alternative of either intrinsic progress or boredom. The
latter prospect has weighed heavily on many who have
taken too literally the traditional pictures of unending
songs of praise to the Creator. We can only doubt
whether to listen to interminable encomiums or to declaim
them would be the more wearisome. This thought,
however, only illustrates the contradiction of translating
eternal life into terms of duration. On a higher level is
the doubt whether any sempiternal existence, apart from
creative activity, can possess any value or fulfil any purpose. This objection is felt still more strongly when we
think of endless torture, an idea which in the Middle Ages

seems to have presented no difficulty. For St. Thomas
Aquinas, the sight of the torments of the damned will
actually contribute to the felicity of the beatified
spirits, and the awful line of Dante, " Questi non hanno
speranza di morte " was not, in the mind of the poet,
inconsistent with the " giustizia " and " primo amore "
which contrived this horrible abode.

There has been much discussion among Christian
theologians whether the soul is naturally immortal, or
whether it acquires immortality. The question depends
partly on whether a life destined for eternity can have
a beginning in time. But there is no agreement here
among early Christian writers. St. Paul is convinced that
flesh and blood cannot inherit the Kingdom of God ; he
says that a " spiritual body," on the nature of which he
does not speculate, is being prepared either for every one
or only for the elect. The bodies of those who happen
to be alive at the second coming of Christ will be changed
into this spiritual substance. Tertullian, the Christian
Stoic, takes a very materialistic view of the relation of
soul and body, and seems to believe that the soul, which
cannot be separated from the body, dies with it, till both
are raised again together by miracle. Theophilus says
that the soul is naturally neither mortal nor immortal ;
" it is capable of becoming either." The Christian
Platonists followed the Greeks in teaching that the soul
is naturally immortal ; Origen takes what seemed to him
the logical step of asserting the pre-existence of souls.
He does not easily believe in the resurrection of the flesh.
Can we really suppose, he asks, that God will provide
new teeth, which we shall not require in the next world,

" for the wicked to gnash with " ? We may perhaps agree with Whately when he says " that the natural immortality of man's soul is discoverable by reason may be denied on the ground that it has not been discovered yet " ; but obviously it is not the kind of truth that could be discovered by " reason." Justin Martyr, Tatian and Irenæus all denied that the soul is naturally immortal. Augustine only insists that the human soul was created by God, and not consubstantial with the Father like the Second Person of the Trinity. Arnobius clearly teaches that the souls of the wicked are annihilated; but he stands almost alone in this belief. Aquinas will not allow that any real existence can ever be annihilated. In immaterial beings " non est potentia ad non esse." Even a miraculous annihilation is not to be thought of. The Lateran Council of 1513 condemned the theory that the soul can literally die. Spinoza, though in his early books he holds the old belief in an imperishable soul-substance, came later to believe that the destiny of the soul, life or death, depends on the objects of her love and interest. In modern times the theory condemned by the Lateran Council has been revived under the name of conditional immortality, the main motive being humanitarian. But, as von Hügel justly points out, we may as Christians hold almost any views about hell except its temporary character; this is plainly barred by the teaching of the New Testament. Nevertheless, the theory has been maintained not only by Hobbes and Locke, but by Isaac Watts, Rousseau, Henry Dodwell (in an elaborate work published in 1706), and by a Congregational minister named Edward White in 1846. A very

strong objection to it is that it implies the sharpest of
all possible bisections in the next world, a view which
though favoured by traditional eschatology is surely incompatible with any kind of justice as we understand the
word. So far as we can see, not only some persons but
the large majority are " over bad for blessing and over
good for banning."

Belief in survival has no necessary connexion with
religion. There is an irreligious belief in it, and there
is a religious disbelief in it. If I wish for another life
because I have enjoyed myself here and wish to go on
enjoying myself, or because I have been miserable here
and think myself entitled to compensation, or because I
have made certain investments in good works and hope,
in the words of a popular hymn, to be repaid a thousand-
fold, that has no more to do with religion than if I invested my money on the strength of one of the similarly
worded circulars which I used to find on my breakfast
table. Such motives for desiring another life have obviously nothing to do with religion. On the other hand,
as Clutton Brock has well argued, much avowed disbelief
in the popular eschatology is really a faith in absolute
values which refuses the support and comfort of any
dogma. It is the supreme example of man's passion
for disinterestedness, the last asceticism of which man is
capable. But probably the unbelief is not so absolute as
it seems to be. It may be a self-denial which the mind
imposes on itself in order to be certain that its values are
pure. There is a real danger that the " will to power "
which is present in all religion may deceive us, expressing
only our desire for rewards for ourselves and perhaps

punishments for others.   These irreligious beliefs, especially when they embody either a snobbish arrogance at belonging, as we fancy, to a privileged corporation, or our hatreds and our selfish desires, empty the doctrine of its real values, and soon make it either intolerable or incredible.   The nemesis of an immoral and unworthy eschatology is the decay of faith in eternal life altogether. Nor can we really regret that such pictures of the resurrection, of heaven and hell, as were painted on the walls of churches in the Middle Ages, can no longer attract or frighten us.   If our beliefs about a future life are tainted with egotism, pride, and hatred, they lose their foundation in God ; and other foundation have they none.   It is therefore not surprising that several saints are recorded to have wished that heaven and hell were blotted out, that they might serve God for Himself alone.   In truth, however, no separation can be made between " heaven " and the vision of God.

Such thoughts lead naturally, not to belief that bodily death is the end of all things for us, but to a different conception of eternal life, from which both the thought of future rewards and punishments and the mental picture of immortality as merely a succession of moments drawn out to infinity, are absent.   That virtue is its own reward, and that this reward is not deferred, is a belief which we have found vigorously asserted by great philosophers.   " In the midst of finitude to be one with the infinite, and in every moment to be eternal, this," says Schleiermacher, " is the immortality of religion."   It is the old counsel of Aristotle, that we should " be immortal as far as may be."   The Fourth Gospel is full of this doctrine of eternal life as identical with the knowledge of God, as a higher state of existence into which we can enter, at least in a measure, before we pass through the gate of death.

This is the noblest and truest way in which eternal life can be thought of. The more we can make it our own, the purer will our religion be from any selfish or mercenary taint. And yet the warning is needed that it is possible to spiritualise our religion overmuch. It is not, as a matter of fact, the saints, who have discarded the desire for heaven and the fear of hell, as unworthy emotions. It is fatally easy to call ourselves disinterested when we are only uninterested. Strong beliefs express themselves in vivid imagery, and when we are deeply stirred we cannot remind ourselves that what floats before our mind's eye is " only poetry."

A French critic of St. John of the Cross has said that " by purification and the dark night of the soul *la sensibilité sera en fait reçue dans l'esprit.*" In the life of devotion, as in the poet's study of nature, imagination may be " reason in her most exalted mood." And therefore I think it is a mistake to deny ourselves pictorial images which cannot possess literal truth. We know that some of our beliefs are symbolical and mythical, but we do not thank our friends for reminding us of it in season and out of season. For instance, when we think of our reunion with those whom we have loved and lost on earth, our deep conviction is that " love is stronger than death," and that in the spiritual world nothing will separate us from each other except discordance of nature. But we picture to ourselves something more human and personal than this, and I do not think we need forbid love to speak in its natural language.

The Greek Fathers spoke of the whole " process of Christ " (as our divines used to call it), the whole history of the Incarnation, Passion, and Resurrection, as a mystery or sacrament. A sacrament is something which in being what it is, means something more, something universal, permanent, and spiritual. It seems to me that the whole of nature is best understood as sacramental in this sense. Earth is a shadow of heaven, but the " shadow is a true shadow, as the substance is a true substance." Here is the answer to that type of spirituality which falls into antinomianism, a kind of religion which seems to be very prevalent in India. Why should we keep our bodies morally clean ? Why should we abstain from actions which please us and hurt nobody ? St. Paul says it is because we are temples of the Holy Spirit. " Whether we eat or drink or whatever we do," it is all part of a divine service, " a living sacrifice."

Art is the attempt to apprehend reality by giving sacramental expression to it. Expression, as Whitehead says, is the one fundamental sacrament. Science in its own way follows the same method. But neither art nor science is the supreme sacrament. Religion in its highest form is an attempt to express reality sacramentally by living in harmony with it.

If this is the character of the whole creation, no scientific discoveries can destroy our faith. But there is a thin, pure, bracing air about natural science which blows away a great many cobwebs from the mind, and stimulates the imagination to wander through strange seas of thought. This is especially true of astronomy. We can sympathise with the American who, after hearing a lecture on the stars remarked, "Then it does not matter very much, after all, whether the Republicans or the Democrats win the election."

As for philosophy, with which so much of this book has been concerned, I ask my readers to consider whether the following words of Bosanquet are not true: " In so far as the religious consciousness at its climax comes to include the vision of all that has value, united in a type of perfection, philosophy is little more than the theoretical interpretation of it."

SUBJECT INDEX

A

Absolute, the, in Bradley, 117; the Absolute and God, 218, 251

Acosmism, 42, 70.

Evum, the intermediary between Time and Eternity, 278-282.

"Annihilation" of Matter, 39, human fear of, 293.

Astronomy, effects on the mind, 3-5; importance to philosophy, 6.

B

Beauty one of the absolute values, 191-202.

Becoming and Being, 126.

Biologism—the laws of life normative for the whole of creation, 108, 113, 234.

Biology in revolt against mechanicism, 51-56.

Body, Soul, and Spirit, 264

Buddhism, 288 *sq*

C

Causation, 87, 88, 250.

Chance, attempts to rehabilitate, 33, 34, 105.

Change and stability, 78.

Christianity, cosmology of, 81, fate of the world in, 25-28; view of Time, 124, view of Evolution, 127; absence of idea of progress, 146; ultimate values, 211; a definite religion, 213; its two main affluents, 215-217.

Civilisation, prospects for, 156-173.

Conditional immortality, 296.

Conservation of value, in Hoffding, 142, 210, 211.

Cosmic rays, 66.

Cosmological argument, 225.

Creation in Time, 11; prejudice against the idea of, 233; various theories of, 235-245.

Creative evolution, 57, 107.

Cycles, theory of, 99-101, 144, 148.

D

Degrees of reality and value, 7, 48, 183.

Deism, 248.

Deity, in S. Alexander, 112.

Determinism, 97, 135.

Dualism in moral valuation, 187.

Duration (*durée*) in Bergson, 73-75; Hegel on, 83; Spinoza on, 84-92; von Hügel on, 121; relation to *evum*, 280-282.

Dysteleology, 21, 24.

E

Emergent evolution, 107, 140, 141.

Entropy and progress, 8-10; the law stated, 19; attempts to find an escape from, 25-68, 227.

Eschatology, Hebrew, 282, Greek, 282-287; Christian, 214.

Eternity and perpetuity, 79; Spinoza on, 84-92; 271, 272; the eternal world, 257-301

Evolution, two meanings of, 125, 126; absence of the idea in historical Christianity, 127-131.

Expansion of the universe, 37, 49, 50.

F

Fear of death, 293, 294.

Free will and divine foreknowledge, 135.

Future life and eternity, 81; the future, 85-92; Broad on, 116.

302

NAME INDEX

A

Adams, Henry, 21.
Æschylus, 143.
Alexander, S , 9, 78, 110 *sq.*, 185.
Aliotta, 19, 30, 109
Aquinas, 170, 208 , 241, 279, 295, 296
Aristotle, 75, 126, 155, 221, 254, 298.
Arnobius, 296
Arrhenius, 65, 100.
Athenagoras, 237.
Augustine, 28, 71, 83, 97, 129, 179, 200, 204, 208, 278, 296.
Averroes, 221, 286

B

Bacon, Francis, 148.
Bacon, Roger, 147.
Balfour, Arthur J., 26, 193, 230.
Barnes, Bp., xi.
Barrow, 93.
Bavink, 67, 131, 137.
Bergson, 21, 22, 72, 75, 104, 108, 282
Berkeley, Bp., 41, 94, 193.
Blake, 202.
Boëthius, 279.
Bonaventura, 277.
Boodin, 141.
Bosanquet, 21, 68, 118, 154, 155, 201.
Bouillet, 260.
Boutroux, 57.
Bradley, F. H., 7, 67, 99, 114, 117, 132, 207.
Bragg, Sir W., 59.
Braithwaite, 34.
Broad, 86.
Brontë, E., 16.
Browning, R., 291.
Brunkes, 52.
Bury, 148.

C

Carnot, 2.
Carpenter, Edward, 160.
Carpenter, Estlin, 279.
Carr, Wildon, 106
Charles, Archdeacon, 282.
Clausius, 2.
Clement of Alexandria, 194.
Clifford, W. K , 114.
Clough, 145.
Clutton Brock, 192, 297.
Comte, 51, 65, 152
Condorcet, 134, 149
Coué, 143.
Coulton, 148.
Cousin, 151.
Croce, 11, 22, 96, 153.
Crozier, 133.
Cudworth, 194, 252.

D

Dante, 278, 295.
D'Arcy, 196.
Darwin, Charles, 131, 142.
Dawson, Christopher, 146, 149, 200.
Descartes, 99, 149, 181, 195, 252.
De Sitter, 50.
Disraeli, 171.
Dodwell, 276.
Driesch, 137.

E

Eckermann, 150.
Eckhart, 130, 271
Eddington, Sir A., 2, 8, 33, 35, 41, 243.
Einstein, 50, 100.
Emerson, 65.
Empedocles, 134, 287.
Eucken, 121, 200.

PRINTED IN GREAT BRITAIN BY THE UNIVERSITY PRESS, ABERDEEN

CPSIA information can be obtained
at www.ICGtesting.com
Printed in the USA
BVHW04*1017120418
513191BV00008B/49/P